'What an extraordinary, beautiful and inspiring
group analysis, art and paintings in a totally ⌣ _
masterpiece. The author, Morris Nitsun, both a psychotherapist and ⌣
throughout, adding a personal narrative to the paintings and sharing a courageous
life story. What is most impressive, however, is how much he lets the paintings
speak for themselves, coming alive through the eyes of the observers. Their
memories, associations, phantasies and projections, all in response to the paintings,
are fascinating and moving, and form a continuing thread through the book. A
further pleasure are the author's insights woven from these biographical threads
and reminiscences, creating a text that is full of interest and resonance for others.

Nitsun has succeeded in creating something entirely new, a new format for
applying group analysis and a new way of understanding paintings. No longer
separate pieces of art, the paintings are given a social and cultural context. Their
stories are both personal and universal. But the paintings are full of contrast. There
is beauty but also the uncanny: the embrace but also loneliness; colour and light
but also dark and suffering. This book will touch many readers and I recommend
it very highly and widely.'

Professor Elisabeth Rohr, *PhD.,*
Institute of Group Analysis, Heidelberg,
formerly Professor of Intercultural Education
at Phillips University, Marburg, Germany

'This is a fabulous book, a tour-de-force. Through the lens of his wonderful
paintings, Morris Nitsun takes us on his journey from South Africa to the UK and
from artist to therapist. He moves effortlessly from the consulting room to his
artist's studio and through a powerful narrative draws us, openly and intimately,
into his life. The book is rich in psychological theory, deeply personal reflections
and artistic prowess. It is unique. As with his previous books, this will become a
classic.'

Professor Dame Clare Gerada,
President of the Royal College of General Practitioners,
Director of Practitioner Health Service, UK

'Morris Nitsun's latest book takes us on a personal journey that chronicles the
author's unique ability to nurture a symbiotic relationship between psychotherapy
and painting during Covid times. The extraordinary artworks that evolved from
this meeting of cultures offer the reader a vivid insight into a wider life of both
struggle and fulfilment.'

Tim Benson, *President,*
Royal Institute of Oil Painters, fine artist and tutor, UK

'Nitsun has exceptional powers of depiction in his art, in his therapeutic and self-
narrative and in his exploration of the mysterious spaces in between. The result is
an absolutely extraordinary book that speaks with deep compassion to distress and

pain and celebrates the spirit liberated by creativity and imagination but brings fresh psychoanalytic understanding to the creative essence of therapy. A profound and wonderful achievement.'

Professor Peter Fonagy, *OBE, Chief Executive,*
Anna Freud National Centre; Professor of
Contemporary Psychoanalysis and Developmental Science, UCL, UK

'*A Psychotherapist Paints* is a visual and conceptual presentation of stunning beauty. Being the artist that he is, Nitsun beckons the reader to join a compelling journey of personal and social discovery, weaving together strands of autobiography, analytic acumen and pure talent. This highly original book is not only a major contribution to psychotherapy: it illuminates the world of the arts and suggests exciting possibilities for cross-fertilization.'

Richard M Billow, *Clinical Professor and*
former Director of the Group Program at Adelphi University,
USA and author of Richard M Billow's Selected Papers
on Psychoanalysis and Group Process (2021)

'Congratulations on a wonderful book. Morris Nitsun gives his readers a rare gift: the reproduction of fifty of his paintings (the paintings themselves are worth the price of the book), as well as a deep appreciation of the obstacles, inner and outer, he had to overcome to achieve the artistic freedom and devotion to truth that are so evident in this book. In his evocative presentations of his paintings, he touches on poignant themes: childhood identity, loss and trauma, oppression and shame, and more. Offering a vivid portrait of himself as a psychotherapist and artist, he does not flinch from sharing the pain of self-doubt and the problems of ageing and loneliness. He writes with courage and clarity. Painting and writing through the pandemic years, his capacity to integrate beauty with the dark side, to face fear, to find hope in despair, and to remain resolutely creative throughout, shines through this book and offers inspiration to many others.'

Jerome S. Gans, *MD, Distinguished Fellow,*
American Group Psychotherapy Association,
Distinguished Fellow, American Psychiatric Association.
Former Associate Professor of Psychiatry, Harvard Medical School, USA.
Author of Addressing, Challenging Moments in Psychotherapy

'In this unique and compelling book, Morris Nitsun treats us to a beautiful portrait of the mind of both the artist and the psychologist. An esteemed group analyst and a talented painter, Nitsun reveals the rich complexities of the human mind in a generous fashion, helping us to appreciate even more fully the ways in which each of us – whether clinicians or patients – can aspire to lead richer and more integrated lives.'

Professor Brett Kahr, *Senior Fellow,*
Tavistock Institute of Medical Psychology, and
Honorary Director of Research, Freud Museum, London, UK

'This is a unique book. Weaving together twin passions – painting and psychotherapy – Nitsun's vivid artwork and lucid writing invite the reader, like a late-comer to his online exhibitions, to be both witness and participant in the "artist's matrix". Through this matrix we comprehend what is both an artistic and psychological journey; a journey where "The Deserted City" (a "dark" exhibition prompted by Covid's lockdown) is gradually re-animated: with nature's bounty and resilience, with dancers, with the spirit of a woman's courage, with the search for transcendence: all testaments to what Winnicott calls "creative living". Movingly, this journey emerges as rooted in Morris Nitsun's relationship with his own mother, a "place" of absence as well as love. Inspiringly, the journey of art and reflection demonstrates the profound and purposeful engagement we must all make, especially in later years, if we are to choose integrity over despair.'

Professor Nick Barwick, *Group Analyst and*
Head of Student Counselling, Guildhall School of Music & Drama

'A magnificent book, inspiring and moving. It is not just to be read: it is to be experienced. Through the paintings and the commentary, the author stimulates the senses. You are entranced by the dolls, shudder at the sight of the deserted cities, smell the earth in fragile nature, and dance with the dancers. As in art therapy, Nitsun creates a safe but transformational space in which readers can project themselves, find a mirror in the images and find themselves in the process. The language is intimate and lyrical. It prompted an unforgettable personal journey. In line with his own concept, the author illustrates how art can deepen "the group as an object of desire". A must read!!'

Marcia Honig, *PsyD, group analyst, art therapist,*
Chair of the master's degree in Art Therapy at
Seminar HaKibutzim College, Chair of the
Transcultural Section of the International
Group Psychotherapy Association, International group facilitator

'In this unique combination of social experiment and personal history, Morris Nitsun takes the reader on a journey, traversing the territory between art, art therapy and group psychotherapy. Personal biography is woven with the author's paintings to form a rich tapestry. Nitsun combines his deep knowledge of group analysis and a lifetime of making art to create an innovative approach to working with groups. At conferences, exhibitions and online during Covid lockdown, he offered his paintings as catalysts, courageously exposing his process to the gaze and associations of audience members. Self-analysis, art and group process combine in this engaging personal memoir A compelling read for art psychotherapists and analysts and all who are interested in the links between art and psychotherapy.'

Professor Joy Schaverien, *PhD, Jungian analyst,*
art psychotherapist and author of Boarding School Syndrome:
The Psychological Trauma of the 'Privileged' Child and The Revealing
Image: Analytical Art Psychotherapy in Theory and Practice

'This is the story of a man who wanted to be an artist and a psychotherapist, and this book is his answer to the question 'Can you be both?' Morris Nitsun is that man; someone who has excelled as both an artist and a group analyst. In this book, Nitsun uses his paintings, and accounts of how groups of people have responded to those paintings, to explore how art and psychotherapy can bring something into being that wasn't there before. Both art and psychotherapy give us a frame in which we can think new thoughts and maybe change our minds in so doing. This process of change is not always comfortable or easy, and Nitsun never avoids that challenge, whether in his work on the Anti-Group, the disturbing image, or the associated painful thought. This is a rich and complex work, wonderfully illustrated with Nitsun's work; and that alone makes this book an essential purchase.'

Gwen Adshead, *consultant forensic psychiatrist and psychotherapist Broadmoor Hospital and HMP Bronzefield; co-author with Eileen Horne, The Devil You Know*

'This book is truly exceptional in every sense. It is the remarkable distillation of the wealth of insights from a long and illustrious career of a psychotherapist and artist. Dr Nitsun's highly accomplished paintings interweave with his therapeutic sensitivity to construct, in respectfully understated tones, a most moving tapestry of the human condition that will touch deeply not only therapists and artists but also all those who can open their heart to the wondrous complexities of suffering and fortitude. The masterful interplay between his visual images and perceptive narrative, his personal journey, group experiences and wider collective, usher the reader into painful and exhilarating caverns of the psyche.'

Professor Renos K Papadopoulos, *PhD, University of Essex. Clinical psychologist, Jungian psychoanalyst, family therapist and author of 'Involuntary Dislocation. Home, Trauma, Resilience and Adversity-Activated Development'*

'This is a very special and creative book. Whereas art and psychotherapy both release unconscious imagery, Morris Nitsun integrates these two processes in his highly original book. He creates a transitional space, which he calls 'the artist's matrix', into which the reader is invited to share his paintings and reflections. Joining this matrix, I became captivated by the images, words and ideas. The way Nitsun merges his two callings, as a well-known group analyst and an experienced artist, into one narrative is powerful and evocative. Therapists, artists and anyone who is open to new learning and experience, will be fascinated by this book.'

Haim Weinberg, *PhD, psychologist and group analyst, past President of the North California Society of Group Psychotherapy and the Israeli Association of Group Psychotherapy. Author and co-editor of several volumes on the social unconscious and the spread of online groups*

'I enjoyed reading this book immensely! In his highly engaging and deeply evocative text, Morris Nitsun eloquently integrates the powerful and reciprocal dimensions of his life: art, identity, creativity, psychotherapy and human relationships – all illuminated within the matrix of group analysis. Replete with his original and beautiful paintings, Nitsun's narrative demonstrates the rich and transformative unfolding of personal development, shaped both by adversity and by opportunity.'

Molyn Leszcz, *MD, FRCPC, CGP, DFAGPA, Professor,*
University of Toronto Department of Psychiatry; Past President,
The American Group Psychotherapy Association

'There is so much in Morris Nitsun's new book that is valuable, moving, and inspiring. Reading about his creative and emotional journey and seeing the rich and varied examples of his powerful, symbolic and beautifully executed paintings, is emotionally stirring. I was gripped as it all unfolded. It is an intellectually nourishing read, bringing together rich and deep experience across psychology and the arts. And all this in the context of worrying world events, particularly the pandemic and climate change. The pandemic is an important background to the book and part of Nitsun's achievement is the wave of creativity it unleashed in him. He illustrates on many levels how in leaning into the shadows, in the free associations of 'the artist's matrix', and in the mourning of loss, we can find light. His book will be a lasting reminder of the benefits of online groups, using art as a creative medium to reflect and connect at a time of threat and isolation. The wide audience this book will reach is too long to list, but it certainly will be of great interest to art psychotherapists. It is exciting to think how this approach could develop in the future. This is a book for now and for the future.'

Sophie Fletcher, *art therapist and psychotherapist,*
in the NHS and private practice, trainer, workshop conductor and lecturer

'Nitsun's latest book *A Psychotherapist Paints* is a courageous and personal account that weaves together the world of an accomplished artist, psychotherapist and group analyst. His concept of the "Artist's Matrix" is an important new contribution, inviting an intersubjective dance between the maker and viewer in a way that is original and unprecedented. Nitsun's visual research journey taps into and recognises the rich potential of the image in the group analytic discourse. Challenging the usual privileging of words over images, he deconstructs hierarchies of practice, offering a rich and expansive resource for all psychotherapists, particularly those in the arts psychotherapies. At a time of such global fragmentation, his creative group matrix, whether online or in person, opens up the potential for renewal, belonging and connection.'

Hayley Berman, *PhD, senior lecturer in art therapy at the*
University of Hertfordshire, visiting professor at the
University of Witwatersrand, and founding director of Lefika La Phodiso,
a psychoanalytically informed art therapy training in South Africa

'I am amazed by the beauty and wisdom of this book. Morris Nitsun has written a compelling work, a testimony to the depths of the creative spirit. The book is richly laden with Nitsun's clinical experience and his stunning, breath-taking paintings. It emphasises how his life journey as a psychotherapist helps to understand the painter in him, and vice versa. Processes that go into making art can shed light on psychotherapy. Nitsun uses his deep knowledge and clinical sensitivity as a group analyst in order to enrich his – and our – insight. The clinician and the artist come together in his exploration of what he calls "the artist's matrix". He highlights dimensions of the creative mind that add to our appreciation, no less, of being alive. The clarity of Nitsun's writing and our delight in the connections between his paintings and his personal and professional odyssey make this an extraordinary book: a sophisticated gift to clinicians at all levels, artists and everybody who reads it.'

Gila Ofer, *PhD, psychologist, psychoanalyst and group analyst.*
Co-founder and past President of Tel-Aviv Institute of
Contemporary Psychoanalysis, founding member of the
Israeli Institute of Group Analysis. Editor of 'A Bridge over Troubled Water:
Conflict and Reconciliation in Groups and Society' (2017)

'In his new book, Morris Nitsun takes us on a journey of discovery in territory that ranges from interpersonal, intra-psychic and artistic regions of the author's life. Nitsun delineates the route of discovery as a fine artist alongside his development as an exquisitely attuned group leader. This is a tale that weaves Nitsun's development of a projective group technique that employs his paintings as the stimulus for group dialogue. Nitsun's work as a psychologist, painter and group conductor organically comes together in a vivid presentation of paintings and rich description of group members emotional responses to the work. This is pioneering work presented in prose and paintings rendered by the artist/analyst. I highly recommend it!'

Elliot Zeisel, *PhD, Distinguished Fellow of the*
American Group Psychotherapy Association,
Founder and Faculty Center for Group Studies, Psychoanalyst,
Executive Producer of GROUP – The TV Series

'Through his latest paintings, memoir and group imagination – a highly original form of travel – Morris Nitsun takes us on a fascinating journey through art and psychotherapy. From the despair and frozen states of the pandemic, he initiates a shift for himself and for us all. Touching on loss, the losses of past and present, of personal and transpersonal, the shift awakens the heart of our being. We take a leap of faith into the freedom of discovery and rediscovery. Through the matrices of art, performance and group dialogue, we discover the possibility of transformation. As if in the dance of the group he describes, we encounter a new joy, a deeper meaning and integrity of being. The book itself becomes a significant transformational object, embracing the infinite, the uncertain, and the wonder of the human condition.'

Marina Mojović, *psychiatrist, psychoanalytic psychotherapist, training group analyst in Belgrade, founder of the International Reflective Citizens Koinonia*

'It is a great pleasure to read this book, it is written with such wisdom, humanity and clarity. It is absorbing to read and has helped me understand the influences of Morris's life on his work. He has a gift for communicating personally and universally, which gives us, his readers, permission to allow honesty and purity in the expression of our own life stories.

I attended one of Morris's online presentations and loved his work. This led to an ongoing creative collaboration between Morris, his paintings and my cross-art dance/theatre group, SpiralArts. We have had two exploratory sessions inspired by The Dancers, Deserted City and Fragile Nature. The images in the paintings are evocative and triggered an outpouring of spontaneous improvisation in dance, music and voice. Inanimate, timeless paintings became the trigger for living expression, seeming to create an extra dimension through mutual creative communication.

This book illuminates the creative resonance and underlying connections between art forms that can cross boundaries and create a new dimension for the expression of life experience in the present time.'

Bryony Williams, *FHEA, Dance/movement teacher, choreographer and co-founder and director of SpiralArts Dance Theatre Company*

A Psychotherapist Paints

A Psychotherapist Paints is a unique account of an internationally known psychotherapist and group analyst's struggle to bring together his psychological experience and his interests and talent as an artist.

This book describes a body of painting that was responsive to a major existential challenge, the COVID-19 pandemic, but which also comes from deeply personal experience; the paintings are a mirror of life through the decades. These paintings, fifty of which are included here in full colour, were mainly presented online to groups both small and large, who were invited to participate in a dialogue that became a vital part of the developing project. The value of this dialogue is reflected in the author's concept of the "artist's matrix", describing the social context in which an artist produces and presents their work. The paintings, together with the autobiographical narrative and the groups' generativity, combine to produce a moving testament to our times.

Intrinsic to *A Psychotherapist Paints* is a question about what makes us creative and how creativity transforms our lives. The result is a work of both artistic and psychological power that will inspire psychotherapists, art psychotherapists and artists themselves, and will point to exciting new possibilities in all these fields.

Morris Nitsun is a consultant psychologist, psychotherapist and group analyst. He is the author of the books *The Anti-Group* (Routledge, 2014) and *The Group as an Object of Desire* (Routledge, 2006), which have been described as classics in the field. In 2015, he was awarded the President of the Royal College of Psychiatrists medal for services to mental health. He is a practising artist who has regularly exhibited in London, and his paintings are in collections across the world.

The New International Library of Group Analysis (NILGA)
Series Editor: Earl Hopper

Drawing on the seminal ideas of British, European and American group analysts, psychoanalysts, social psychologists and social scientists, the books in this series focus on the study of small and large groups, organisations and other social systems, and on the study of the transpersonal and transgenerational sociality of human nature. NILGA books will be required reading for the members of professional organisations in the field of group analysis, psychoanalysis, and related social sciences. They will be indispensable for the "formation" of students of psychotherapy, whether they are mainly interested in clinical work with patients or in consultancy to teams and organisational clients within the private and public sectors.

Recent titles in the series include:

Psycho-social Explorations of Trauma, Exclusion and Violence
Un-housed Minds and Inhospitable Environments
Christopher Scanlon and John Adlam

Sibling Relations and the Horizontal Axis in Theory and Practice
Contemporary Group Analysis, Psychoanalysis and Organization Consultancy
Edited by Smadar Ashuach and Avi Berman

From Crowd Psychology to the Dynamics of Large Groups
Historical, Theoretical and Practical Considerations
Carla Penna

A Psychotherapist Paints
Insights from the Border of Art and Psychotherapy
Morris Nitsun

For more information about this series, please visit: www.routledge.com/
The-New-International-Library-of-Group-Analysis/book-series/KARNNILGA

A Psychotherapist Paints

Insights from the Border of Art and Psychotherapy

Morris Nitsun

Routledge
Taylor & Francis Group

LONDON AND NEW YORK

Cover image: *Bess as Bride*, Morris Nitsun, 2021 (page 139)

First published 2023
by Routledge
4 Park Square, Milton Park, Abingdon, Oxon OX14 4RN

and by Routledge
605 Third Avenue, New York, NY 10158

Routledge is an imprint of the Taylor & Francis Group, an informa business

British Library Cataloguing-in-Publication Data
A catalogue record for this book is available from the British Library

Library of Congress Cataloging-in-Publication Data
Names: Nitsun, Morris, author.
Title: A psychotherapist paints : insights from the border of art
    and psychotherapy / Morris Nitsun.
Description: Abingdon, Oxon : Routledge, 2023. | Includes
    bibliographical references and index.
Identifiers: LCCN 2022021179 (print) | LCCN 2022021180
    (ebook) | ISBN 9781032140773 (paperback) |
    ISBN 9781032140766 (hardback) |
    ISBN 9781003232230 (ebook)
Subjects: LCSH: Nitsun, Morris. | Psychoanalysts as artists. |
    COVID-19 (Disease) and the arts.
Classification: LCC ND1096.N58 A35 2023 (print) | LCC
    ND1096.N58 (ebook) | DDC 701/.15—dc23/eng/20220803
LC record available at https://lccn.loc.gov/2022021179
LC ebook record available at https://lccn.loc.gov/2022021180

ISBN: 978-1-032-14076-6 (hbk)
ISBN: 978-1-032-14077-3 (pbk)
ISBN: 978-1-003-23223-0 (ebk)

DOI: 10.4324/9781003232230

Typeset in Times New Roman
by Apex CoVantage, LLC

To my mother

Contents

PART 3
Reflection and review   165

Paintings

Foreword

Forewords, Prefaces, Prologues and even Introductions are bridges over chasms, obstacles and gulfs of one kind or another into a space of new information, new ideas, new possibilities and even new relationships. In the context of psychoanalysis and group analysis, bridges are often discussed in terms of developments from dyads into "relational thirds" (Benjamin 2004). I also think about these bridges in terms of the creative tension between theories of transference and beliefs in transcendence, the fulcrum between them being the willingness and ability to exercise the transcendent imagination (Hopper 2003). Mature hope is inherent in the notion of imaginative perception, which is rooted in both the Independent tradition of British psychoanalysis (Mitchell and Parsons 1993), and in the Foulkesian tradition of group analysis with which it is closely related.

Imagination is always subversive. It violates the epistemology of classical science. It involves a kind of destruction of those boundaries which inhibit and oppress in the context of those which facilitate and construct. However, creativity is always located in the space between these two realms of experience. The paradox of creativity involves the continuing destruction of the material instruments of it and changes in the relations between the artist and his audience and, in turn, their relations to each other.

This impressive new book by Morris Nitsun, who is a senior group analyst and a well-known author and painter, can be located within this subversive – if not rebellious – tradition. I hardly care whether his book is by a painter about the psychoanalytical and group analytical experience or a book by a psychoanalytically oriented psychotherapist and group analyst about the world in which he lives, sees, interprets and paints. His book is "really" about the transformation of personal experience of the world into a reflection of it, which can, in turn, become part of the experience of others. Morris empowers his patients to see him and use him as they wish and need.

During this time of Covid, many analysts have focused on the unconscious connections between the "China Virus" and social violence (Hopper 2022). These responses to the existential threats of social trauma and the fear of annihilation bring to mind a variety of "plague literature", ranging from *Death in Venice* to *The Plague*, to *Nemesis*, which is suggestive of the experiences of such diverse writers as Mann (1912), Camus (1947) and Roth (2010), and the cultures of 20th century Europe and the United States. Nitsun's paintings are rooted in his experience of the current twenty-first-century pandemics, and much of the narrative is influenced by the alternation of despair and hope that has pervaded this momentous period of time.

As an ex–South African growing up in the apartheid years, Nitsun has also evoked the society and cultures of colonial South Africa, with its burdens of social Darwinism and British eugenics (Busetto In Press). The exploitation of indigenous peoples and their lands, involving not only horror and cruelty but also passion and colour, was punctuated by waves of immigrants from India and Europe in search of economic and political freedom. Inevitably, attempts to master this environment and to build a brave new world were based on the values and technologies of the old. The "Great Mother" (Neumann 1955) was both so near and yet so far, and the brutality of male power was omnipresent. In the absence of a father who rescues, it is rarely clear if one should seek to rescue or to be rescued.

It is hardly surprising that in this context, Nitsun searches for the feminine and the female, which do not always reside in the mind and body of one's personal mother, but must often be discovered and co-created through and with others. This is explored in both a painful and a liberating way in his series of doll paintings. However, he also elucidates the dynamics of gender fluidity in the figurations and configurations of the dance, shifting the singular object of the doll into the interpersonal subject of the dancer and sometimes into the dancer and his/her partner. It is not generally known that Norbert Elias, one of the fathers of the theory of Group Analysis, was preoccupied with the history of dance, in both its courtly and its popular forms, and in particular with the combined themes of gender and power within figurations of movement with others.

These paintings might be compared and contrasted to that of Kurt Schwitters, who was one of the founders of experiential art, and whose collages demanded that the audience assume an active role in the signification of them. In the context of abundance in juxtaposition to extreme inequality within industrial Europe, *object trouvé* had a particular meaning. Nitsun's painting and writing are also a creative response to the conditions by which he was constrained and restrained. Yet, in the exploration of the vitality of decay, he has not limited himself to exotic flowers of South Africa. In his wanderings of Covid-stricken London, he has not lost himself in the canyons of concrete and asphalt. He has taken the risks demanded by the portrayal of the human form, not only alone but also with an "other".

I am reminded of the very English book *On not Being Able to Paint*, in which Marion Milner (1950) shares the vicissitudes of her creative processes. Several other analysts have shared their transference processes to the subject matter of their work and to the work itself, for example, the Jungian analytical psychologist Joy Schaverien (2003). I am also reminded of Ferenczi's early ideas concerning "mutual analysis" (Falzeder and Brabant 2000). Ferenczi's efforts ran aground in the context of core Freudian ideas of abstinence and pathological countertransference within an increasingly institutionalised psychoanalysis. Of course, psychoanalysis has changed since Ferenczi began to work in this way, partly as a result of his innovations and attempts to realise them.

I (Hopper 2003) tried to do something of this kind in "Wounded Bird", in which I recounted my interpretation of the group's relations to a painting in the room in which our group was meeting. This painting was not only a "self-object", but also a "mediating object", similar to what Volkan (1981) called a "linking object", which can be a concretisation of a traumatic experience of loss and mourning that can be held and shared. We now realise that linking objects can be expressions of chosen glories as well as chosen traumas (Friedman 2019). The failed dependency of traumatic experience must be understood in terms of the social unconscious, and specifically in terms of what Kaës (2018) discussed in terms of the failures of unconscious pacts, alliances and guarantees within the "meta-social".

Nitsun's new book is a fascinating and courageous attempt to link the work and the objects of painting, psychotherapy and group association into one whole. The paintings are like Winnicottian transitional objects in that they must be both discovered and co-created, but in this project, they become "collective transitional objects", perhaps as displacements from the group and its conductor, which is almost certainly how the various founders of Group Analysis would have seen them. It is important for us to explore this development. Using the paintings and their stories within the clinical encounter allows the analyst to relate to his patients and his patients to relate to him in a mutually playful, transparent and new exploratory way. This also involves learning more about their socio-cultural-political worlds, allowing a consideration of how these worlds both intertwine and overlap.

Especially coming late in Nitsun's career, this painterly book is a very bold – if not radical – move. I feel privileged to be able to include such a book in the New International Library of Group Analysis (NILGA). Outside the confines of art therapy in dyads and in even in groups, Morris Nitsun is the first to introduce the use of the group analyst's own work into the clinical experience. All books in NILGA are intended to be of interest and stimulation to colleagues and students of Group Analysis and related disciplines. However, this book invites us to see our mutual reflections within the group mirror, to hear our thoughts about them, and to try to move beyond them.

Earl Hopper
Series Editor

References

Benjamin, J. (2004). Beyond doer and done to: An intersubjective view of thirdness. *Psychoanalytic Quarterly*, LXXIII.

Busetto, P. (In Press). Sex, custom and madness: A case study of a psychiatrist in the tripartite matrix of South-Africa. In Hopper, E., and Weinberg, H. (Eds.), *The Social Unconscious in Persons, Groups and Societies. Volume 4: Clinical Implications*. London: Routledge.

Camus, A. (1947). *The Plague (La Peste)*. Paris: Gallimard.

Falzeder, E., and Brabant, E. (Eds.). (2000). *The Correspondence of Sigmund Freud and Sandor Ferenczi*. Cambridge, MA: Harvard University Press.

Friedman, R. (2019). *Dreamtelling, Relations, and Large Groups: New Developments in Group Analysis*. London: Routledge.

Hopper, E. (2003). Wounded bird: A study of the Social unconscious and countertranference in group analysis. In *The Social Unconscious: Selected Papers*. London: Jessica Kingsley Publishers.

Hopper, E. (2022). From remorse to relational reparation: Mature hope, communication and community in our responses to social conflict and to the virus as a persecuting object. *Contexts*, Issue 95, March.

Kaës, R. (2018). *Linking, Alliances and Shared Space*. London: Taylor & Francis.

Mann, T. (1912). *Death in Venice*. Frankfurt: S Fischer Verlag.

Milner, M. (1950). *On Not Being Able to Paint*. London: Routledge.

Mitchell, J., and Parsons, M. (Eds.). (1993). *Before I Was I: Psychoanalysis and the Imagination by Enid Balint*. London: Free Association Books.

Neumann, E. (1955). *The Great Mother: An Analysis of the Archetype*. Princeton: Princeton Classics.

Roth, P. (2010). *Nemesis*. Boston: Houghton Mifflin Harcourt.

Schaverien, J. (2003). *Desire and the Female Therapist: Engendered Gazes in Psychotherapy and Art Therapy*. London: Routledge.

Volkan, V. D. (1981). *Linking Objects and Linking Phenomena: A Study of the Forms Symptoms Metapsychology and Therapy of Complicated Mourning*. New York: International Universities Press.

Preface and acknowledgements

In 2020, faced with the closure of galleries but keen to show my paintings, I embarked on a series of online exhibitions. What started as precisely that – an online vehicle for my art – transformed into a series of substantial events in which art, memoir and group dialogue came together unexpectedly, powerfully, revealingly.

This book is very different from anything I have written and published previously. Readers who know my writing may be expecting a further treatise on *The Anti-Group* (Nitsun 1996, 2015a) or *The Group as an Object of Desire* (Nitsun 2006), probably my two best-known publications. That I have written such a different book reflects a late life-stage, as well as the likely last years of a long career: reaching eighty years of age with almost sixty years of clinical practice under my belt and wanting to reconcile some of my abiding interests, notably in psychotherapy and art. Insofar as it is a book about groups, it reflects a movement away from the abstract constructs of theory and the complex link between theory and practice that I have spent decades trying to unravel and understand. Stepping back from my hybrid professional identity as a clinical psychologist, psychotherapist and group analyst, and with the perspective of long experience, I am struck by the density and intensity of theoretical debates that populate these fields, coupled with competition to advance the newest, best, most profound, most original contribution, as well as fuelling controversies about what is right and wrong in psychotherapy, even allowing for the fact that in such a complex field there is hardly a clear, unambiguous right or an absolute, incontrovertible wrong (apart from obvious misdemeanours in the consulting room). I recognise that I have been as much a part of this fray as anyone else – I have muscled in with the rest, staking my claim to originality and authenticity. I have no regrets. It has been a stimulating, enriching, if in some ways hazardous, journey and, in many ways, I feel privileged to have been a part of it. But it no longer captures my interest with the same freshness and conviction that it once did, and I am happy to move on to territory that more fully reflects who I am now and what I wish to express and share.

Having qualified my current interest in theory, particularly the anti-group, there are aspects of the concept that are an important part of my recent journey.

Having spent decades formulating the concept, reflecting, researching, writing and lecturing on it, I believe that I have emerged much freer in my approach to groups. In part, this may be a function of the greater ease and tolerance that comes with age, an increased capacity to be oneself, to play. However, I also think that by confronting my doubts and anxieties through the prism of the anti-group, by examining the link between myself, my personal group history, and the concept, I have found a more comfortable place in the universe of groups. Much of the personal examination was difficult, touching on my existence in groups since early childhood, but, as I have emphasized in my writing, recognition of these links, particularly in oneself, is vital in one's growth as a group analytic practitioner. I believe that by this working-through process – grappling with my own anti-group – I came much closer to the group as an object of desire, the group that is alive with energy, potential and creativity. I have maintained this throughout my writing: that my interest in the anti-group was not for the sake of indulging the destructive aspects of groups per se. It was/is to free the group from the sediment of the past and the grip of unconscious traces that obstruct the creativity of the group.

It is in this area of the group as an object of desire that my present project takes root. Of course, the main subject of the book is the forging of a creative link between my artistic and psychological initiatives, what this will mean for my continuing development as an artist and what implications it has for others working across similar borders. The prospect of making this connection is hugely meaningful, and the artistic side of me is at its core. But this is also very much a book about groups. I could not have made the leap of faith without my interest and engagement with groups. Every project I describe has an important group component insofar as groups were my consistent audience and source of feedback and stimulation. As such, I delve more than previously into the imaginative and creative potential of the group and see my project as a marriage of sorts between the sometimes egocentric world of the artist and the interpersonal world of groups.

A theme that traverses the fields of psychotherapy and art is that of human development, with the challenges of existence a key preoccupation. My interest in this theme weaves through the pages of this book. Loss figures prominently: the varieties of loss, ranging from the loss of a toy in childhood to the loss of youth and the ultimate loss of life through mortality; the small losses that are large in their poignancy and the profound losses that are almost too large to countenance. The threatened and actual loss augured by Covid intensified the spectre of loss. This book was written in the throes of lockdown and the waves of anxiety generated by the pandemic, the prospect of illness and death a looming presence. My absorption in painting was one of my ways of surviving, of using time, of drawing on my creative energy. What I learned in my journey through painting is that the loss can be faced, mourned and, further, transformed. Through my various visual themes, I found myself revisiting the past, my own historical and ancestral past, and the present moment continually, relentlessly, irrevocably, becoming past. Yet, increasingly, in the book, my perspective changes from one of dread and near despair to one of hope. Surviving loss is reassuring, and the promise of a future, however fragile and uncertain, is life's greatest gift.

The importance of painting, for me personally and for the project, must not be underestimated. The impetus for the present project came more directly from painting than anything else. The pandemic and ensuing lockdown not only released time to paint but added a new challenge and sudden urgency to my artistic initiative. I embarked on a series of paintings that were significantly different in mood and message from my previous work. That I was able to do so, gain the momentum, and produce a body of work was an essential part of what gave me hope. Psychotherapy, particularly group analysis, came in more as a consequence, advantageously, serendipitously, but as a development of the painting, particularly in my decision to open a dialogue about the work and, more particularly, to do so in a group context. Once this happened and more than confirmed its value, I initiated more dialogue, more groups, and keenly welcomed psychological and psychotherapeutic thinking. But painting was the mainspring, the fount of the journey, the start of the inquiry.

This book is unusual not because it concerns a psychotherapist who paints. It is unusual because it concerns a psychotherapist who *writes* about painting. To my knowledge, there are many psychotherapists who paint – to varying levels of proficiency or public recognition – and for some, as for me, it is an important if not essential part of their being. However, very few have ventured to write about the convergence. One exception is Marion Milner, whose book *On not being able to paint* (1950) is a classic treatise on a psychoanalyst's excursion into visual art. Much of the book describes Milner's struggles to realise her artistic vision, the blocks she experiences and the suggested unconscious factors that mitigate against a freer, more confident use of the painting medium. I mainly differentiate myself from these constraints insofar as I prefer to see myself as *able* to paint. I have my difficulties and disappointments, but I am productive and have had sufficient affirmation to support my belief that I can paint. My challenge, however, is similar to Milner's in bringing analytic exploration to bear on the artistic process and knowing how far to take this, drawing strongly, as I do, on group feedback as well as self-reflection. In any case, Milner's book, *On not being able to paint*, was written many decades ago, in the 1950's, and it is time to revisit this area of convergence, selfishly for my own edification, but also for the many psychotherapists who make art and may wish to communicate more openly and discursively about their work.

This has felt like a lot to accomplish in a single book: bringing together two major career interests; selecting and organizing the artwork; choosing fragments of my biography; integrating the psychological perspective; documenting and analysing the process and feedback of groups; and putting it all together in a coherent, readable package. There were very few precedents to follow, and it was necessary to create a framework that had some conceptual basis while eschewing too great an allegiance to academic proprieties. To some extent, I found what I was looking for in a qualitative research approach – the heuristic model of Moustakas

(1990) – that lies outside the conventional psychotherapeutic sphere, allowing me a greater freedom of movement and interpretation than I might have had with a more tightly structured research or clinical framework. As will be seen throughout the book, freedom of expression is the single most important criterion for me, not only in the book, but in the paintings and in the emergent sense of self that is the byproduct of the book.

Linked to the artwork, a further challenge was the representation of my paintings in the text. How could an essentially visual output, with a considerable artistic yield, be incorporated into a professional text within the framework of an academic publisher such as Routledge? This includes adequate reproduction of the paintings themselves since the text is meaningless without the corresponding images. Five series of paintings are at the centre of this book. Each must be illustrated, and the illustrations must be up to scratch. Here lies another challenge, adding to the already complex set of requirements to fully realise the book. Fortunately, Routledge was generous in its appreciation of this requirement, enabling the reproduction of fifty paintings. While not of the standard of fine art reproduction, the images are relatively clear, serve the text well and make this an unusual book that crosses the conventional boundaries of art and academia and hopefully will inspire similar ventures.

While struggling to find a framework for the book and resolve the dilemmas in its production and publication, I have been fortunate in having the consistent support and feedback of a solid network of friends and colleagues who have been engaged with the project and warmly supportive of me personally.

I want first of all to thank Earl Hopper, who, as editor of the Routledge New International Library of Group Analysis, was affirming and supportive from the beginning. He read an early draft of the chapters and responded immediately. He keenly grasped what I was trying to say, resonating with the themes and offering insights and advice. Since this book is so different from my usual group analytic interests and publications and was somewhat difficult to place in a publishing framework, his support has been invaluable.

Linked to Routledge is Susannah Frearson, senior editor, who, with a steady hand, steered the book through to production, not just providing guidelines but showing warmth, clarity and flexibility. She was very ably assisted by Jana Craddock, editorial assistant, who brought further sensitivity, support and coherence to the project.

I particularly want to thank a group of close friends, some of whom are also colleagues, who were with me on my journey from start to finish.

Marc Kingsley, a wonderful friend and psychologist of great acumen, was fully engaged with the project, responding with heartfelt admiration and support throughout. He introduced me to the heuristic approach, which strengthened and deepened the project. He gave unstinting time to reading and rereading drafts and responded with consistent appreciation and encouragement.

Bibi Brown, my wise and spiritual friend, offered surprising, novel and far-reaching suggestions that profoundly helped to shape the project, ranging from her passionate response to the early doll paintings to suggesting the first studio discussion in Hove, and to initiating my highly creative collaboration with the SpiralArts Dance Theatre Group. These were all her ideas. The dance improvisations have been an unexpected and exciting development, strengthened by Bibi's engagement and commitment.

On the subject of the dance, I also wish to thank Bryony Wiliams, the director of SpiralArts, who responded keenly to the idea of the paintings as a stimulus for dancing and gave me the opportunity to work with a sensitive and talented bunch of dancers, musicians and singers (and a circus performer).

My partner, Tony Fagin, was supportive and patient through the vicissitudes of the project. An outstanding editor, he went through the early drafts with a fine toothcomb, highlighting errors, large and small, and commenting strongly and constructively on style. An excellent cook and writer himself, he fed me in more ways than one.

Sue Einhorn deserves special mention for consistently reading the text and offering astute and challenging comments, especially on complex issues of identity and belonging.

Numerous people attended my online presentations. A good number contributed in specific ways that I wish to acknowledge, whether participating in the groups, supporting the initiative, reading and discussing drafts of the book, or staying friends through the ups and downs. Amongst these, many of them in different countries, I wish to thank Catherine Bercusson, Sheila Damon, Hana Danor, Judith Ganem, Clare Gerada, Bracha Hadar, Marcia Honig, Ronnie Levine, Irene Newton, Michael Nolan, Wil Pennycook, John Schlapobersky, Phil Schulte, Maureen Ryan, Mookie and Roget Tabakin, Liat Warhaftig-Aran and Leah Zinder.

Special thanks to the Hassocks Honeys – Lou Beckerman, Reina James and Mike Reinstein – for love and support.

In Chapter 3 of the book, I develop the idea of the artist's matrix: the social context in which artists work. All those mentioned here constituted "my artists' matrix" in the last two or three years and, without them, the project and this book would not have happened. I was fortunate indeed to have had such a rich matrix.

Introduction

This book represents a radical departure from my previous work, interests and writing as a group analyst. While holding true to the spirit of group analysis in its regard for the value of group communication, the book describes a much more experimental journey than any I had previously undertaken. As a practising artist over several decades, I had largely kept my artistic interests separate from my group analytic and psychotherapeutic interests, inhabiting two rather different worlds with different incentives and rewards and different patterns of interpersonal communication. In 2019, on the occasion of a large exhibition of my recent paintings, these worlds unexpectedly began to come together, significantly through the insights of a group invited to discuss the exhibition. This set in motion a series of events, starting in real space and transferring online, in which I presented my paintings to groups of different sizes with the aim of facilitating a discourse that would stimulate awareness and further inquiry. In part, I presented my paintings as a form of visual memoir, touching on key aspects of my personal development that were reflected symbolically in the painted images. These events were richly rewarding, prompting me to pursue the approach with several different series of paintings and different groupings of people, each focusing on a theme of some existential significance.

This spirit of inquiry, actively pursued in all these events, is one of the distinguishing features of the approach. The bringing together of three distinctly different modalities – painting, memoir and group exploration – was novel, untried and risky. Each event required a vision of how to present the paintings, how to structure the event and how to anticipate what might unfold. Each posed a challenge in terms of the complexity of the task and the unpredictability of the outcome. How would it work? What impact would the exhibition have, particularly in an online form? Beyond the bedding in of a new approach, establishing the nuts and bolts, and seeing how they worked, a deeper process of inquiry became evident. In part, this was my own inquiry, one that felt intense and compelling, demanding what meaning my paintings have in the current world, what they say about me as an artist in later life, and how this new format would clarify these concerns. Further, what would the event mean to others and what mutual learning might be gained in the process? It was this emerging sense of inquiry, the hopes and doubts in my own

DOI: 10.4324/9781003232230-1

mind about the venture, the questions recurring from one presentation to another, and the accumulating and illuminating feedback from the groups that was perhaps the most powerful and fruitful aspect of the events.

Part of the difficulty of writing about this experience is how to give it a conceptual frame. Although a descriptive account might be adequate, I found myself reaching for a framework of some sort to provide a container, to make the venture communicable to others. The link between myself and others has always been vital in my thinking, and, in writing a book, the communicative link becomes all the more relevant. Looking at different frames of reference, I began to realise that I myself was the starting point. Here was I risking a very different venture from anything I had attempted before, finally bringing together two major aspects of my life, keen to create some form of integration and fuelled by a drive to forge something new. I was also seeking the participation of others in a process of inquiry that would hopefully help me to understand and further my quest while giving my audience something of value, of meaning, in the struggle we all share to know ourselves and our world.

It became apparent that I would need to find a frame of reference outside the usual psychotherapy or group analytic discourses. Conventional psychotherapeutic frames, either theoretical or research, were restrictive. They did not fit the more idiosyncratic nature of my project. Increasingly, I became aware of the *heuristic* nature of my inquiry: heuristic in the sense of starting an inquiry spontaneously based on a current initiative that merits study and that, if pursued on its own terms, might open new doors of awareness and initiative. This approach, which I consider under-utilised in psychotherapeutic research, is to a large extent associated with the heuristic model formulated by Moustakas (1990) and refined by Sela-Smith (2002). Moustakas (1990) broadly describes heuristic inquiry as a "phenomenological research method that focuses on investigating human experience". He emphasizes that, throughout the inquiry, the inquirer and participants must stay as close as possible to the phenomena they have experienced and that, in recounting their stories, they deepen their understanding and insights into the phenomena. The heuristic process is based on autobiographical experience, the research question or point of inquiry ideally being of profound personal significance to the researcher who remains integrally involved in the continuing process. The data originates with the researcher, and through dialogue with others, a story can be created that reflects the qualities, meanings and essences of universally shared experiences and concerns. Moustakas encourages "self-dialogue", particularly at the beginning of the study, a form of introspective inquiry and self-discovery that provides the initial guiding steps. The self-dialogue is intended to unearth implicit or tacit dimensions of experience that can be made explicit to others. Implicit knowledge made explicit is germane to the development of a coherent overall narrative.

The heuristic method, as described earlier, is similar to the process of psychotherapeutic inquiry. That too begins with the experience of an inquirer, possibly both therapist and patient in their respective roles, with the aim of developing a meaningful life narrative. The difference is the research orientation of the heuristic inquiry, aimed not so much at helping with problems but the discovery of themes that are both unique and universal. Knowing relatively little about heuristic inquiry, I was impressed when introduced to it more fully by my friend and colleague, Marc Kingsley (2021). What excited me immediately was the idea that the passionate concern of the inquirer was not just a legitimate focus of research inquiry but the core, indispensable component of the inquiry. This not only resonated with me: it also made me aware of how powerful my engagement with my developing approach was and how much significance it had acquired at this stage of my life. The unexpected convergence of my life-long interests in art and psychology had captured my imagination, not just as the ground for creativity but the acquisition of a new sense of purpose and direction in my coming years. I was preoccupied with the project, but rather than seeing my preoccupation as excessive, intrusive, or even neurotic, I could now see it as generative, conducive to further development and further inquiry, and of benefit not just to myself but to others.

Moustakas describes several stages in the development of the inquiry. The initial stage, as described above, is the identification of the main research topic or question. This is followed by a period of immersion in the question, phenomenon or subject, requiring the inquirer to be as fully engaged as possible with the phenomenon, to the extent of it "being lived in both waking and sleeping states" (Sela-Smith 2002). In the next phase, the researcher gathers this knowledge, insight or awareness, organizing the information into themes. These are then shared with the other participants or researchers, often in the form of a narrative depiction, inviting responses, affirmative or otherwise, from participants. Finally, there is a period of creative synthesis that can take a variety of forms: a story, artwork, prose or a poem. Above all, Moustakas encourages the inquirer to be fully present and open throughout a time-consuming period of sustained immersion and focused concentration on a central question, "to risk the opening of wounds and passionate concerns and to undergo the personal transformation that exists as a possibility in every heuristic journey" (Moustakas 1990, p. 14).

The idea of stages in the above outline is not meant to be rigid but to suggest processes that can be flexibly employed in the implementation of the inquiry. In fact, the description, barring some sequential differences, is the process I was already intuitively pursuing in the genesis and evolution of my approach. The main difference is that I used my paintings at the start of the group presentations as part of the process of inquiry rather than at the end of the research as a form of creative synthesis. The paintings, and their present and past origins, are the main substance of both the inquiry and the immersion in that inquiry. The days, weeks and months of painting, which happened mainly during lockdown, were a very full immersion. The creative synthesis in my inquiry is this book. The book aims to bring together the journey I undertook via painting, memoir and group inquiry and to forge an overall understanding of this new venture. This synthesis also suggests a further inquiry: whether the method I followed, combining the separate modalities, has the potential for further such projects across psychology and the arts.

A further, and crucial, context was the pandemic of the years 2020–2022 and still a worrying phenomenon at present. Although I had started the series of paintings in 2018 and had my first group presentation in 2019, the preponderance of the work and the online presentations were in the Covid years, triggering an intense impulse in me to create, to use the extra time during lockdown to grapple with unresolved aspects of my development, to actively address the tension between my identity as a psychotherapist and an artist. The pandemic faced us all with challenging questions about the world we lived in, what sense we made of our existence and how we would deal with a radically altered post-Covid environment. Caught up in the waves of anxiety generated by the pandemic, I wanted both to catch up with who I was and to anticipate who I might be in a fast-changing and tumultuous world.

Readers who know my publications in group analysis may be wondering where my previous writing fits in, in particular the concepts with which I tend to be associated: *The Anti-Group* (Nitsun 1991, 1996, 2015a), *The Organizational Mirror* (Nitsun 1998) and *The Group as an Object of Desire* (Nitsun 2006). The anti-group, while not the focus of this book, exists in the shadows of all that I am exploring. The concept sets out the negative, potentially – and sometimes actually – destructive forces in groups. It highlights typically group antagonistic processes: doubt, mistrust in the group, attacks on the group, retreat from the group. It is relevant to group psychotherapy since it challenges and potentially undermines the forward, therapeutic thrust of the group. It is also applicable more widely to social groups, family and organizational groups, and political processes. The afore-mentioned pandemic, for example, can be seen, hypothetically, as an anti-group force, attacking not just individuals through disease and death but laying waste to communities at many levels of organised society. Climate change, similarly, whatever its ecology, can be understood in anti-group terms, wreaking chaos and devastation on the environment, both the physical and social environment. Further, both the pandemic and climate change can be seen as *symptoms* of an underlying, self-destructive social tendency, reflected in rampant individualism, excessive consumerism and waste, amongst other disintegratory forces. Although the concept of the anti-group has a negative connotation, it also suggests the awakening of creative processes through recognition of our contribution to social destruction, through taking responsibility, and through reparation. The dark light of the anti-group potentially yields to the light of awareness, of gratitude, of wonder. It is this more optimistic spirit which inspired my concept of the group as an object of desire: the group that is passionate, forward-looking, hopeful. While not exploring either concept in detail in this book, the dialectic of creative and destructive, of dark and light, weaves through much of the material in the forthcoming pages.

The three main sections of this book broadly follow the stages of the inquiry.

PART 1 establishes the frame. It identifies the convergence of my artistic and psychological interests as the predominant line of creative inquiry: an ambitious, hopeful undertaking, highlighting the struggle I had in previous years to be myself. It raises the question of what value to myself and others this development heralds and how it might influence the rest of my working life.

Chapter 1, "Can I be both?" describes the biographical background to the project: the intense, almost lifelong struggle I had balancing my dual interests and the tendency for art to drift to the margins, with psychology as the dominant force. My upbringing in South Africa in a traumatized Jewish family in the throes of apartheid goes some way to explaining this: the constraints on finding myself, my confusion about sexual orientation, and my shielding behind a safe, conventional choice. However, my perseverance as an artist paid off, following me to London, where I actively pursued painting as a calling. Gradually, my two interests became friends, not foes. Starting a radically new series of paintings pre-Covid in 2019, paintings with much more conscious psychological intention than in my previous work, the process intensified during lockdown, yielding a considerable body of work that spanned the worlds I have travelled. A momentum builds up.

Chapter 2, "Early stages", delves more fully into the new series of paintings and the decision, in the face of art galleries closing due to lockdown, to show my work online. This soon becomes more than an online exhibition: content not just to show paintings, one of thousands of artists grasping the newly emerging online opportunities, I wanted to share the accumulating significance of this work in my life, including my personal back-story and the symbolization of psychological preoccupations through art. I have resources that might help to facilitate the process. An experienced group analyst, having run groups of different sorts over the years, I am comfortable facilitating groups of people. As a lecturer, I have experience in talking to many audiences, including self-presentation as a key component. I had the wherewithal, it seemed, to make something meaningful of the opportunity. But uncertainties abound: will it work; am I exposing myself too much; will people be engaged, stimulated, moved? Will the integrated approach impress, or will it fall flat on its face?

Chapter 3, "The artist's matrix", steps slightly to one side to explore the importance to the artist of an audience and the different ways this can be achieved. It includes the notion of the visual field as more than a simple act of perception, of looking at a painting. It involves the artist and the viewers in a dialogue, whether in reality or symbolically, in which a psychological space is created where questions of symbolic meaning are debated. I suggest that for many artists, this communicative field is missing, that they work in a vacuum and that neither they nor the public are able to benefit from a process of mutual communication. This touches on issues of "the transitional space", the way art operates between object and other, symbol and reality, self and environment (Winnicott 1953). I suggest that in the approach I developed, the process came much closer to this form of dialogue than I have previously known. This was also my way of drawing others into the heuristic inquiry, progressing the project through a further stage of engagement and feedback. The outcome was a sense of co-creation.

PART 2 of the book is a detailed description of each of the five painting series, providing a personal and social background to the work. Since these descriptions are repeated in several parts of the book and largely depend on the reproductions of the paintings to bring them to life, I offer here a summary of each presentation.

Chapter 4– "Dolls and demons". Images of vintage dolls inspired a series of paintings in which the dolls are personified with a name and a suggested character but with sufficient ambiguity to elicit a wide range of perceptions of the figures and interpretations of their individual stories. The link to childhood was key, both through the similarity of the dolls to children and the relationship of children to their playthings, especially dolls. Gender differences were highlighted in the group discussions, but even more powerful was the recall of childhood experience against the background of cultural history in which loss and trauma are resonant themes. My sharing of my own family history appeared to stimulate others' recall, which in turn deepened my own awareness of links with the past, creating considerable synergy in the group discussions.

Chapter 5– "The deserted city". This series of paintings was a response to the exponential spread of the pandemic in the first half of 2020. The paintings depict the emptying out of European towns and cities in the wake of the pandemic, the deserted streets and embattled buildings serving as a metaphor for the erosion of human life and social connectedness. The most dysphoric of my presentations, coming at the height of the pandemic, it impacted strongly on the groups attending the online presentations. The themes that emerged included a sense of the overall environment, the natural world and the human world, being under threat. Linked to that was a theme about home, the importance of people's homes during the pandemic, as refuge and container. But the corollary was a sense of imprisonment: the claustrophobic experience of being confined, isolated, forced to retreat.

Chapter 6– "Fragile nature". Striking a different note, the paintings in this series were a celebration of the woods in the area in which I live in north London, but more than that, a paean of praise for the natural world. In line with many others, I experienced a more profound contact with nature during the pandemic than ever before. The lasting beauty and solace provided by nature were contrasted with its fragility, its cycle of birth and death, its vulnerability to changing conditions, its struggle within its own ecology. This was presented as a parallel to human life and our vulnerability at the time of a raging pandemic, yet with the hope of survival and human resilience.

Chapter 7, "Dancers". Departing even more from the bleakness of lockdown, this series depicted dancers in an explosion of energy and expression. They included both female and male dancers and focused on two main forms of dancing, ballet and Spanish dancing. Although portraying the exuberance of dance, the paintings also touched on the painful aspects of dancing: the immensely hard work, the exhaustion, the competition in a tough, demanding milieu. This series was accompanied by a strong personal narrative concerning my childhood wish to be a dancer and the relinquishing of my hopes in a context of oppression and conformity. The series highlighted the body as a site of self-and-other experience, the struggle to live comfortably and pleasurably in one's body – and with other bodies.

Chapter 8, "Four women". This was the most different, thematically and in execution, of the five series: an exploration in the painting of four women's quest for identity. Originating in a very personal way with my own mother and her difficulty in establishing a sense of herself beyond her domestic role, to some extent even within her domestic role, it contrasts her with three well-known women who, in very different ways, achieved a powerful sense of identity: Rosa Parks, the early black civil rights activist, Mother Teresa, the nun who was canonized, and Jan Morris, who in the early 1950's transitioned from a man to a woman. Raising questions about female identity and fulfilment, the narrative embraces culture and history as components of the search for self. The paintings were all based on photographs, making this the most representational of the series. But the questions posed go beyond the representational: to the challenges and constraints of personhood for men and women.

PART 3 draws together some of the main themes of the book, evaluating the fruits of the heuristic inquiry but also re-appraising some of the themes yielded by the study.

Chapter 9, "A deeper view", revisits the five series of paintings, asking whether they can be understood as a totality. Is there a binding theme, a trajectory, that explains the sequence? While some of the ideas are reported in my descriptions of the presentations, a fuller picture comes to light. I believe the mother-child relationship is key. I now see the doll paintings as starting a symbolic exploration of my relationship with my own mother. Were we real or dolls to each other? Was she real or a doll? Was I a doll? These questions highlight the question of attunement in our relationship against a historical background of trauma and loss. The deserted city paintings were overwhelmingly about a real environmental and human disaster, but I believe that the threat to survival, the empty streets and houses, also represent a depressed, anxious mother, a mother who has endured persecution and deprivation. Fragile nature ascends from the trough of depression to a real, green, earth-bound encounter with nature, symbolically the rediscovery of an alive, surviving, containing mother. *Dancers* takes the life-force further. Here is the pulsating body in full sway, possibly the reanimated mother, but also at times vulnerable, exhausted. Finally, *Four Women* goes to the heart of the theme – my mother's depression and her struggle to find herself. Putting her alongside three women who have achieved a powerful identity helps to repair her, to give her strength and grace.

Chapter 10, "Concluding thoughts", highlights the main questions of the inquiry and the answers that emerged, some more clearly than others. The convergence of my two main interests is seen as generative and affirming.

The central role of painting is emphasized, as is the positive impact of showing my work online and the way this created a new visual field that I have titled "the artist's matrix". The group events had a highly generative function, not only providing feedback but opening up vistas of history and the social unconscious. The place of memoir in adding substance to the narrative is described. Finally, an elusive phenomenon, the uncanny, is brought to light, discovered through the paintings and reflected in the discussion. This links the paintings analytically with early emotional development. On a wider level, it symbolizes the traumatically ruptured environment of the Covid years and the sense of weird, nightmarish existence in lockdown.

The chapter also suggests ways in which the findings could be taken forward: a more expansive framework for psychotherapy and a new direction of travel for artists seeking greater dialogue with the public. This attests to the synergy achieved in a multi-dimensional approach: the creative friction generated and the liberation from rigid boundaries of theory and practice.

Part 1

Background

Part 1 describes the autobiographical background of the project that is a major part of this book. The focus is on myself and the pressures of growing up in South Africa in mid-20th Century South Africa, then emigrating to the UK in 1968. It explores the problem of thwarted artistic interests and the tension between my major interests in psychology and art. It describes how the project took off on the eve of the pandemic.

Chapter 1 is rooted in childhood and early adulthood in apartheid South Africa, family history, and life in a small, isolated rural Cape Province town.

Chapter 2 describes life as an emigrant in London, the development of my career as a psychologist and the struggle to keep artistic interests alive, but with some success.

Chapter 3 is more discursive, considering the potential of an extended visual field – "the artist's matrix" – in which there is greater social interaction between the artist and the public in which group feedback is an active influence.

DOI: 10.4324/9781003232230-2

Chapter 1

"Can I be both?"

This book celebrates the coming together of two life-time interests, separate though interconnected – psychology and art. It was as if an unusual marriage had taken place. But it took until I was nearly eighty for this to happen. For most of my adult life, these two interests had co-existed in a largely competitive, even combative relationship. Then, in the space of about two years, a merging, a union, began to occur. My painting embraced a more psychological dimension and my psychology opened up to art. It resulted in a series of paintings that started before the Covid lockdown, continued through the bleak months of 2020 and 2021 and became the focus of regular online presentations to groups of varying sizes, the group itself given the opportunity to discuss the themes in some depth, at both personal and social levels.

The almost life-long tension between my predominant interests can probably be understood in the context of growing up in South Africa in an embattled Jewish family environment. I was born in 1943 in the throes of World War Two. Although as a child I knew nothing about the war, I believe that its impact rippled through society at every level and affected my parents deeply in ways that were hardly acknowledged. They were both immigrants from Lithuania earlier in the 20th century, knew each other as children and met again in the early days of Johannesburg history. My father lost half of his family, who had remained behind in Lithuania, in the Holocaust. My mother, as a child, had been exiled with her family for years for spurious political reasons to the fringes of Siberia, where they endured privation and hunger. I grew up in the depths of apartheid, a doctrine that divided South Africa not just between black and white, but across all society and demanded a high degree of conformity to social norms. In this environment, it is perhaps understandable that I chose the relatively conventional path of studying psychology at university and training to be a clinical psychologist. But the artist in me burned from early on. I knew from childhood onwards that I had artistic talent. I could draw, capture likenesses, compose landscapes with perspective, design posters and cards, and make all sorts of objects, from plaster of Paris portraits to puppets that moved and danced.

The problem was that art was unrecognised and unappreciated in the environment in which I grew up. It was not taught or encouraged at the Jewish day school

DOI: 10.4324/9781003232230-3

I attended for most of my schooling, and although my sketches and elaborate patterns were noticed and sometimes admired at school, there was a sense that this was not serious stuff. The school was heavily geared to academic achievement. I bought into the competitive spirit, vying to be the smartest student in the class. This lack of regard for art was also reflected in my parents' value system and the community of which they were part: a conventional, close-knit Johannesburg suburban Jewish community anxious to protect itself from the crossfire of South African politics. Eager for their children to excel at school and graduate into a respectable profession, my parents had no idea what to do with a son who wanted to be an artist (as well as a ballet dancer and a dress designer). The only support I had was from an older brother who later became an architect and who, with his keen visual sense and eye for design, remained interested and a source of encouragement for my painting until the present time. My mother, as will be explained later, was validating and encouraging to me in a general sense, but only later became interested in my painting.

The already complex challenges of my youth were exacerbated by growing up gay in a deeply repressive environment. Having to conceal who I was, infused with a sense of painful, bewildering difference, harbouring what felt to be a guilty, dangerous secret, reinforced at several levels by religious and social sanctions (in Jewish Talmudic lore, it is recommended that homosexuals be stoned and banished), was difficult enough for a sensitive teenager. It undermined my sense of self, but more perniciously, it challenged a belief in the separate facets of my personality and my interests. Nothing could belong together because it was all invalid, because I was invalid. It was as if I was "born a crime" (Trevor Noah 2016).

As a difficult adolescence ended and an uncertain, anxious adulthood started, I began painting seriously, quietly, at home, experimenting with watercolours and oils, often copying impressionist or post-impressionist artists. I was usually surprised by what I produced. The paintings looked competent, yet also artistically sensitive. I remember copying a Van Gogh painting of a straw hat on a table and being struck by its vividness. It looked not just like a copy but an original painting. Even to my untutored eye, it had quality. But I was entirely self-taught. When it came to formal studies after school, there was no question of even considering art. I was expected to go to university to lay the foundation for one of the "good" professions, medicine, law, even dentistry. None of this appealed to me, but I was interested in the arts generally, not just visual art, and I ended up doing an arts degree, majoring in English, psychology and history of art. The latter, the history of art studies, was the only concession to my continuing interest in painting. I remember wandering through the fine arts block at the University of the Witwatersrand in Johannesburg, a modern building with an art gallery in which hung the work of well-known, vibrant South African painters of the day – Baldinelli, Cattaneo, Battiss, Skotnes. I loved this work, the textures, the compositions, the colours. I went back to look at the paintings many times. They were me. They were everything I wanted to be. I should have been in one of the university fine arts workshops, painting away, a voice told me. But this constituted a secret, elusive, unattainable life, away from the rigours of academic studies, from the "good" profession I was expected to choose.

The choice of post-graduate training as a clinical psychologist was propitious. It was a way of pursuing my keen interest in people, the drama of individual lives and the social processes that steer them. Although struggling with my own difficult issues of becoming an adult, I took to the profession with some confidence. Possibly, the conflict issues in my life and, paradoxically, my artistic sensitivity made me an intuitive listener and sympathetic clinician. In later years, when I emigrated to England and made a career out of psychology, the journey was challenging but rewarding. The problem was that it pushed further back my longing to be an artist. Back in South Africa, before London, though, I was not prepared to let the dream go. I continued to paint, attending part-time classes in art, immersing myself, whenever I could, in the atmosphere of the visual arts. I had unexpected early success. Two years running, I entered the prestigious South African Artists of Fame and Promise competition, and both years my work was selected for exhibition. How exciting it was to arrive at the smart top floor of the Johannesburg Adler Fielding Gallery with its spectacular view of the city and beyond, and see my work hung close to some of the big artists of the day – Lionel Abrahams, Sydney Goldblatt, Pranas Domsaitis, Louis Maqhubela, and others. The third year I entered the competition, an even more exciting surprise awaited. I won the prize as best student artist, the criterion being an artist under age 32, rather than being a formal art student. I went to the opening of the exhibition one evening, milling around with other artists, art lovers and the Johannesburg glitterati.

My prize-winning painting was a very large canvas (probably the largest painting I have ever executed) called "Party". It showed a group of white figures in evening dress huddled together on one side of the painting. On the other side, a crystal chandelier suspended from above pierced a large, empty space. The contrast between the social group and the empty space was deliberate. Only dimly aware of the symbolism at the time, despite the deliberate composition, I recognised in later years that it was a sharp socio-political statement. Possibly, the empty space reflected the absence of blacks. Further, the group of people, although standing close together, were not in communication but a group of isolates, the empty space in the painting reflecting the fear of emptiness and abandonment: possibly a statement about alienation in white South Africa. The smart men's dinner suits and sparkling jewellery on the ladies' costumes concealed their anxiety and disconnectedness. But I was also in this: a young adult struggling to find himself in a troubled, split society, not at all sure that he wanted to join the party.

I had, in the interim – before winning the prize – started an informal studio apprenticeship with a well-known South African artist, Aileen Lipkin. Having painted in isolation for years, I doubted myself as an artist. Although my selection for Artists of Fame and Promise had temporarily buoyed my confidence and given me a brief, exciting exposure, I was still very cut off from the art world. I was all the more aware of how much there was to learn. Aillen was an artist I admired greatly, and I initially joined a small art class she had started. Later this turned into something closer to an apprenticeship in her large studio in the leafy suburb of Observatory. She was a great teacher, knowledgeable, enthusiastic, brimming with excitement about contemporary developments in painting. However, she was highly critical. If she liked my work, she gave generous praise, but this was somewhat rare, and if she didn't like it, which was rather more common, she was unflinching in her criticism. In some respects, this was helpful. To this day, about sixty years later, I value and use what I learned from her in technique and composition. However, she was not only critical of flaws in my painting: she was profoundly challenging on the overriding issue of my dual interests: studying/practising psychology and pursuing painting at the same time. "You can't do both", she insisted, "if you want to be any good as an artist. You can't pick and choose. Art is a commitment. You can't dip in now and then, as you please". Her challenge affected me deeply. To this day, in moments of doubt about my painting, I hear her words, loud and clear, still fearing – in spite of success – that she was right. No doubt, in those early days, this echoed the sense that I shouldn't have been an artist in the first place: that I should be a conventional, conforming Jewish boy proving my worth in aspiring, materialistic white Johannesburg. Looking back now, I am shocked at how susceptible I was to Aileen's challenge, to her rigidity, to my not having a countervailing voice that said the opposite: "You are fine. You can be both. You can be a psychologist and an artist."

I have often pondered the strength of Aileen's judgment. Why was it important for her to be so dogmatic? Did she believe that there was something unethical, something greedy about wanting both? Was it envy? Or did she actually think highly of me as an artist and want to protect my artistic integrity and potential? She once told me that her elderly father, who visited her frequently, referred to me scoffingly as Picasso. "So, how's Picasso getting on?" he would inquire with a smirk. She had said to him – she told me – "He is not Picasso, but he's pretty good".

Returning to the painting award, the prize was a year's study at an art school of my choice in an overseas country. It was a complicated coincidence. I was already planning to leave South Africa to go to England in order to pursue further psychotherapy studies. This was at a time when many in the helping professions, particularly psychotherapy, were leaving SA to study or practise abroad. London was the favoured destination. My plan was to get a job as a clinical psychologist and simultaneously undertake a more specialized psychotherapy training. This was challenging enough. Aged 24, I had never left South Africa, was still living in my parents' home and had never earned a living. I was both excited and daunted, if not terrified, by the prospect of London. To add to the challenge, I now had a year's art study on offer. Where, how, would I fit this in? Leaving my plans fairly loose – I had been preoccupied with finishing a PhD in psychology before leaving Johannesburg – I arrived in London feeling overwhelmed and lost. The psychotherapeutic training plan was more complicated than expected, and at the same time, I found it very difficult to penetrate the art world. Yet, there were possibilities. In fact, a unique opportunity came up, which I entirely bypassed. I was talking to a number of people about my plans, seeking advice on where and how I might undertake the year's art study. I managed to get an appointment to see Maurice Kestelman, then principal of the Central School of Art in Holborn. I took a painting to show him my work. He was not only praising of the work (a flautist shown in close-up) – he said he admired its intensity – but very sympathetic to the choice I was facing. He suggested the prestigious MA in Fine Art at the Royal College of Art. Unsure whether I was eligible, given my lack of a first degree in art, he there and then telephoned a colleague at the College and asked about this, explaining that I was an academically accomplished South African psychologist who had won a bursary to support a year's art study. Was I eligible for the Royal College MA? The answer, and I heard it on the phone, was an unhesitating yes.

I did not pursue the opportunity. I have never fully understood why. I think I felt out of my depth. It wasn't entirely credible that, without any academic art study, I could be enrolled on such a high-powered course. The old doubts had resurfaced. Adding to this was the intense disorientation I was now feeling in London. I was lonely, vulnerable, adrift in a huge city. I simply lacked the guts to risk everything and study art for a year. I had another good profession at my fingertips, which I hadn't even started post-qualification, that could provide an income, familiarity, status. I decided to apply for a job in clinical psychology and either put the art study on hold or find a compromise solution. I opted for the latter, asking the bursary funders whether I could use the money to study art part-time, and they agreed. I enrolled on various evening classes over time and benefited from these, but to a limited extent. In later years, I realised what a fantastic opportunity I had missed. This was in the heyday of the Royal College. Famous artists such as David Hockney and John Craig Martin had studied there around that time – and there was I, about to start a job as a National Health Service research/clinical psychologist working with schizophrenics in a dilapidated Victorian psychiatric hospital.

The story that followed was one of success in my chosen profession. Although by then very anxious, homesick and very uncertain, I had made the right decision. The feedback in the first few months of my work was validating. The work was difficult and demanding, but my understanding of the field and the complexity of patients' lives was evident: a sense that I knew what I was doing. That I was valued and appreciated was greatly affirming. Within a few years, I became head of the psychology department. This was a time of increasing funding in the health service in the UK – so different from the present – and there was a growing demand for psychological services. This enabled me to innovate in several directions and what started off as a small department in a backwater on the eastern fringes of London gradually became a large, expanding department that attracted a generation of outstanding psychologists. My own clinical interests remained in psychotherapy, then group psychotherapy, and this was one of the distinguishing features of the department – an openness to a broad range of therapies within a psychodynamic frame that emphasized interpersonal relationships. I was particularly interested in the use of projective techniques, sets of pictures or other stimuli that elicited patterns of anxiety and defence within the interpersonal field, identifying both the conscious and unconscious roots of the individual's emotional development. In the 1980's I invented a new projective technique called "The Hospital Relations Technique" that assessed patients' attitudes to help and their expectations of treatment: fears and fantasies of illness and their relationship to carers. Unfortunately, projective techniques were not absorbed into mainstream psychology in the UK at the time, and I was somewhat out on a limb. But these were creative years in a different, though possibly connected way, to artistic creativity. I was seemingly not only a competent clinician but an able leader, building up what became a renowned psychology department. In 2015 I was awarded the Royal College of Psychiatrists President's medal for services to mental health. I eventually worked in the Health Service for 51 years, retiring in 2020.

Here was more than enough evidence that I had made the right choice of career. However, success was just a part of the picture. As I progressed up the professional ladder and the departmental staff base expanded, my work as an NHS (UK National Health Service) head of department became increasingly managerial, with administrative and budgetary concerns dominating my day-to-day role. I became more and more estranged from the source of my clinical training and the lifeblood of my psychotherapeutic interests. The work became increasingly tedious, burdensome and stressful. Added to this was the weight of interprofessional rivalry generated by the success of the department, with a powerful phalanx of psychiatrists opposing much of what I did and the increasing bureaucratization of the NHS further destroying clinical freedom and initiative. The job increasingly lost its freshness and enjoyment.

Where was painting in this dense tapestry of organizational stress? In fact, I had continued to paint, once again in something of an artistic vacuum, but surprisingly productive considering the obstacles. I began exhibiting my work in London galleries, starting in 1974 at a gallery in Islington. I held exhibitions every three to four years, and they were all successful in terms of attendance and sales. I started acquiring a following, people who purchased my work. There was talk of a "The Nitsun Room" to describe rooms in purchasers' homes in which hung a significant number of my paintings, usually acquired over years. There were also overseas buyers. Yet, the work was never actively promoted by London galleries. This was one of the curious features of smaller commercial art galleries: they were generally inept at reaching a wider public, usually confining themselves to a gallery list of interested parties, mainly from the geographical vicinity of the gallery. But through my own networks, the sphere of buyers expanded. This was all gratifying. The packed private viewing of the exhibition prior to the official run, the buzz of excitement and admiration of the work and the rising number of sales over the weeks added to a highly affirming experience. What was especially meaningful was what quite often happened after an exhibition when I, perhaps unexpectedly, bumped into someone who had bought a painting/s. "I still love that painting", they might say. "We hung it above the fireplace in the living-room and I look at it every day. It brings me so much pleasure". This sense of my work making a lasting impression and of it bringing joy touched me each time this happened. I would comment, "I wish my psychological work would make others so happy!" reflecting on how challenging psychotherapeutic could be, with its complex rationale and ambiguous outcomes. In psychotherapy, we work in the realm of unknowing. A painting on a wall in someone's home is a known object, an incontrovertible fact, whatever its content or worth.

It was this discrepancy between the simpler, self-contained process of painting and its tangible rewards, and the complexity of organizational life with its volatile and antagonistic forces, that led me to consider that I had done my time in the inter-professional fray of the NHS. By the late 1990's, the degree of bureaucratization and technological intrusion, with arduous computerization of all work records and clinical data, was becoming increasingly burdensome. I began to plan an early retirement and left my full-time NHS job in 2000, in time for the new century. I continued working part-time in the NHS in a different health trust in a far less demanding, consultative capacity. I also started working in private practice, joining a well-established set-up in central London. It was liberating to relinquish the mountains of NHS administration and focus on what I most enjoyed: the clinical work. This also freed up time to paint. My artistic output expanded and I continued to have successful exhibitions.

Another change came with my decision to seek specialized training in group analysis, the main approach to group work in the UK. Having been trained in an individual therapy model, I had come to realise the power and effectiveness of groups in clinical settings and the wider world. I undertook the four-year training at the Institute of Group Analysis in London and emerged with a qualification and an identity that came to transform my life. Struggling myself with the volatility, unpredictability and sometimes destructiveness of groups, I wrote an essay called "The Anti-group: destructive forces in the group and their therapeutic potential" (1991) that won The Fernando Arroyave Essay Prize and was described as a "historical and ideological breakthrough" (Tuttman 1991). This and my next book, *The Group as an Object of Desire* (2006), were described as "classics in the field" (Gans 1997, 2006). My third book, *Beyond the Anti-group: survival and transformation* (2015), is less well-known but is a collection of essays on contemporary manifestations of the anti-group. In this book, there is a chapter titled "Group analysis and performance art" that explores the role of performativity in groups and makes a case for a much closer convergence between group analysis and contemporary art. To a large extent, that chapter anticipates the present book. My various publications led to numerous invitations to present keynote talks and workshops nationally and internationally. For about twenty-five years pre-Covid, I travelled extensively, visiting places I might otherwise never have seen. During Covid and lockdown, the invitations and presentations continued online.

My group involvement is very relevant here as the group audience became a vital dimension of the online painting presentations that are the subject of this book. I did my best to maximize group participation so as to share the themes and impact of the paintings and to get the audience associations and explorations, aiming at a socially engaged event that went beyond the paintings themselves. As will be seen in subsequent chapters, this considerably enhanced the approach, adding to the breadth and depth of the presentations.

There then arose a crisis in my direction as a painter. I had for many years painted well-liked landscapes, seascapes and still life, with scenes of Mediterranean countries a common theme. Houses featured prominently: often a single, modest dwelling in a vast landscape. Colour and light were vibrant, brushwork vigorous, textures tactile. The popularity of this work and the brisk sales reinforced my tendency to repeat these themes. My investment in this kind of painting reached a zenith in my last gallery exhibition pre-Covid. I had titled the series of paintings "In Praise of Beauty". The title was emblematic of my striving at the time to defend the value of beauty in art. For some years, an anti-art, anti-painting, anti-beauty mentality had dominated the contemporary art world, with conceptual art threatening to replace painting as both serious and "cool". In the eyes of many, especially critics, painting was dead and beauty was dead. Finding this dictum alienating, I was determined not just to continue painting but to celebrate painting beauty. I sought and loved beauty. The title "In Praise of Beauty" stood boldly on the cover of my 2017 exhibition at the Highgate Contemporary Art gallery. The irony was that, of all my exhibitions, this was the least successful. I never knew whether it was the quality of the work – it seemed not – but the overall response was more muted than usual. There were problems with the gallery where I was exhibiting. The ownership of the gallery had changed, and there were tensions in the mounting and running of the exhibition, probably resulting in its diminished impact.

Whatever the effect of difficulties with the gallery, the exhibition triggered my own doubts about my painting. I became aware that my popular themes were leaving me dissatisfied. I was tired of the repetition, of the surrender to other people's taste and admiration, of the emphasis on sales. I felt a degree of disgust at my obsession with the market value of my work, particularly since, having a more than adequate income from my psychological work, I did not have to depend on art to make a living. To be fair to myself, however, I believe that it was not the money itself that spurred me on: it was more that exhibiting my work and selling paintings had become a way of affirming my identity as an artist. This touched on my old doubts about my authenticity as an artist, sharply expressed in Aileen Lipkin's warning, "You can't be both". The public event of an exhibition was a way of proving that I was an artist, that I *could* be both. It is a great experience to show one's work, to briefly be the centre of attention, to be acclaimed. There is little to beat the excitement of a preview with crowds of admirers who have come to see one's work. While chatting to the many people eager to make contact, a warm feeling of celebrity suffusing the atmosphere, I could see the gallery director engaging with buyers and little red "sold" stickers appearing, as if by magic, all around. Which artist would not revel in that? Or would others *not* require quite this degree of public validation?

The theme "In Praise of Beauty" became a paradox of conflicting values. On the one hand, I wished to affirm my love of beauty and, in parallel, the universal love of beauty, despite the scepticism of the cognoscenti about its place in art. On the other, beauty as a core value may have outrun its course as the leitmotif of my own painting. Did I really need to continue pandering to buyers' taste in order to justify my claim to be an artist? There was an additional question that had nagged at me for many years. How did my art relate to my psychological work? For most of my career, I had kept these interests largely separate. This served a purpose: my psychological work, particularly in-depth psychotherapy, was serious, difficult, demanding, interpersonally charged and often stressful. Painting was a form of therapy, *my* therapy. Alone in my studio, I could escape the intensity of disturbing relationships and dysfunctional organisations into a world of my own creation, a quieter space in which I could roam freely. The painting had a kind of dreamlike quality, not without its frustrations and challenges, but providing an environment that offered a much-needed reprieve. It suited me to escape into a world of beauty, of rich colour, vibrant texture and glistening light. It would be wrong, I believe, to say that the work was superficial. People of discernment saw depth, emotion and mystery in the paintings. A whole tranche of paintings, depicting solitary dwellings in empty landscapes, spoke of isolation and loneliness, existential conditions I had battled much of my life. People seemed attracted to these qualities as much as to the lure of sensuous landscapes and sumptuous still lives. But still, there was an urge to move on.

As an artist and psychologist, I was, of course, one being, and there couldn't *not* be some link between the two sides of myself. Perhaps the gap grew larger in my mind when I recognised that my predominant interests in psychotherapy were in the deeper and darker aspects of human psychology. The book for which I became well known, *The Anti-Group*, focused on very problematic, primitive, potentially if not actually destructive, tendencies in individuals and groups. I was not one for quick fixes and easy solutions. I believed that it was through reaching into deeper personal and social unconscious processes and the spoils of archaic history that meaningful progress could be made. It was this more sober, possibly pessimistic view of human nature that I felt was missing in my painting. Not that it was an obligation. Painting images that appealed to people, that would bring colour and light to their lives, was no idle achievement, given the struggle most of us have to survive the confusion and conflictual areas of life. In a way, I was offering another kind of therapy through painting. But, increasingly, I wanted to see a link between painting and a deeper, more disquieting psychology. More and more, as I grew older, did I want to find a thread to unite them. More and more I wanted to prove not only that I was both an artist and a psychologist but that a new synergy and power could be generated by their coming together.

In 2012 my beloved sister Shirley died. She was 72, four years older than me. We had been life-long friends. She was perhaps the person I felt closest to, loved most, depended on to explore the most painful aspects of being human, in addition to the minutiae and travails of everyday life. We were kindred spirits. She died suddenly, very unexpectedly. My difficulty coming to terms with her death, in a state of frozen emotion, led me to seek psychotherapy myself. Having had several therapists over many years, including a 4-times a week psychoanalysis and a five-year twice-weekly group analysis, I opted this time for a Jungian analysis. Dealing with later life issues and feeling that something essential had been missed in my previous years of psychotherapy, I was keen to try a different approach. It was a wise choice. My analyst, himself quite elderly, was in various ways more attuned to me than any other therapist I have known. The area we focused on most strongly was my childhood, going back to the dusty South African town in which I grew up and the embattled family of my youth. What he understood, and highlighted, was the painful lack of mirroring I had experienced as a child: "mirroring" refer- ring to the sensitive recognition and affirmation of a child's existence. My parents were preoccupied with a demanding business and their own troubled relationship against the shadows of traumatic family history, and they had little time or inclina- tion to understand the highly sensitive, artistic, troubled boy that I was. They were loving parents but of a generation that lacked a capacity to attune psychologically. Hence, from early on, my struggles as a child went unrecognised, and my artistic talents unnoticed. It is not difficult to see in this the origins of the self-doubt that dogged me throughout life, of feeling under almost relentless pressure to conform and please, of shying away from risk. My analyst not only understood this: he was able to mirror me in the way I needed at the time. He was able to recognise and rejoice in my creativity while fully grasping the lost, painful child inside.

The analysis was instrumental, I believe, in helping me to move out of the zone of comfort, to take the risk of painting what was more hidden, more troubling, more unconscious. It is probably not a coincidence that my first breakout series of paintings focused on vintage dolls as symbols of childhood, highlighting the theme of mirroring in childhood. The paintings were like portraits of the dolls, evoking the ambiguity of what was real and what was unreal. In the mutual gaze of the dolls and the viewer was embodied the drama of childhood and the fundamen- tal, life-giving requirement of mirroring and attunement. More significantly, this series of paintings heralded the coming together, finally, promisingly, excitingly, to be repeated in further series, of the two core aspects of my being – psychologist *and* artist.

Chapter 2

Early stages

The project begins

In this chapter, I explore the context and influences of my new initiative. This is a dense tapestry, a tangle of threads, from deeply personal concerns to the sweep of a worldwide pandemic. Rather than attempting to present these phenomena in definitive order, I present a story in the making, perhaps closer to life as we know it than to a prescribed structure.

The project began in Brighton in 2019, the East Sussex town where I had bought a house as a coastal retreat from London, which is where I normally live and work. The sea has always been a great inspiration, and solace, to me. I chose this house because it had a large, unconverted loft, perfect for converting into a studio. This done, I found my creative juices flowing. My first series of paintings was based on vintage dolls, the story of which I explain more fully in Chapter 4. Briefly, it was owning a Victorian house and being surrounded by antiquarian Brighton that stimulated an interest in Victorian artefacts, including dolls, which were a significant feature of Victorian childhoods. I mounted an exhibition of this work in my studio as part of the Brighton and Hove Artist's Open Houses in 2019. Not only was the reaction to the paintings strong, eliciting a wide variety of reactions, but an invited group discussion of approximately thirty-five people in my studio at the end of the exhibition was highly stimulating. I led the discussion, taking the audience through the paintings and talking about the cultural background and impetus for the paintings. I brought in aspects of my own childhood, linked to family history, that were germane to the theme. Whether this was the reason, the paintings themselves or the combination of visual images and narrative, the effect was powerful. The spontaneity and directness of the group were striking, with feedback from several participants after the event confirming the value of the experience. Having chosen to specialise in group analysis in my clinical practice in the past few decades, my antennae were out for the dynamics of the group discussion. I was amazed. Everything I valued about groups was there: a freely associative process, open, resonant, searching, revealing, moving. I felt gratified on two equivalent levels: as an artist and group analyst/psychotherapist. The prospect of bringing my two main interests together, in a way that was quite unexpected, was beginning to take shape.

DOI: 10.4324/9781003232230-4

I was invited to give a talk the following year, 2020, at the annual conference in New York of the American Group Psychotherapy Association (AGPA) within the framework of "The Ormont Lecture", a prestigious annual event. The invitation highlighted my publications in the field and requested that I speak about one of my well-known subjects, particularly *The Anti-Group*. Having spoken on this theme many times, including at previous AGPA conferences, and feeling tired of the repetition, I decided to do something different. Fresh from the excitement of the Brighton group discussion, I decided to offer *Dolls and Demons* as my lecture theme. With two and a half hours of lecture/workshop time at my disposal, I saw this as a valuable opportunity to test out the material with a new audience in a different context. The conference organizers initially didn't know what to do with the offer. It was not what they had in mind, and it was difficult for me to convey the substance of the presentation. But they eventually agreed, and I delivered the presentation on 7th March 2020. The audience reception more than justified the decision. Once again, the group discussion was open, vivid and touching. The presentation confirmed a growing sense that the approach had considerable potential.

The presentation took place in New York in the first week of March 2020, a fateful time in the history of the worldwide pandemic. The atmosphere of manic denial I experienced at the conference is described more fully in Chapter 5. Suffice it to say that having had a very close brush with Covid in New York, I returned to London to find the city in the grip of fear. Aged 76 and doubly vulnerable because of an underlying lung disorder, I was advised by my respiratory consultant to go home immediately and strictly isolate. Like many others, I realised I was facing a sudden and dramatic life-style change, with no end in sight. I quickly established that I could continue my clinical work online, mainly individual and group psychotherapy, becoming familiar with Zoom as the predominant platform. This gave a welcome structure to the days and a reassuring element of continuity in a scarily transformed universe. Moreover, the new structure also allowed me much greater free time. Not having to travel to central London and back each day for work freed up precious hours. Whereas friends and colleagues described casting around for activities to keep them occupied, I had hardly a moment's doubt about how I would use the time. I would paint. Not only that, but I would pick up the new thread I was developing, weaving the paintings into a narrative that could be shared with others in groups. Realising that I could no longer do this in a physical space, the option of transferring to an online space soon became apparent. I was using Zoom regularly to run my psychotherapy groups, and, in spite of some shortcomings, I could see that it worked surprisingly well. In fact, I enjoyed the medium. The tableau of faces on the screen in this new configuration was, for me, a novel and intriguing experience.

The paintings

It seemed to be coming together. I was beginning to paint a lot, relishing the additional time at my disposal. Used to planning physical exhibitions but knowing that I would not be able to exhibit the work in a three-dimensional gallery for the foreseeable future – like so much else, the art gallery world had completely closed down – I committed myself to the online project. The online platform offered a valuable means of showing my paintings, with the advantage of an extended event combining biographical narrative and group feedback. This challenging and exciting opportunity ushered in what was possibly the most creative period in my life. Ideas swarmed into consciousness, suggesting salient themes that merited whole series of paintings. These, it seemed, would organise my work for some time, leaving me with a clear direction of travel. I was no longer floundering in a quagmire of ideas, struggling to realise vague, tentative plans, giving up on half-baked work. The paintings emerged in bold succession. There was an intensity of purpose that I have seldom felt. The atmosphere of a new venture, the coming together of long-standing separate strands of interest, as if previously living in two worlds, was highly motivating. I was living now in one world.

What a strange time it was. The world outside, which I shunned, was a dangerous place. The daily statistics in that first spring of 2020 confirmed that the epidemic was spreading rapidly worldwide and, closer to home, it was creating havoc in London. Yet, it was an oddly exhilarating time for me. My studio is at the top of a tall house in north London overlooking woods, with a commanding view of the trees and the city beyond. The skyscape is constantly changing, and I can see both the sunrise and the sunset from the studio windows. Clouds drift past in their myriad forms. Birds fly by. Planes glide across the sky in the far distance. Classical music could be playing, and I might, for just a moment, feel I was, metaphorically, in heaven. I could move freely across the room, often poring over sketches and Google images, trying out new compositions, rummaging through materials, experimenting with techniques, browsing through art books, but mostly painting: getting on with the work. If I did leave the house, it was to go for walks, almost always in the woods, where I felt a renewed and powerful contact with nature – the subject of my next online presentation, *Fragile Nature* (Chapter 6). Then I would return home and usually go straight back to the studio. Although in a safe bubble of my own (shared with my partner), I was aware of the terrible disparities between people at this time. Television and newspapers drove home the grim daily statistics, the rising number of cases and the mounting death toll – and, beyond the actual body count, the lives of isolation, fear, impoverishment, and in many cases, the confinement to cramped spaces with no outside access, while I could roam through the generous spaces of a suburban home with a verdant garden and the woods a moment away. I felt relieved to have all this at my disposal, lucky, but feeling guilty at the inequalities that were more and more revealed.

While describing an atmosphere of initiative and optimism, the themes of my painting were nonetheless in tune with the prevailing mood of fear and confusion. Although I was safe and well in my studio, I was aware of a sense of desolation, not just in the world outside but somewhere in myself, that nagging fear of damage and desertion that hides behind the struggle to remain hopeful and creative, that stubborn vein of nihilism and despair that haunts the human psyche. The second major series I painted, titled *The Deserted City* and described fully in Chapter 5, was a direct expression of this theme. Alarmed at the speed of the spreading virus, still somewhat shaken by the brush I had with Covid in New York and observing the escalating images in the media of empty cities and towns around the world, I was moved to put this into paint. But it was not cities in general. It was the cities of southern Europe that I was most aware of. These were cities that I loved. The way Covid manifested itself initially in southern Europe, particularly Italy, gripped my imagination.

The paintings of this period heralded a dramatic shift of subject matter. Having for many years painted mainly sun-filled European landscapes and seascapes, work that was well regarded and marketable, I was aware of a much darker vein creeping into my painting. This was not altogether fortuitous. As noted previously, I had for some years grown restless with my customary subjects, worried that I was pandering to my buyers' tastes rather than following my own inclinations. Wanting to experiment, I had in earlier years tentatively taken risks, only to retreat, to return to familiar, comfortable territory. Now, in the face of lockdown and with the world teetering on disaster, I felt compelled to paint in a way that reflected the sense of environmental crisis and inner turmoil that was so prevalent. The doll paintings, produced before Covid took hold, had presaged a change. Now, in the eye of the pandemic, there was no turning back.

Having painted for many years on a white ground, relying on this background for luminosity in my work, I began to paint on dark backgrounds. Most paintings were done on black. I continued to use mainly the palette knife, or knives, my preferred medium, but I was painting more loosely than before, more concerned about mood and less about detail and refinement. All subsequent series, *The Deserted City*, *Dancers* (begun pre-Covid but completed during lockdown), *Fragile Nature* and *Four Women*, were painted on a black background. These were not necessarily sombre paintings, as in many cases the focal point stood out vividly from the dark background, animating the scene, but underlying that were the shadows of a seared, frightened world. People who knew my work from before were often surprised, taken aback by the paintings. Words such as "sombre", "scary", "very serious" peppered their reactions. Some harked back to the "beautiful paintings" they loved. "Why the change?" one or two asked, rather irritably. But others welcomed the new work, seeing the value of a new departure, particularly in the context of a pandemic. I was oddly relieved myself, knowing that I was painting in a way, and on subjects, that were long in abeyance, sheltering in my unconscious, waiting to come up for air, hungry for expression. The pandemic had lifted the lid.

The new work was also directly in line with my values as a psychotherapist and writer. I had a great interest and belief in the forces of "dark" humanity, not for the sake of pursuing the dark in its own right, but as a route to reparation and creativity. Much of my writing in the field of group analysis had focused on the disruptive, disintegratory forces in individuals and groups. My concept of the anti-group epitomized this interest, but with a clear vision of the creative potential of destructive tendencies recognized and harnessed. "Every act of creation",

Picasso once said, "is also an act of destruction". I would add to this that every act of destruction has the potential to trigger the creative. This link, between the creative and the destructive, is to my mind an ontological given, seen at many levels of existence. Although I sensed that my previous painting had hidden depths, often commented on by viewers, the work nevertheless, in my estimation, was too easy, too comfortable to sustain itself, to have relevance in an embattled world. It seemed that to forge a synthesis between my psychological work and my life as a painter, paintings that were darker in colour and content, more ambiguous, more challenging, were a necessary point of departure, a signpost on a different journey.

Understanding the change

While the circumstances of my changing approach to painting were in some ways clear, I was aware of an inner pressure that was not so easily explained. I was obsessed with this new project. There was an urgency to progress, to paint, to complete whole series of work on a particular theme, then move on to another theme. I painted like a demon. I completed at least forty paintings on *The Deserted City* in less than four months. My output was prodigious.

In hindsight, it is not difficult to see how the isolation of lockdown created a pressure to generate, to fill the void with product, with material, with ideas, with images. Whereas some people were paralysed by lockdown and the fear of illness that haunted daily life, others thrived in unexpected ways, finding new energy, new bursts of creativity. I was one of the latter. But I was also conscious of my age and life-stage. At seventy-six, although relatively healthy and fit, I was undeniably in the older age category. If this was ordinarily an age for reflection, for fears of fragility and decline, for the dread of mortality – for the hourglass of time running out – then the threat of the virus circling invisibly around cities and towns, transmitting itself mysteriously from person to person, hovering in the air like some ghoulish apparition, added hugely to the anxiety. Given my age and underlying lung problem, a form of chronic pneumonitis, I was officially classified by the UK government in the "extremely vulnerable" category. Letters, texts, and emails from a government source repeatedly put me in this category, usually with very strict warnings to shield. My respiratory consultant, on my return from New York in March, had emphasized that if I contracted Covid, I would be at grave risk. Everything pointed to a very high level of vulnerability. Ironically, I believe that I had had a mild form of Covid, contracted in New York but undiagnosed, and a subsequent immunity test confirmed this to be the case. But at the time, in those dark, terrifying early days, it was difficult to know what to believe. So, I think that the urgency of my painting reflected a heightened sense of transience, an accelerated fear of death, evoking a determination to prove that I was still alive and productive, to use the time remaining in as purposeful a way as possible. The material I was choosing to paint, representing bleakness and emptiness, the spectre of mortality not far away, was probably a way of mastering the anxiety, of confronting dread, of taking charge of the existential crisis that was threatening to overwhelm and to decimate.

In the background of this crisis was another slow-burning challenge, if not crisis – the prospect of retirement. I had, in 2000, already retired from a thirty-year, full-time position in the NHS as head of psychology, and in June 2020, I "retired" a second time from a twenty-year post-retirement job as an NHS consultant psychologist-psychotherapist. In toto, I had worked in the NHS for fifty-one rich, rewarding years. These years were filled with event, learning, experimentation and intense professional and social engagement. The NHS had become a home. I had found it extremely difficult to retire from this job. I had become very attached to the service, the people, the institution: the "brick mother". The anxiety of separation, the fear of facing a vacuum, remained with me for years afterwards, raising doubts about any further retirement plan. I stalled any immediate decision, feeling fit and functional enough to continue to practice for some time. Working now more and more in private practice, I discovered, happily, the joys of going back to my original choice of profession: to be a practising clinician, focusing on psychotherapy, dealing in depth with one person at a time or with a familiar, cohesive group. At the start of lockdown, I was able to transfer my entire practice to Zoom and, after the initial adaptation, found this very workable. In fact, because of their isolation, most clients were keen to meet virtually. This was especially the case with the groups. The opportunity to meet regularly with a familiar, supportive group of people gained a new momentum. My groups had seldom been as committed and cohesive as they were in the months of lockdown. The work deepened, social isolation in participants triggering a host of anxieties but also new insights and an increased willingness to risk psychic awareness, to go the full mile of the psychotherapeutic journey. I found the work immensely meaningful.

I emphasize my enjoyment of psychotherapeutic practice during lockdown in order to highlight that I was not seeking simply to replace this work with painting. I was not looking for a substitute. The excitement was in the potential to link the two, not in an additive way but in an altogether new synthesis. And, since time was rapidly moving on, with the prospect of waning years and diminishing energy, a new project, with new learning and new opportunities, was enormously energizing. Based on the writing of James Grotstein (2004), we can discern three main challenges of ageing: libido, the death instinct and the epistemophilic impulse. The first two are self-explanatory, representing the inescapable tension between life and death, but the third, the epistemophilic impulse, requires clarification. In essence, it is about curiosity: curiosity as a sign of aliveness, a reminder that life and the world we live in are ever interesting, that there is inexhaustible richness and variety to explore and apprehend. I so appreciate and subscribe to this vision. It sums up what I believe, and it describes the thrust, the pulse, the life-blood of my initiative. It links up too with the heuristic inquiry that was becoming a driving force.

These are reasons enough, I suggest, to elucidate my motivation. Another, more complicated reason, and more difficult to communicate, is the fact of my gayness. This ties up with ageing and the dread of isolation and loneliness. In a stable partnership with a man for over forty years, I was nevertheless without children and any substantial family network. Most of my family, and long-standing friends, had died. Active and busy as I was, I could feel very alone. I have sometimes wondered whether my intense creativity over the decades, in terms of the sheer quantity of my creations in painting, writing, publishing and practising psychotherapy, were symbolically my children. I had come from a family in which childbearing was regarded as an urgent necessity, a way not just of bringing life and joy but of ensuring the continuity of the family and the survival of the race. While not having wanted children for most of my life and being to some extent critical of the unreflective ease with which some people slide into parenting, I couldn't deny a nagging doubt: that I was transgressing a biological imperative, that I was failing my family and my people. Was the pressure to paint, building up again in this fraught time, not just a way of filling an artistic void, but a struggle to make sense of a deeper purpose, of justifying my place in the world?

The online challenge

The successful transfer of my clinical practice to an online platform is relevant not only to the continuation of my psychological work. As highlighted, it offered a whole new way of exhibiting my paintings. I was not one for painting without an audience, for hiding my work in my studio or obscure corners of my house. I wanted to show what I had done. In fact, each of my series was done with an audience in mind. Particularly since I was developing themes that had wide relevance at such an unusual time in our history, I wanted to show my work, speak about it, touch people, hear their feedback. I wanted to offer my painting as a vehicle for self-awareness and discussion, and to get back from the audience insights that might help me, that might expose unconscious areas, open up new possibilities, create new vistas. Above all, I wanted to communicate.

The valuing of communication is strongly related to my psychotherapeutic work, particularly group analysis. I explore this more fully in what follows since it is at the heart of what I was attempting, but I could not have done it without the opportunity provided by an online platform. It was serendipitous that it occurred at the very time I was looking for an audience. My Zoom groups, not only psychotherapy groups, but also conferences, webinars and the whole gamut of online meetings, convinced me that this was a medium suited to my artistic aims. Suddenly, it no longer mattered that galleries had locked down and that I couldn't show my work in physical space. I had discovered a novel way of bringing people together: not only people living in London but others from the rest of the UK and people from abroad. My audience widened considerably.

The advent of an accessible online platform gave interested parties a ready opportunity to join, but additionally, in the throes of lockdown, there was a hunger for stimulation, an aching wish to make contact with others. The epistemophilic impulse referred to above was probably as true for others as for me. In the midst of a pandemic, foreclosing horizons in many directions, people were particularly curious about their world, the histories that had made them, the culture that had moulded them, maybe even more curious than usual because of the threat to human life and civilisation as we know it. People were thirsty for knowledge and debate. The gift of additional time in lockdown made this all the more possible. Creativity, and an interest in creativity, boomed. People wanted to make art, to see art, to participate, to contribute.

The power of the image

The paintings, grouped into themes, were the framework for each of the presentations. Gripped myself by the themes I had chosen, each touching on an existential dilemma or preoccupation, my paintings were imbued with a particular intensity. I was no longer painting casually, content to see what emerged as the composition began to take shape. I was painting purposefully, wanting to reach the viewer, to share something about what it was like to be living in the present time, battling with known fears and unknown forces. While in some respects I was not surprised at viewers' responses – and there was a complex range of reactions – in other respects, I was stunned. People were engrossed, moved, disturbed, sometimes baffled. Viewers' associations as individuals and their resonances as a group were powerful. Although intuitively I knew that visual images can be affecting, I became increasingly aware of their impact. The visual is important as a foil, or contrast, to verbal communication, which is often elevated to supreme status in the universe of communication. I had from early on in my career been suspicious of the overweening emphasis on verbal communication, which is part of the psychotherapeutic tradition. In many psychotherapists' minds is the belief that words are all: an assumption that everything inchoate and unconscious is translatable into words: the goal of psychotherapy is to realise this potential. In group analysis, for example, the founding father SH Foulkes (1948, 1964) emphasized the importance of verbal communication above all else. Much as I agree with the value of verbal articulation in therapeutic settings, I am also wary of the idea that words are the whole story. In my own writing, I have repeatedly argued that words are limited in the extent to which – and what – they can reveal, that people's underlying capacity to use words is variable, that words sometimes fail to convey complex and confusing states of mind and that words can be separating and alienating rather than uniting us all in understanding (Nitsun 1996, 2015a). I agree with Daniel Stern (1985), who described words as double-edged swords: they provide a valuable way of communicating, yet they can also be limiting and misleading. I argue these points so as to highlight the potential of visual images to penetrate conscious barriers, to stir up forgotten or repressed memories, to evoke feelings in the raw: to feed communication. Of course, the use of words to describe reactions such as these is valuable, if not essential: they do enhance communication. But the source of the emotion must come from a more visceral depth than words alone.

Projection

Since the images in my paintings are often ambiguous, sometimes deliberately so, sometimes fortuitously through a slip of technique or misplaced intention, they tend to evoke wide differences in viewers' perception and interpretation. The dynamics of projection come strongly into play here. Projection, understood psychologically, refers to the perception of ambiguous stimuli in a way that reveals unconscious or unrecognized aspects of a personality (Piotrowski 1950). Visual images have been used extensively in the administration of so-called projective techniques (for example, the Rorschach inkblot test, The Thematic Apperception Test and my own research instrument, the Hospital Relations Technique (Nitsun 1988)), aimed at unearthing and elucidating anxiety and defensive systems in individuals, their interpersonal patterns, and their inner, imaginative life. Some of my paintings seemed to function strongly as projective devices, notably the doll series. While this was not their primary aim, the material added depth and dimension to the group discussion, loosening verbal associations and resonances, unearthing unconscious imagery, and evoking the dynamics of similarity and difference.

In part 2 of this book, in which I describe the presentations in greater detail, there are selected illustrations of the paintings as well as accounts of viewers' reactions, demonstrating the power of projection more fully: how the visual and the psychological came together in a new synergy. At the same time, as Bollas (1987) points out, the aesthetic object is not just a passive vehicle for people's projections. It has a power of its own to stimulate and move. We are arrested by good art. We are struck by art, and we enter into it with our being.

Story telling

While emphasizing the visual component of the approach as a *sine qua non* and questioning the value of an overly verbal approach, it is nevertheless important to highlight the impact of the narrative that accompanied the paintings. The themes I chose were aimed at everyone in the sense that they explored shared existential preoccupations: they offered a broad metaphorical canvas. However, I brought myself directly into the narrative. Every presentation had a story to tell. I began each presentation not only with the wider scope of the theme, but with myself, what preoccupied me, present and past, what particular concern was puzzling me, what elusive answer I was seeking. Additionally, I risked sharing some of the more hidden areas of my life, some of the troubling, unresolved dilemmas of childhood and later development. This varied, of course, from theme to theme. In the Dolls series, for example, I spoke about my attraction to dolls in childhood and how I abandoned this for fear of censure. In the *Fragile Nature* series, I shared fears of mortality in the wake of the pandemic and how contact with nature helped to put this in perspective. In *Four Women*, starting with my mother and her unresolved struggle, I explored the different ways women were able to establish their identities and how this paralleled aspects of development in general. Themes mirrored across the presentations included loss, trauma, the passing of time, intergenerational transmission, and the journey to find oneself. Looking back on my overall agenda, I can see that in some respects, the paintings, and the presentations as a whole, were fundamentally a way of revisiting my own development while offering the opportunity to others to share theirs. It was this personal element, in some ways undisguised, that, I believe, imbued the presentations with their impact. In subsequent chapters, I describe more fully how the personal aspect animated the project.

The act of storytelling is itself an art, an aspect of our shared humanity, that merits attention (Weisel-Barth 2020). Telling one's story is a core component of psychotherapy. Everyone who comes for psychotherapy has a story to tell. However inarticulate, the story demands attention and understanding as the first requirement of therapy. In some ways, psychotherapy is about creating a better story, ideally a more congenial story with a more favourable outcome, but since this is not always possible, generating a more coherent story that is owned and understood by the teller is a worthwhile achievement in itself. I did not aim at such development in my presentations – they were not psychotherapeutic by design – but as I am generally aware of people's striving to deepen meaning in their lives and to heal the broken parts, therapeutic intent could not have been far away. Telling my story, usually in a way that imparted hope, was a way of touching the wound, the "basic fault" (Balint 1968) in others – and doing this by example. This probably accounts, in part, for the strong statements by two participants following my New York dolls presentation that they had learned more about themselves from this event than from years of psychotherapy. I believe that I modelled openness for others: this facilitated a helpful, if not healing, discourse.

The narrative intrinsic to psychotherapy has in recent years become a major focus in both theory and practice. A distinct school of narrative therapy has emerged in recent decades (e.g., Combs and Freedman 1996: Denborough 2014), focusing on the narrative at the heart of every life: the way people construct stories about themselves from birth to old age that mould how they function in the world. Often, the stories are negative, undermining personal strengths and potentials. The capacity to "re-story", to build a more life-enhancing narrative, is at the core of the therapy. Apart from this highly structured narrative approach, the idea of the narrative is currently explored widely in different approaches to both individual and group psychotherapy. These are not necessarily described as narratives that accurately mirror a past reality or imagined present: they are often a tangle of memory, imagination and invention. Weisel-Barth (2020) describes the "intimate fictions" created jointly by patient and analyst in psychotherapy. Golinelli (2021) emphasises the mysterious and the ineffable in the life narrative, infused with the workings of both the personal and cultural unconscious. A sense of the uncanny, the inexplicable, hovers, evading full comprehension.

The narrative literature, of which the above are examples, resonates strongly with me as I contemplate the body of work I produced in this project. Here, the narrative was told in the parallel form of paintings and memoir, expanded by the many contributions of the groups, together weaving a larger narrative that became clearer and sharper in some respects and remained elusive in others.

Is this psychotherapy, group therapy or art therapy?

Although my approach to some extent overlaps with psychotherapy, it is, in one respect, very different. In traditional psychotherapy, there is a clear division of roles. The therapist is the authority, the expert, the one who listens and understands: the patient brings the problems in order to get help from the therapist. It is an asymmetrical relationship, reinforced by years of institutionalised practice, often with strict injunctions to practitioners to maintain this form of the relationship. Self-disclosure on the part of the therapist is, for the most part, proscribed. It is regarded as unprofessional, unbounded, irresponsible. In my presentations, I step out of tradition as a psychotherapist by opening up publicly about myself. It is a kind of therapeutic turn-about, an analytic *volte-face*. Not only that, but I am inviting responses to my story and the images that illustrate the story, reversing the usual therapist-patient feedback process. The approach is reminiscent of Ferenczi's attempt at "mutual analysis" (Rudnytsky 2021). In this, he experimented with levelling out the relationship between analyst and patient: each would take turns in analysing the other. Ferenczi's experiment ran aground, failing to create a sustainable psychotherapeutic process. More recently and successfully, relational analysis and the intersubjective approach have closed the conceptual and existential gap between patient and therapist, propounding a more democratic approach that involves both parties as more equal players (Mitchell and Aron 1999). The change in my approach was a spontaneous direction of travel. I did what came naturally. But I am aware of the potential, if not need, to challenge psychotherapeutic convention, risking an approach that is more open and mutually participative.

The issue of managed role reversal described above is relevant to both individual and group psychotherapy, and I dwell on this briefly here, given the overlap. Group analytic psychotherapy, my chosen approach, is more democratic in its structure than most other therapies, given the emphasis on the group and the therapeutic function of the members in relation to each other. The role of the group analyst as the therapeutic authority is accordingly diminished. On the positive side, there is potentially greater scope for flexibility. A well-known definition of the process by Foulkes, the founder of group analysis, states: "therapy of the group, by the group, including the conductor" (Foulkes 1948). This highlights the position of the conductor as a group member him/herself, not a remote authority. It allows for the possibility of judicious role shifts and gestures of creativity. In my experience, most group analytic therapists remain strongly bounded, careful not to disrupt the therapeutic frame, erring on the side of caution rather than risk. However, Foulkes' description of the approach as a more open-minded, egalitarian therapy accords with my own inclination, and it is in this spirit that I undertook the present project. I was not undertaking psychotherapy but remained mindful of underlying psychotherapeutic principles and the implications of modifying conventional boundaries.

Where is the overlap with art therapy? Clarity is needed here. Art therapy is a different and distinct practice with a strong tradition and literature of its own (Waller 1999). It is a form of therapy that uses art production as a source of personal expression and communication aimed at emotional and creative growth. It started within a one-to-one format, but in recent decades has become much more group orientated. There is now a strong tradition of group interactive art therapy, which draws heavily on Foulkesian group analysis (Waller 2014; McNeilly 2005). Although there is some overlap with what I do, there are clear and important differences. In art therapy, the art is produced by the participants, with the therapist as guide and facilitator. The therapist does not usually produce art him/herself. In my approach, I am the artist, and the participants are invited as an audience to an exhibition of my paintings. They are not patients, and they do not paint or draw. If anything, I am the one under scrutiny and the group at times has a therapeutic function for me. In this sense, what I do could be seen as the *reverse* of the art therapy process.

Having differentiated my approach from art therapy, it is worth recalling a time when I ran art therapy groups myself. This was in the 1980's when I was working as a psychologist on psychiatric wards and initiated a large-group art therapy programme. At the time, I was interested in gestalt psychotherapy and ran the groups along gestalt art therapy lines (Rhyne 2021). This encourages participants to identify with the painting or drawing they have produced by using the first person "I" to describe the contents of the art piece: "*I* am a big tree and *I* have many branches." and so on, usually revealing important aspects of self as embodied in the image. I found this a productive way of working, surprisingly amenable to very disturbed in-patients, and I have a remaining fondness for the work. Reflecting on why I didn't pursue this further, since it was an effective approach, I realise that I preferred at the time to keep art and psychology in separate areas of my life. The separation had a purpose. I wanted my own art practice to remain sovereign, free to exist in its own right, unaffected by the demands of work in a psychiatric institution. This was a way of protecting my own art. Somehow, practising art therapy muddied the waters, putting me in the position of art facilitator or tutor when what I really wanted to do was paint. It was only in later years that it seemed remotely possible to combine the two approaches in such a way that they would generate something new rather than detract from each separate practice. This was the spirit behind the present project.

The group process

I touch on this subject in several parts of the book, but it merits a place at this early stage. This project reflects my complex, ongoing relationship with groups as a phenomenon, both groups of belonging in a social sense and groups as a medium of psychotherapy. There is a history to recount, some of which is mentioned in the Preface to this book and described more fully in the Introduction. My doubts about the value of analytic psychotherapeutic groups marked my initial post-qualification period as a group analyst. In part, this was a reaction to the idealization of groups I encountered in my training. It was also a reflection of unexpectedly difficult experiences that both I and others met in running groups. This led me to write my first essay on the anti-group (Nitsun 1991), followed by a book publication in 1996. Writing about the anti-group was, for me, a rite of passage, a way of working through my ambivalent relation to groups, as well as exploring and elucidating the destructive potential of what I saw in groups. But immersing myself in the anti-group also enabled me to flip the coin – to see the positive, hopeful, inspiring aspects of groups. It brought me closer to the phenomenon I later called the "group as an object of desire", the subject of my second book (Nitsun 2006). While focusing on sexuality in the group as an area that had been neglected in the group analytic literature, the book more generally celebrated the well-functioning, life-enhancing group, the group in which there is a high level of engagement and commitment, in which there are "deep resonances from heart to heart as well as from mind to mind" (Nitsun 2006, p. 1). By the time I came to initiate the present project, I had become more and more familiar with the group as an object of desire – including my own desire. This is why I had no hesitation in setting up the online events with the full involvement of groups, believing that the group imagination would animate the presentation, adding a depth of awareness and diversity of perspective. Having emphasized the positive value of the groups, however, I need to bear in mind the challenge of the anti-group. Looking at my own development over the decades, I see the operation of anti-group forces in formative ways – from my family's background in traumatic 20th-century European history, struggling with displacement and immigration, to the impact of apartheid South Africa, to the problems of difference and alienation in my childhood and adolescence. The present project can be seen as being born out of these social and personal disjunctions and disruptions, which may have fuelled the intensity of the project – to survive, to live, to create.

Reflection

Reflecting now on the role of these groups, it strikes me what a powerful experience they were for me personally. The impact went beyond the task of the group. It wasn't just that I was the artist showing his paintings and talking about himself or that the group responded with questions and comments. Something in the encounter went deeper. The group fulfilled a need in me, something more like a family or friendship group that is holding and containing, attentive and affirming, a hedge against the memories of displacement and non-belonging. Very possibly, this symbolically was the family I missed out on as a child: the open, fearless family that recognised the artist in me: the family that, rather than turning away in doubt and bewilderment, turned towards me in recognition and appreciation.

Chapter 3

The artist's matrix

The traditional and the new

A work of art needs an audience to realise its existence, to come alive, to have meaning beyond its existing as an object, unseen, unheard, in a vacuum, in a remote gallery or on an unremarkable wall. A little like a human being: we realise our humanness through communication with other humans. Without it, we may wither. Although some artists practise art without expecting recognition, either because they don't need it or won't seek it, most artists depend on the reaction of an audience. This is not necessarily about selling art. It is about recognition and appreciation of the product. It is the oxygen of the artist's air. The function of a live audience has, to some extent, been overtaken in recent years by social media, in which artists post their work, potentially to be seen by thousands, if not millions. But this is usually a fleeting contact, quickly superseded by a flood of other images, competing on a virtual stage of unbounded proportions. There is the illusion of recognition in a quick-fire universe without end, in a crazed merry-go-round that never stops. Some artists do gain recognition through this process, but this tends then to be inflated and hyper-cathected, creating another chimaera, while the preponderance of artists' work is drowned in a deluge of images.

Part of my struggle to realise the artist in me was to be known, to be seen, but in a way that was not simply a cursory viewing, a nod to a painting on a wall. I wanted to encounter the viewer in the visual field, to communicate, to have a mutual interchange. My experiment with an online platform unexpectedly opened such an opportunity. This raises questions about the construction of the visual field more generally: questions about how artist and viewer(s) are positioned in an aesthetic matrix. I set out to explore what this means to me and to other artists who question the meaning of their art in the wider social context.

Showing my work online means showing a reproduction of the painting, not the real image. It is a photograph in a slide show rather than the actual work which can be seen, touched, that exists in a three-dimensional world. Does this matter, that it is an image of an image? Walter Benjamin (1935), the German philosopher, famously debated the advantages and disadvantages of the reproduced image. Through the media of photography and printing in Benjamin's time, and currently with the mass reproduction of images, the work of art can be seen by millions.

DOI: 10.4324/9781003232230-5

There is the advantage of bringing art to the masses, to be seen, enjoyed by many, even fostering the illusion of ownership: "*this is my Picasso*". The disadvantage is that the work of art loses its "aura", its uniqueness in time and space, its singularity. Is there a way through this dilemma? Can the image seen by many still retain its integrity, its sense of origination? Yet, paradoxically, the image is not "real" anyway: it is an impression, an interpretation. In this chapter, I describe how the online process I pursued, with the addition of an autobiographical narrative and generous audience reaction, gave the work a new dimensionality, an extended meaning: several dimensions in depth if not space. This was achieved not through the manic exposure of social media but through interaction with a committed audience. The experience has led me to ponder more generally the construction of a visual field in which artist and viewer can meet, not just as distant cyphers, but in dialogue.

The artist has long held a fascination for psychoanalysts and psychotherapists: the inner workings of the artist's mind and its creative expression as a focus of inquiry. This has led to a considerable literature, all the way from texts such as Freud's analysis of the symbolic meaning of Leonardo's creations (Freud 1916) to the existential analysis of 20th-century artists such as Rothko (Schama 2009b) and the contemporary exploration of psychological parallels in the work of Louise Bourgeois (Storr 2016), amongst many others. However, there remains a gap between the artist and the commentary, as if the artist is an object of inquiry rather than a living being possibly eager for contact and appreciation. With today's technologies, there is much greater potential for a mutual interchange, but how far have we gone with forging the link?

There have been analysts who themselves are artists, although this is usually a background interest or hobby, not necessarily shared publicly or written about. Amongst the minority of psychoanalysts and other therapists who have documented their own artistic experiments, Marion Milner is perhaps the best known. A psychoanalyst in mid-twentieth-century England, she had close links with some of the key figures of the time, Anna Freud, Winnicott and Melanie Klein, amongst others. In her famous book, *On not being able to paint*, Milner (1950) describes her struggle to produce a series of drawings/paintings through a spontaneous process of experimentation. Dealing with blocks and resistance in the creative process, she focuses on art as an expression of the artist's inner world, including unconscious fantasy, with particular reference to the body and the intra-psychic experience of bodily states. In this sense, her analysis is very much of its time: the detailed observation and analysis of the individual psyche, with art seen as an expression of a profoundly subjective internal world. Although she shares this openly with the reader, there remains a sense of a private, almost clandestine experiment. Valuable as the exercise is, it has, by today's changed standards, an anachronistic ring, quaintly solipsistic. Our perspective today is much more linked to the wider universe, to a wider field of interaction and interpretation. The hermeneutics of twentieth-century classical psychoanalysis have given way to the heuristics of contemporary psychotherapy, with its much greater emphasis on the relational world, the interpenetration, indeed indivisibility, of individual, group and society. Accordingly, art is seen not so much as the creation of an individual separate from their world, but as a person deeply contextualized in the full dimensionality of social reality.

Towards an artist's matrix

I intend in this chapter to formulate a way of conceiving a visual field that hypothetically would facilitate a closer dialogue between the artist and the audience. In part, this reflects my own journey as an artist, what I needed to know at the start of my project and what I now understand better, though imperfectly, at the summation of the project. I am not the first to tackle the subject. The idea of an aesthetic field of the sort I describe is the subject of a recent study by Snell (2021), who links the work of Cezanne with the field theory of post-Bionian psychoanalysis, originated by a group of Italian psychoanalysts (Ferro 1999). With commentary on Cezanne's work and many references to the "new" field theory, this offers a theory of the visual field that embraces artist, audience and world in a "multiverse" of sensation and meaning in the process of being and becoming (Snell 2021). An expansive and intriguing idea, it is largely theoretical, focusing on a revered artist of the past, Cezanne, whose voice, although captured in quotes and commentaries, can no longer be heard. This differs from the experience-near model that I intend to pursue. I am interested in the here-and-now of the communicative space, allowing, of course, for theoretical and cultural considerations, but involving artist and audience in an alive discourse. Another theory that offers potential is group analysis, and in particular, the concept of the group matrix (Foulkes 1964; Roberts 1983; Nitsun 1996). The group matrix could be described as the cornerstone of group analysis. Originally regarded as a rather vague, arcane concept, not easily defined, the group matrix has in recent decades come into its own. Highlighting the network of connections in which we are all embedded, the influence of layers of social history, past, present and future, the concept has gained clarity and meaning. This is the essence of the group matrix (Hopper 2018; Hopper and Weinberg 2016; Schlapobersky 2016). Applying the concept to specific contexts, there are proposals for a "medical matrix" (Gerada 2019) and a "soldiers' matrix" (Friedman 2015), while further matrices suggest themselves as the containers of segments of society and culture. As yet, there has been no suggestion of an "artists' matrix", but there is good reason to consider that artists are themselves embraced in a network with historical roots and contemporary potentials. The artist's matrix I suggest could be seen group analytically as both the *foundation matrix*, that which already exists in the historical sphere of experience, and the *dynamic matrix*, a matrix that undergoes changes in the course of time. (Foulkes 1964; Hopper and Weinberg 2016). The initiative I describe in this book can be seen as the creation of a matrix that draws on a *foundation matrix* and evolves in the course of the presentations as *a dynamic matrix*. The group evolves, as I do with it. If this idea of an artist's matrix holds ground, it positions me not as an isolated artistic being in a vague, indefinable context but as an artist in a community of artists, viewers, traditions and potentials. If this seems obvious at one level, at another, it gives substance to what we intuitively know. It creates a framework for the project I describe in this book, linking with the aforementioned heuristic model of inquiry in which the artist's matrix becomes a crucial component of the evolving field.

While the matrix described above tends still towards the meta-psychological, remaining in the hypothetical sphere, it is important to recognize that it has real, creative properties that may yield tangible products. The matrix is not just static, especially in its dynamic form. It is itself generative. There is a poetic aspect to it: the idea of birth, of foetal development, is a cogent metaphor for the group matrix. Deriving from the Latin word "mater", the matrix symbolizes a womb or container in which something grows and is held in a nurturing way (Roberts 1983). Rather than being a purely passive container, it is productive. In a group, this happens through the synergy created by the contributions of all those who constitute the matrix, but it is facilitated and transformed by the implicit "maternal" container. Although explicable in these interactional terms, there is at the same time a kind of magic that occurs, rather like Jung's alchemical analogy of separate forces converging to create something new – the "conjunctio" (Jung 1956). In the process of change, there is a mysterious component that may be beyond full understanding. We are in the territory of Winnicott's transitional space (1953), describing the creative potential of a field of participants in which something different emerges, transcending the membership and creating a new dimension. This is the creative spirit of the matrix. It is the version of the matrix that, I believe, is relevant to my project, linking the participants with my paintings and the autobiographical thread that informs the narrative. Together, these elements create something new. I see it as the basis of the artist's matrix, both in a general sense and specifically in my own case, searching for a place in the artistic universe, spurred on by those who have shared my work and responded from hearts and minds.

We tend to see creativity as emanating from an individual. True: the history of art is built on the seminal contributions of individual artists through the ages. However, no artist exists in a vacuum. Even if the artist works alone, there is always a context that in some way influences their creation. This is not an easily definable context that unambiguously nurtures the artist's creativity – it often presents obstacles – but a configuration of culture, zeitgeist, artistic trends and constraints that permeates the world in which the artist lives and breathes. This applies not only to the wider artistic matrices of history but to the smaller matrices, such as a group of people working together on projects, installations, performances, which may have a strongly creative trope, impulse or drive that facilitates creative expression. I have touched on the generative aspect of the matrix in several of my publications, and it is an aspect of what I describe as the group as an object of desire (Nitsun 2006). I felt this process coming alive in the present project. Although I was officially the artist, the presentations stimulated a creative spirit in the groups in attendance, the images evoking many rich associations and turning the existing matrix into something fertile and productive. This had a binding effect on the groups. Many people attending were strangers to each other, but through connecting with the group, they came closer, responding to the artwork and adding thoughts, images and allusions, literary and otherwise, to the unfolding matrix.

Viewed in these terms, we can see the value of painting and other art forms as seminal in the formation of a developing artist's matrix but also the corollary: how the matrix as a container facilitates the creation of the artistic object.

A historical view

The artist's matrix has a historical dimension: the presence of figures from the past who have grappled with the fundamental questions of being an artist. The quest to be known, one's work to be seen and appreciated, is a theme that runs through the history of art. The vicissitudes of this quest are the stuff of legend. Consider one of the best-known artists of all time, Van Gogh. In his lifetime, Van Gogh's work was either unseen or, if seen, largely repudiated, ridiculed. The tragic fact of his selling only one painting in his lifetime to a client other than his brother, Theo, says it all. Although there were various reasons for Van Gogh's mental anguish, including the searing tensions in his personal relationships and his isolation in a provincial town in France in the last years of his life, the failure to attract interest in his work must have added fuel to his breakdowns, self-harm and eventual suicide. The irony: a century after his death in a field in Provence, van Gogh is possibly the most widely known artist of all time, revered and adored, his paintings selling for many millions, his work in countless reproductions. A contrasting example is Picasso. From early on, his work was seen, admired, bought. Increasingly secure in the art network, he is able to experiment, take bold steps, break new ground, initiate trends (Schama 2009a). Visibility and recognition in the artist's matrix are reinforcing, motivating. The theme of recognition and feedback is a leitmotif in the social history of art.

There are artists whose concerns about the interactional dimensions of the visual field are germane to their work. They desire to draw the viewer closer to the art so that the relationship between the two is amplified, the viewer in the embrace of the work – *as if the viewer could be sharing the visual space with the artist*. Cezanne, as Snell (2021) points out, was preoccupied with presence in his motifs. In some ways, a traditional painter, he at the same time sought to bring a new dynamism into his work, animating the image in such a way that it could be seen and experienced more fully and deeply by the viewer. The object in Cezanne's paintings, be it a mountain, a still-life, or a portrait, evokes a deeper and wider human field.

A more recent artist with similar preoccupations is Mark Rothko, the American abstract expressionist. Famous for his monumental paintings with their grid of abstract shapes playing off against each other, his work is rooted in an existential-ist perspective concerned with being, the passing of time, and loss. Given these themes, it is not surprising that his work has been the subject of much psycho-analytic commentary. In part, this refers to his acute sense of an audience, the relationship he sought with the viewer. Schama (2009b, p. 420) states of Rothko: "No other painter in the history of modern art – perhaps in the entire history of painting – was so obsessed with the relationship between the artist and his audience". Rothko regarded his work, each painting, as in an ongoing state of evolution. No work was finished as such: each piece was shrouded in the illusion of perpetual becoming. Not only did he want to share this with the viewer, but he wanted the viewer to participate in the living process of the painting's immanence. In this sense, the work was co-created by the viewer. Schama compares this to the mystery of foetal development, where we may hold something as it unfolds into throbbing life (not at all unlike my description of the group matrix above). We, the viewer, are partners in its creation, in a sense, auxiliary artists inhabiting and co-constructing the artist's matrix.

The online opportunities of today's world considerably extend the scope of the artist's matrix. Sheer exposure is an aspect of the internet-driven world, but more so, the potential for interaction with an audience, fostering connection, validation, discussion, amplification. This does not rule out gatherings in real-time and -space, and there is indeed a debate to be had about the dominance of the virtual and how it subserves – or not – the artist's agenda, but we now have a more complex, richer potential field of feedback than ever before.

Paintings as symbols

Much has been written psychoanalytically about the symbolic meaning of art, how painting and other art forms reflect, capture and interpret psychological experience, including distal and unconscious experience. This usually relates to individual intra-psychic experience, with reference to early experience in relation to significant others, the early sensual, holding experience of infancy providing a platform for the later evocation of aesthetic imagery. There is much less written about its relation to groups, which is why I go to some length in this chapter to address the gap. Because of the relative dearth of writing in this sphere, it is useful to look at some of the relevant psychoanalytic literature and to see what can be extrapolated to groups.

Christopher Bollas (1987) touches on issues that are integral. His notion of the transformational object, while being linked to the "vertical" emphasis of the early mother-child relationship, highlights the wider symbolic significance of art, whether in an individual or group context. Arising in the form and quality of a mother's presence and attention in infancy, creating an "idiom" of the self-other experience, a search arises in later life for a transformational object that revives the early experience. Bollas links this to a notion of the "aesthetic object", or a moment of aesthetic encounter in which there is a powerful connection with an object of beauty that embraces the viewer in a heightened experience of self-in-the-world. This happens spontaneously, and often unexpectedly, in the appreciation, for example, of nature, landscape, flora, the sea, a beautiful person. The arts similarly evoke the transformational object: painting, music, a fragment of literature can all have this effect. They may all touch the viewer/listener/reader in a way that is transformative, if only for moments in time. In the present project, I wanted to create an experience for an audience, bringing painting and narrative together in a way that would reach and move people. Through the groups' reactions and the intersubjective depth achieved, there was an aesthetic encounter that transcended the separate elements of the initiative.

That much of this happened during the dark days of Covid, and during the deprivations of lockdown, meant having an audience that was eager to be nourished, to be transformed, as well as helping to transform. Hence my sense that the groups were powerfully engaged. Given the pandemic, I have wondered whether I was undertaking this work and offering online presentations in part to provide stimulation and solace to fellow travellers in a beleaguered world. This, too, was an important part of the artistic matrix I was developing: the coming together through images and narrative at a time of fear and stress.

Bollas' writing tends to emphasize the life-enhancing potential of the transformational object. However, he suggests that the impact of the early mothering relationship is by no means always growthful and that frustrating early experiences are also formative in the search for a transformational object, possibly to correct but also mirror the early problem. In chapters 8 and 9, I explore the transformational aspects of my complex relationship with my own mother, including her frustrations in realising herself as a person.

A different emphasis on the significance of objects in emotional development comes from Volkan (1981), an expert in the psychoanalysis of trauma who attempts to make sense of the enduring and processing of trauma. This includes the relationship to objects, be they literally objects such as a book or toy or item of clothing, or a relationship with another. "The linking object" (Volkan 1981) refers to something that connects the traumatized individual with aspects of previous experience that may be comforting. It helps to endure and possibly overcome the trauma. An example is the teddy bear in my painting "Laura and Teddy", described in Chapter 4 on the doll series. The painting was seen by one viewer as a child at boarding school holding her beloved teddy. The child, in this narrative, was traumatized by the boarding school experience but took comfort from the teddy bear that linked her to memories of home and family in another country.

The paintings in my presentations can be seen to have similar functions. As linking objects in the years of the pandemic, they elicited a dialogue with the fear – and hope – that many people experienced. As mediating objects, they facilitated making sense of the overall experience while evoking surprising insights – the "unthought known" (Bollas 1987). Although the viewers, people in the audience, were not necessarily traumatized as such, everyone struggled with anxiety and confusion during the pandemic. In some cases, there were direct connections with illness or the loss of a friend or relative who had succumbed to Covid. Lockdown was a time of retreat and refuge, a time of heightened anxiety, with the shadow of trauma hovering in the background, sometimes intruding sharply into the foreground. I hoped in some of my presentations, with the paintings as mediating or linking objects, to provide a framework in which the experience could be shared openly and meaningfully.

These ideas help to give further substance to the concept of the artist's matrix. The artist creates a world within the scope of a particular piece of art. This is shared with others as an aesthetic or evocative object. I suggest that this is more fully realised in dialogue with others than is the sovereign, immutable object, a painting or a sculpture that exists in splendid isolation. In Part 2 of the book, detailed descriptions of my presentations illustrate this point more fully.

The group process

There are other aspects of the group process that merit recognition, that add to an understanding of how the groups functioned and helped to fashion the artist's matrix. One aspect is the distinction between the vertical and horizontal axes of the group. The vertical axis refers to the linear, hierarchical relationship to the psychotherapist/analyst: more typical of dyadic analysis or therapy with its limited interactional sphere. The horizontal axis, which is specific to the group setting with its multiple membership, describes communication and influence across the group membership. This may include the analyst but as part of the group rather than as a separate authority. The strength of group analytic therapy is largely vested in the horizontal axis, bringing in a much greater diversity of thought, history, and opinion than the dyad, and hence considerably enlarging the therapeutic frame. Psychotherapy aside, it is the horizontal axis that I believe is so valuable in the construction of an artists' matrix, the enrichment of understanding that comes through the participation of not just one viewer or critic but a group of people representing different perceptions and perspectives. Yet, the importance of the vertical axis and its implications for the leadership of the group should not be denied. Different needs and requirements are met by the group facilitator. He/she holds the group boundaries, contributes from a wise and informed position, and enables the horizontal axis to emerge, consolidate and thrive.

Deleuze and Guattari (1987) have formulated the influential notion of trees and rhizomes. This, by analogy, describes the distinction between the vertical (trees) and horizontal (rhizomes) highlighted above. The tree is an apposite image for the vertical axis, and rhizomes, a colourful analogy for the spread and clustering of creative thought that occurs in a well-functioning group. Echoing my view, Berman and Avrahami (2022) highlight the need for both processes in effective groups. In my presentations, there was a crucial interaction between the vertical axis (myself as presenter, group analyst, artist, narrator) and the horizontal axis (the eyes, ears, hearts and voices of the group members).

Performance art

Of the various art forms that are akin to my project, performance art is one of the most relevant. Having started as a marginal body of expression in the early 20th century, performance art has gained considerable presence and influence in the art world (Goldberg 2011). Its relevance to my work is debatable, but it is worth exploring the principles inherent in this art form. I have previously written about performance art. Impressed by its ascendance in the art world and its implications for other fields, including group analysis, I included a chapter entitled "Performance art and group analysis" in my 2015 book, *Beyond the Anti-group* (Nitsun 2015a), which is a collection of essays on contemporary issues, including art in the 21st century. It is useful to revive some of my ideas in this context.

The chapter in my 2015 book highlights profound cultural change in the 21st century as an important backcloth. Reflecting a world in which many familiar boundaries have disappeared, there is a growing interpenetration of disciplines and schools of thought. Quoting from my chapter: "such penetrating change that diverse spheres of thought, action and imagination may be expected to collide in unexpected, even radical ways. Performance art is at the epicentre of many of these changes, drawing on a multitude of cultural forms . . . and crossing boundaries." (Nitsun 2015a, p. 185). Possibly, back in 2015, I was anticipating my own attempt to challenge the traditional boundaries of psychology and art, albeit doing so in a more exploratory way than some of the radical excursions of performance art.

Performance art tends to break with established traditions of "static" visual art, notably painting and sculpture, by creating live art forms that attract an audience and encourage participation between performers and spectators. Goldberg (2011) describes the history of performance art in the 20th century as the history of a permissive, open-ended medium executed by artists who are impatient with the limitations of more established forms and are keen to take their art to the public. Some performance artists seek to directly involve the viewer/s. Tino Sehgal (2012), for example, has experimented with large-scale groups. He regards the participants as powerful assets, an audience who should be drawn directly into the creative process rather than remaining passive observers. His most well-known piece, "These Associations", invites large numbers of people to participate in a series of interactions that are essentially group relational processes, with an emphasis on sharing and feedback.

Another aspect of performance art is storytelling, often in autobiographical form. I touch on the subject of memoir throughout this book, and it is useful to consider its place in performance art. In the contributions of well-known performance artists such as Marina Abramovic and Cindy Sherman, the personal story, in its many guises, is often at the core of the performance. In the work of both Abramovic and Sherman, themes of self, identity and existential status are embedded in the fabric of the performance. I would not claim to be a performance artist, but there are aspects of the approach that I value. The idea of a presentation to an audience that combines artwork with a biographical narrative – my chosen format – is close to the spirit of performance art. The audience's response is not just a mirror of the presentation but, through engagement and interaction, adds to the meaning of the event, enlarging the artist's matrix. Although I tend to be a "straightforward" presenter, in the sense that I deliver a talk without embellishments and actions, there is inevitably an element of performativity in the way I communicate. I am not averse to arousing people's feelings and sympathies, to touching them personally.

While not aiming to be a performance artist, I locate my project within the realm of contemporary artistic forms that situate performativity within a multi-dimensional, interactive approach: another way of construing the artist's matrix.

Conclusion

I have argued in this chapter for greater recognition of the group as a context for both the creation and appreciation of art. Traditionally, the artist has been regarded as somewhat separate from society, leading a mysterious, self-enclosed existence on the margins of the community and relating through art but largely at a distance. This may reflect a romantic-tragic vision of the artist that may have its place in the history of art but is out of keeping with the contemporary world with its enhanced social links. I have called this configuration "the artist's matrix". It anticipates the exploration of my own presentations in Part 2 of the book and derives from insights I have gained in the course of undertaking this work. The visual field I describe is enriched by bringing together different elements such as painting and narrative and encouraging a group response that is active and participatory rather than passive and observational. That the gatherings in my project took place during the pandemic added depth and poignancy to the discourse.

Part 2

The paintings

Part 2 of the book is devoted to a detailed presentation of the five series of paintings that make up this book. These are: *Dolls and Demons*; *The Deserted City*; *Fragile Nature*; *Dancers*; and *Four Women*.

The paintings in each chapter are embedded in a narrative. With some variation, the chapters follow the same sequence – an introduction to the theme, a presentation of the paintings and the threads that link the visual images to the narrative. Poetry is introduced in some chapters. Because of publishing limitations, a selection of the paintings had to be made, presenting only key works in each series and describing others. There is an account of the groups who attended the presentations, initially in physical space and later online.

The thematic build-up of the five painting series is highlighted, with a growing awareness of the symbolic underpinnings of the project.

DOI: 10.4324/9781003232230-6

Chapter 4

Dolls and demons

Introduction

This chapter describes the period preceding the pandemic that was the beginning of my excursion as a painter-psychotherapist. I was preoccupied with the theme of dolls and produced a series of approximately forty paintings based on this theme. I held an exhibition of the paintings in my studio in the seaside town of Hove, East Sussex, in May 2019. The exhibition was part of the "Artists' Open Houses" programme linked to the annual Brighton Festival and drew many people to see the work over a one-month period. Although the dominant images were of dolls, the figures were ambiguous. Many of them could be seen as children, blurring the distinction between real and unreal: doll and child; child and adult. Possibly because of this ambiguity, reactions to the paintings were much more varied, intense and contradictory than anything I had expected. I was surprised, at times overwhelmed, by the power of the images to evoke such a plethora of responses.

The differing responses to the paintings started at the outset, as people visited the exhibition. Viewers reacted in distinctly personal ways, often in striking contrast to others' responses. But the main revelations came in a large, invited group discussion towards the end of the exhibition. This generated a rich associative process, touching on themes of emotional significance: childhood identity, the importance of playthings, relationships with parents, sibling rivalry and, beyond that, historical trauma, tragedy and loss. It was the power of this discussion that inspired not just my further painting forays but the addition of an autobiographical narrative and psychological commentary.

The doll paintings started a process of inquiry that I realized increasingly was very personal, culminating in the last series, *Four Women*. These first and last series of paintings bracketed the overall project, the other themes providing interlocking perspectives on a unifying theme that gradually emerged over time. But, for the moment, the dolls themselves take centre stage.

Background

Why, at this stage of my life and painting career, did I embark on the series of dolls, a curious subject that was a marked departure from my previous work? (see

DOI: 10.4324/9781003232230-7

Chapter 2 for a more complete background). Many people enquired about this and often arrived at the exhibition asking, "Why dolls?" As explained earlier, I had begun to feel that my painting was repetitive, too easy. I had felt the danger of stasis, of getting stuck, of settling for the secure and comfortable as an artist. Even the keen sales of the paintings made me question whether my work was too comfortable. I felt a strong urge to return to the human subject. But what sort of figures would I paint? Then, as if by chance, the dolls emerged. When asked by viewers about the change of direction, I tended to give an "objective" reply. I had recently bought a Victorian house in the Brighton area and became interested in Victoriana. I roamed the many antique shops in Brighton and Hove, and there, amongst the stacks of furniture and "objects d'art", were the dolls.

There was a strong fascination with dolls in Victorian times, of almost cultish proportions. The trend was amply reflected in early photographs and etchings of children and their dolls. See Figure 4.1, "Victorian Child and Doll", which is an etching rather than a photograph but conveys the relationship between child and doll. These little groupings are usually carefully and artfully composed, sometimes revealing a striking similarity between children and dolls, in dress and demeanour – although in Figure 4.1 there is a clearer difference between child and doll. The dolls in the Victorian pictures, not unusually, have dolls of their own, tiny little dolls clutched in the hands of the bigger doll. The figures usually form affectionate little groupings, conveying a sense of maternal care and a quality of tender bonding between the figures.

My explanation about Brighton Victoriana seemed to satisfy people's curiosity. But I felt that the reasons were more complex. There was not only my wish for a change of direction but an interest in linking my preoccupations as a psychotherapist and group analyst with the pursuit of painting. As a clinician and writer, particularly in the group field, I had tended to emphasize the darker aspects of human development. Could I, as an artist, now situate myself more clearly in this world; could I produce paintings that would reflect a more quirky, unexpected, challenging, disturbing aspect of humanity? And could I do this without compromising myself as a painter, my love of colour, my interest in form and texture, and my wish to engage the viewer?

I had decided early on that I would not paint images of sweet, pretty dolls – the conventional perception of dolls – but dolls that could evoke differing feelings and associations. I decided to strengthen this aspect, to subvert the apparent innocence of dolls, blurring some of the faces, adding vigorous brush marks in places and exaggerating some of the features. In hindsight, I can see the likelihood that the images would evoke strong reactions. However, as I mentioned, I was in for a surprise. The images elicited wide-ranging and vivid associations, varying from those who saw them as beautiful, evocative figures to those who found them uncomfortably ambiguous, triggering disturbing associations of damage, abuse and loss.

In order to pursue my subject matter, I researched dolls extensively online. I was astonished to find an overwhelming number and variety: dolls of different countries, cultures, eras, fashions, moods: English vintage dolls, French dolls,

Figure 4.1 Victorian Child and Doll

Source: Etching by unknown artist, 14 × 10 cm, Getty Photo Image, with colour wash by Morris Nitsun, 2022

German dolls, Russian dolls, American dolls; tiny dolls, huge dolls, plain dolls, impossibly glamorous and ornate dolls. Mostly these were girl dolls, but there were also boy dolls. Further, there were dolls that represented adults, including a set of Russian aristocratic dolls and others with ballet-dancer attire and elaborate headgear. Even old-age dolls with wizened little faces! Fascinating. Each of my paintings was based on one of these images, mainly the child dolls, using the idea of the doll as a starting point but interpreting it in my own way. By the time of the exhibition, I had produced almost forty paintings on this theme in approximately six months, a high rate of output by most painters' standards, and it felt like a complete and rounded collection. When titling the paintings, a question arose: how would I differentiate the dolls? I decided to personify them – to give them each a name. Faced with the huge range of names, I remained true to the sources of inspiration, whether English or "foreign" dolls such as French and Russian, also trying to bring a Victorian aspect where applicable, and out poured the names: Martha, Natasha, Olga, Rupert, Jenny, Pierre, Hugh, Arabella and so on.

Dolls as symbols

It is useful, before proceeding to explore viewers' responses, to consider the significance of dolls in childhood development, what they represent and what they symbolize. They are part of the magical world of toys in childhood but carry the added significance of their resemblance to people, particularly young children. As such, they act as a bridge between the child and the world, between the animate and the inanimate, between the world of fantasy and the real world (even though these realms are often closer than imagined). They may represent the child itself, but they are also objects of projection. They can be anything you wish, a baby, a sibling, a friend. In your play with them, you can experiment with a host of relationships: mother or father to baby, friend to friend, teacher to pupil, dresser to dressed. They can be good objects or bad objects: loved, adored, indulged; or reprimanded, reviled and rejected. They provide a playground or stage for rehearsing the social and interpersonal challenges that arise in the child's present life and beckon in the future (Stern 1985; Hashmi et al. 2020). The child's sense of growing identity and efficacy, the multiple roles they will be required to play and indeed their place in the world is often played out with their dolls. In many ways, they constitute self-objects (Kohut 2009), providing psychological functions that are germane to childhood development, such as mirroring, twinship, merging and agency. They can be regarded as transitional objects (Winnicott 1953), helping the child to separate from early parental figures, and transformational objects (Bollas 1987), enhancing the experience of self and other.

But dolls are not just imaginary characters. They are embodied: they have little bodies, heads, eyes, ears, noses, torsos, limbs, hands and feet. And of course, they are gendered. Although gender-neutral dolls are now more common, dolls have always been mainly girls, their femininity emphasized in looks and clothes. Boy dolls exist as well, in some cultures more than others, and their gender is similarly differentiated in hairstyles and clothes. Dolls have orifices: even if just the impression of a hole, these minimal signs suggest that they might be able to speak, eat, hear, pee. Recently, these features have become more pronounced and more real: dolls that blink, open their mouths, speak, feed, cry, walk, sing. I remember as a child being fascinated by these possibilities: examining the sense organs and orifices to see what they did and wondering whether, through some magic, the dolls might literally come alive.

An aspect of dolls that I was not in touch with, not consciously at any rate, was their frightening aspect. It was only with people's feedback that I began to recognize the ambivalence towards dolls, mainly coming from fear. Dolls, many people feel, are weird, creepy, sinister. They belong to the realm of the ghostly and the uncanny. The ambiguity between real and unreal that for some is intriguing and playful, is uncomfortable and eerie for others. Some people associate dolls with horror stories. One woman linked the dolls in my paintings to *Annabelle*, a well-known cult film about an evil doll. Another made an association with the film, *Whatever Happened to Baby Jane?*, in which Bette Davis, playing a deranged, ageing actress who was once a child star, dresses up as a child doll to foster the illusion of perpetual youth. At the same time, she carries out acts of frightening domestic terrorism against her crippled sister.

The face

The bodies of dolls are usually obscured by their clothes, pretty dresses concealing their rubbery nakedness. But the face and hair are always prominent and visible, and it's the doll's face, more than anything else, that defines its personality. When painting, I was aware of concentrating on the face. In a sense, these were portraits, portraits of inanimate dolls, but with the potential to come alive, to be characters, characters that told a story, hardly formed in my mind, but open to conjecture, to imagination. As I added brush marks and textures, blurring and sometimes distorting the image, I was aware of a narrative unfolding, a story in the making.

Not only is the human face the main expression of a person's character and individuality: it has a central role in interpersonal communication. The face usually registers some or other attitude or emotion and plays a significant part in mutual understanding. It has a crucial mirroring function. It mirrors the person to whom the face belongs, and it mirrors the interpersonal other in expressive communication. It conveys messages and meaning in the same way that speech does, but often more directly, in a less disguised fashion. People often search each other's faces for a hidden truth or imagined feelings.

The face features significantly in developmental studies and psychoanalytic treatises on infant and child development (Wright 1991). But this was not always the case. Early psychoanalysis tended to emphasize other parts of the body rather than the face. However, Winnicott in the UK made early seminal observations, crystallized in his famous question, "What does the baby see when he looks at his mother's face? I am suggesting that ordinarily, what the baby sees is himself or herself" (1967, in Winnicott 1974, p. 112). Although Winnicott's quote empha-sizes the mother's face – and what the child sees in it – we now recognize both faces as vital, mother's and baby's, in a reciprocal mirroring relationship. Winn-icott went on to describe the destructive effect of failed mirroring on the child, see-ing it as an impingement, an interference with developmental trust and continuity. Searles (1965) in the USA similarly gave the face early recognition in individual and interpersonal development. Like Winnicott, he located it in the mother-infant relationship, describing how the mother is the child's earliest mirror and how her responsiveness imbues the child with their sense of self and emotional knowledge. If the mother's face as a mirror is unreflecting, damage may be done to the child who becomes walled off from their own emotional self.

The gaze

Returning to the exhibition, to what extent did mirroring influence people's reac-tions to the paintings? What happened when visitors came face to face with the figures? As noted, there were striking differences in how viewers engaged with the dolls. Some hardly engaged at all, hurrying through the exhibition, others spending a good deal of time looking at the dolls. A fairly common reaction was the feeling that the dolls were looking at the viewer. Several people referred to the dolls' gaze. They felt that the dolls were inviting them into a conversation of some sort. The dolls were appealing to them, confronting them, challenging them. One viewer was so struck by this phenomenon that she suggested the exhibition be called "The Gaze". For her, this was positive. She felt mesmerized by the dolls' eyes, strongly drawn into a conversation with them, and, although in some cases this was uncomfortable, she wanted to engage. Each doll, she felt, had a different gaze and invited a different conversation. This contrasted markedly with viewers who gave the paintings short shrift: a quick, cursory glance and rushed off or pre-ferred to look at my older paintings downstairs. For them, the gaze was aversive.

Both the face and the gaze specifically have been, and are, the subject of detailed psychological commentary. Kenneth Wright (1991) describes the gaze as a meta-phor for the entire developmental process – how we come to know ourselves and others as separate beings. The face is intrinsic to contemporary developments in psychotherapy, linking with the current emphasis on mirroring, attunement and empathy. Looking and seeing the other is no longer avoided. Whereas in early psychoanalytic practice, and still now to a large extent, the analyst sits outside the patient's field of vision, the face-to-face, eye-to-eye encounter is regarded as intrinsic in contemporary psychotherapy, a source of vital engagement and infor-mation. This is particularly the case in group psychotherapy (Schermer 2018). Here, a number of people, including the therapist, are not only in close physical proximity but face each other in each and every session. Participants are transpar-ent in this setting: their faces, in all their moods and vagaries of interest and emo-tion, on show. Participants' facial expressions are a moment-to-moment reflection of the group process and relationships within the group.

The range of responses

The first painting

In this section, I describe the multiplicity of responses to the paintings, trying to bring some coherence to the outpouring of associations. To start with, I focus on one person's complex responses to the very first painting on show, in the entrance hall of the house at the beginning of the exhibition. This response highlights some of the themes to come. The painting is named "Laura and Teddy" (Figure 4.2) and shows a child in shadowy outline holding a teddy bear. The teddy bear is painted in greater detail and has a stronger presence than the child. The painting differs from all the others in showing two figures – the girl and her teddy – whereas the others are of a single doll. The viewer whose response I outline here is a psycho-therapist working with adults who have been traumatized as children. She brought to the painting her specialist knowledge of individuals who were sent to boarding school as children, some for many years. It is now well-known that the experience of a British boarding school can be emotionally damaging (Schaverien 2015), although in the earlier 20th century, awareness of the problem hardly existed – or was denied.

This viewer was very affected by the painting. She said it haunted her. She felt that the shadowy depiction of the child represented exactly how boarding school children might feel: neglected, unseen, uncared for, and how the vivid teddy bear represented the strong attachment to aspects of home, the child's parents, siblings, toys that were sacrificed in the transition to boarding school. For these children, dolls and toy animals such as the teddy have a special significance as objects of attachment and comfort. This is akin to the "linking objects" that Volkan (1981) described as representing a connection, through person or object, with a traumatic past.

Moving onto the rest of the exhibition and the welter of responses, I have chosen to group them into categories. Initially reluctant to over-simplify the range of responses, I realised more and more that what seemed spontaneous, random differences in people's reactions followed particular lines. Trends emerged. Consistent pictures of childhood revealed themselves as if drawing on shared constructs. Three main categories became evident –

- The lovely/loved doll/child
- The monstrous, frightening doll/child
- The traumatized doll/child

The lovely/loved child

There were a number of viewers who expressed great delight in the images, intrigued by the dolls' resemblance to children and how this evoked impressions and memories of childhood. One person expressed this vividly. She saw the dolls

Figure 4.2 Laura and Teddy
Source: Morris Nitsun 2019, oil, 90 × 60 cm

as exuberant, joyful images of childhood. They looked as if they were contemplating a bright, colourful world, joy reflected in their vibrant faces. They were filled with wonder. Further, she commented, this was an important communication to those, particularly adults, who have lost their sense of wonder. When I mentioned that some viewers had had an aversive reaction to the images, she expressed surprise. The vigorous brush marks and seemingly random colour of the figures that elicited a negative, anxious reaction in some people, seeing these features as evidence of fragmentation or abuse, evoked the opposite response in this viewer: "That's what makes them. That's their beauty. The colours and the marks are expressions of what they see around them, a world of wonder and delight".

Highlighting the difference in viewers' perceptions, Figures 4.3 and 4.4 are images of dolls/children that were perceived by some viewers as likeable, endearing figures and by others as disturbed and disturbing, eerie, lost, ghostlike. Mostly, people's responses emphasized either/or: either the positive, likeable attributes of the dolls or their negative, disturbing attributes. But some viewers shared more complex impressions: the beauty and power of the images as well as the mysterious and more disturbed elements. I asked some viewers to put their thoughts in writing, and here are (abridged) copies of their comments. They both mention the vulnerability of children, as seen via the dolls, but with different associations –

I was so moved to see the paintings. They are extraordinary, and many of the dolls look lost and wistful. They are haunting and so beautiful. They reach back of course into your childhood and everyone else's as well. . . . I am more and more aware of the double lives children live – on the one hand full of joy and ebullience, and yet also so uncertain, anxious, vulnerable. And how hard we try to protect them from all the darkness and how deeply they sense it and how much remains unspoken but it's there in the eyes of your doll/ children . . . all that unspoken sadness, as well as innocent wonder, is there, in the eyes and mouths of your dolls. And I know that for everyone seeing your paintings and certainly for you, they contain other, deeply personal associations. Anyway . . . I think they're absolutely brilliant – and certainly unique.

LZ

These are such powerful images. They're so evocative, so enigmatic. They evoke such tender feelings in me, about my dolls when I was little, and the bodily, quite visceral, even sexual frisson between children and their dolls, but also between children and their parents. They are lovely and I would love them to stay just as they are, for us to appreciate their innocence and beauty. But I am sure they will draw lots of different reactions. I loved my dolls but some people hate dolls. People are so good at putting stuff into children . . . and dolls. I feel sad that they can't just remain there in their costumes and funny hats.

AL

Figure 4.3 Martha

Source: Morris Nitsun 2019, oil, 59 × 42 cm

Figure 4.4 Rupert

Source: Morris Nitsun 2019, oil, 59 × 42

The monstrous doll/child

The positive, affirming, highly appreciative responses above – although hinting at differing attitudes to dolls – stand in marked contrast to those who saw the dolls in a negative, disturbing light. I use the overall category of monstrous in a metaphorical sense to describe these viewers' reactions to the dolls. I considered using the word "evil", but this felt archaic, with its connotations of original evil. The actual words people were used were more like "strange", "sinister", "frightening", "spooky", "creepy", "scary", "ghostly", "horrible" and even "terrifying": words that pick up directly on the dolls' unnerving impact on many people. These responses surprised me as I had not previously regarded dolls as frightening, and I had no conscious sense of wanting to paint sinister figures. But the frequency of this association was undeniable. People were adamant that this is what the dolls were, as if harbouring an intrinsic, malign force. A number of people could not bear to look at them. One young woman, on arrival at the exhibition, expressed an immediate aversion. She associated the images with horror films. She cringed on seeing the first few dolls, her hands rising to her face in fear or horror, and she visibly shrank as she looked around the collection. Not long afterwards, she said, "I must go", and she fled down the stairs. Another person, a friend who was familiar with my previous painting, went upstairs to the exhibition on arrival and almost immediately came back down again, shocked. "I'm sorry", he said, "But I just can't stand looking at them. They remind me of sinister dolls and scary parts of my childhood". These viewers often linked their aversion to the eyes of the dolls, which they saw as blank, staring, or threatening. This was in total contrast to those who perceived vulnerability and sadness in the eyes and regarded this feature as part of the appeal and charm of the paintings.

Figure 4.5 is an example of one of the paintings that were most often seen as frightening, if not terrifying. The doll is called Vicky and is one of the largest paintings in the exhibition, the size possibly adding to the sense of threat. I myself had seen Vicky as a "cute kid", a bit in awe, surprised by the world she perceives, but others saw her as both frightened and frightening.

A different, though possibly linked, dimension is ambiguity. I refer here not so much to the painted images as ambiguous, but rather to the ambiguity of dolls themselves as representations of human figures. Dolls reflect an ambiguity between real and unreal, doll and child, animate and inanimate. Studies have highlighted the confusion and disturbance this can cause the viewer. In aesthetics, the "uncanny valley" is a hypothesized relation between an object's degree of resemblance to a human being and the emotional response to the object. The concept suggests that "humanoid" objects that imperfectly resemble actual human beings provoke uncanny or strangely familiar feelings of eeriness and revulsion in observers (Misselhorn 2009). "Valley" denotes a dip in the human observer's affinity for the replica, a relation that otherwise increases with the replica's human likeness (Wikipedia).

Figure 4.5 Vicky

Source: Morris Nitsun 2019, oil, 80 × 60 cm

It is important, therefore, to note that there is a double ambiguity in these paintings. As dolls, they are ambiguous in their resemblance to human beings: as paintings, they are ambiguous through the particular technique of painting, sometimes intended, sometimes unintended. The theme of ambiguity arises strongly with the doll paintings and appears at several stages in this book since other painting series also evince varying degrees of ambiguity. The phenomenon of ambiguity touches directly on the psychological process of projection.

There is a further aspect of the dolls seen in a negative light that may belong in the category of the monstrous. It's about the dolls as needy. I put this response in the category of "monstrous" because some people described it in a highly aversive way. "I can't stand them", one woman said. "They seem to want something from me and I have nothing to give them. They are demanding something and it makes me want to pull back". It was as if there was a monstrous need in the doll/child, a frightening hunger that repelled the viewer.

The traumatized doll/child

Responses in this category were perhaps the most disturbed and disturbing of all. There were two rather different but interrelated perceptions: the dolls as abused, physically or emotionally; and the dolls as lost, rejected, abandoned. The theme of abuse was striking, vividly expressed. At an early point in the preview of the exhibition, one viewer spent some time looking at the paintings, expressing a growing unease. Finally, when he came to the painting of a boy doll, "Johnny" (Figure 4.6), he said,

> I know what it is. They have been abused. You can see it in his face here, his red cheeks look as if he's been slapped and the red line across his neck looks like his throat has been cut.

Another person saw abuse from practically the first moment she encountered the paintings. The more she looked at them, she said, the more convinced she was. The dolls disturbed her greatly. She saw their expressions as reflecting trauma and suffering. As with other viewers, she was quick to leave the exhibition. "They're pitiable", she said, "I find it very painful to look at them". This person, who worked with children, linked the theme directly to the widespread child abuse in society at large, past and present, both revealed and hidden. The intimation of abuse in the paintings, or perceived as such, became a consistent theme. Once people formed their perception, it was surprisingly definite: this is what the dolls represent, this is what they are. This person added, "There is too much of this around out there, the abuse. I see it here too. What made you paint abused children?"

A different strand of perceptions emphasized loss and abandonment. In this perception, the dolls themselves or the children they represented had suffered loss or had been abandoned. The narrative took different forms. One very articulate response, focusing on the dolls as dolls, described them as having once had a

Figure 4.6 Johnny
Source: Morris Nitsun 2019, oil, 42 × 59

place, a meaning, a significance that was lost. They had belonged to a child or a family, had been loved and looked after, but had since been discarded. Now they were lost in time. They had no place and you could see it in their shabby dress, their mournful expressions. Time was cruel to them. The narrative distressed this viewer. She found the dolls' plight unbearably sad. Her attitude of despair grew as she contemplated the images.

Sadness was a prevailing theme. Many people saw sadness in the dolls' eyes, sometimes deep sadness. There was grief and longing. The perception was again generalized: most of the dolls, if not all, conveyed sadness. This response was sometimes linked to the one described previously in which the doll/child was described as very needy, deprivation and sadness linked in the perception.

A final trend in the responses may relate to both the monstrous child-doll and the traumatized child-doll. It concerned emptiness. In this interpretation, the dolls were seen as manufactured, unreal figures that were hollow. The pretty dresses hid artificial bodies with empty interiors. The dolls had no personality, no claim on life or relatedness. Of course, this is objectively true. But it worried some people more than others. One couple saw this particularly in the dolls' eyes. They were dead eyes, vacant, staring. If the eyes are the window of the soul, one person commented, then these creatures had no soul. Like many of the perceptions, these comments came across as absolute: the essence of the dolls is their emptiness.

The groups

In this section, I describe two very different group events. I treat them separately, including their theoretical implications, but bring them together in the concluding comments.

Group I

The dolls exhibition culminated in a large gathering of colleagues and friends in the Hove studio, surrounded by the doll paintings. This was an invited group, about thirty-five in number, consisting largely of individual and group psychotherapists, as well as people from other professions, writers, musicians, architects and other artists. Group members sat around the room in a rather haphazard circle on chairs, cushions and the floor itself. The group had an explicit purpose – to discuss the impact of the paintings and what this triggered in them.

I was particularly interested in how the discussion in this group would evolve. The presence of many psychotherapists was challenging: how, as individuals and a group, would they respond? I had heard the views of a largely lay public in the preceding weeks and was surprised and impressed. How would the psychotherapist compare?

I facilitated the discussion, beginning with some personal information, including my childhood experience with dolls. I described how as a young child of six or seven, I had been attracted to my sister's dolls and liked playing with them, examining them, dressing them and speculating on their characters. Although not debarred from this contact, I had an uneasy sense of this being an inappropriate activity for a boy and gave up playing with them prematurely because of this anxiety. This was in 1940's/1950's South Africa, when apartheid was well established, with an overall sense of cultural oppression and demand for conformity to a rigid Calvinist ideal of family and gender-specific values. No place for a boy to be playing with dolls. Possibly my painting the dolls series in later life was a way of filling the gap, of revisiting my early interest in dolls. It may have been my openness about this that triggered several gender-based observations in the group. One or two gay men described how as children, they had been intrigued by dolls but avoided playing with them out of a fear of censure. A woman who, as a child, was attracted to boys' toys deliberately rejected dolls in protest against the imposition of feminine stereotypes. Another woman had been concerned about her young son playing with Barbie dolls because they represented a debased version of femininity: she would not have minded had they been the more "typical" dolls. She mentioned that her son had grown up gay.

The "therapists" group was more open about gender issues than I found in other viewers. The group highlighted the imposition of gender stereotypes, confirming the prevailing norms of the last century and, as in the above examples, illustrating the long-standing social constraints on children of both sexes. Comparisons were made with the current greater social tolerance of gender fluidity, yet recognizing that ambiguity often troubles people. Interestingly, too, there were gender-based differences in the communication styles of this group. The group was more evenly balanced for the sexes than is usual in a therapist-dominated group. The men, I found, approached the dolls' theme in a more reserved, distanced way. One or two initiated intellectual discussions about dolls. What was the definition of "doll"? What was its derivation? This question prompted several men there and then to Google the root of the word "doll", and a discussion ensued. Although useful in some respects, the discussion tended to dampen the emotional resonance created by the paintings. The women in the group, by contrast, told emotionally laden stories about their relationship to dolls and expressed more direct feelings in the discussion.

A further theme described the doll paintings as excavating aspects of lost or repressed childhood. This aspect of the discussion was especially rich, perhaps reflecting therapists' interest in early development and the inclination, in some at least, to talk openly about their own experiences. Numerous people recalled childhood experiences, some with dolls and some more generally, getting in touch with both painful and happy aspects of earlier years. The doll images were described as emblems of the distant past, now reviving memories and early fantasies. The word "revivification" was used: the sense of reviving, reanimating the dead or the disappeared: forgotten years, forgotten selves, forgotten toys. These came to life in the discussion.

Perhaps the most vivid example of the above was given by a colleague who grew up in Germany in the aftermath of World War Two. She described how as a child, she would wrap her dolls in cloth or newspaper then bury them in the garden. Some months later, she would exhume the doll and unwrap it to see what effect the burial had had. She wanted to see how the doll had fared, what damage it sustained, whether it had survived. Although she initially gave no specific information about the post-war context, it was difficult not to consider the dolls' burial as a symbolic representation of something to do with the war: more than "something" in fact. Burials on a wide scale were a feature of the war: the mass graves, the people buried dead, alive or half-alive, and the exhumation of the dead at the termination of the war, revealing the dreadful evidence of how many had been slaughtered. Although my colleague performed her own little burial ritual in the early 1950's, her action can be seen as an unconscious enactment of what had happened through the years of the war and had intensified as the "final solution" accelerated in the last few months. Perhaps it was a child's innocent, intuitive attempt to grasp the horror of what had happened and to evaluate the impact on real lives. Her actions would have paralleled the actual exhumation of bodies that continued – and was publicized – in the years following the war.

Struck by the power of this person's associations but concerned that my interpretation had gone too far, perhaps a projection of my own, I contacted my colleague soon after the event. She confirmed the accuracy of my interpretation. She herself understood the burial of the dolls as an attempt to make sense of half-conscious, inchoate, disturbing rumours about the war.

The example of the burial of the dolls not only illustrates the point about "revivification" (the bringing alive of the dead) previously noted. It touches on the process of mourning that is a requisite of dealing with loss. The process is comprehensively outlined in Freud's classic text "Mourning and Melancholia" (Freud 1917), in which he describes the repeated return to the loss and the lost object as a way of gradually mourning the loss. In this interpretation, the little girl in the story is grasping unknowingly at the trauma of war, privately in her garden, collectively through her unconscious identification with an entire society. Both the personal and the social, the private and the public, the conscious and the unconscious – all of which in any case reflect an interpenetrating matrix – vividly come together in this exceptional tableau.

Thematically and affectively, the emphasis in the discussion was dysphoric. The perception of dolls as sinister and frightening resurfaced, some people expressing a degree of distaste for the paintings. "I much prefer your other work, your landscapes and seascapes", a colleague said. Many people had associations of damage and abuse, in a similar way to some of the public's earlier responses but in rather more depth, as in the above example of burial and exhumation, possibly because of resonances across the group that intensified these associations. There were stories of sibling conflict around the dolls, disturbing memories of abuse as meted out to both children and dolls. There were poignant narratives of loss: abandonment of children and abandonment of dolls mirroring each other. The girl burying and unearthing her dolls in the garden symbolized the pervasive struggle to transcend damage and loss.

As noted previously, one of the most striking aspects of the discussion was the degree of projection onto the dolls. Projection was evident in the public responses that had preceded the group discussion in the prior weeks, conveying the impression that this was spontaneous, unconscious, on people's parts. One might have expected that in this more professional group – largely psychotherapists – there would have been a greater consciousness of projection, of the force of subjectivity, and an attempt at least to address or understand this: to own the projection. But this was not the case; the projections came thick and fast. There was a tendency to concretize the images in the paintings, of talking as if the projected characteristics were intrinsic qualities of the doll rather than attributions emanating from the viewer. Impressive as it was that people could associate so freely to the images, there was a quality of unfiltered projection. The associations lacked an "as-if" quality. At one point, the projections were so powerful that a non-therapist member of the group commented, "Don't you realise that these are projections? These are rather sweet, pretty dolls". Another protestor argued, "I think that the dolls aren't one thing or the other. Everything you're saying is being put onto the dolls". In spite of this challenge, the projections continued, sometimes conveyed with clarion conviction: "These *are* damaged dolls", "They *have* been abused"; "They really *are* sinister"; "They are *definitely* lost in time".

The strength and tenacity of some of the responses, even in this aware therapist group, were such that I wondered about the dynamic not just of projection but of projective identification (Ogden 1992; Nitsun 1996). The projections were tangible, and they were welcome in the sense that they brought the paintings alive and generated a lively discussion, but the degree of investment in some of the perceptions had the quality of projective identification: an identification that is so strong that the boundaries between self and other are blurred. Similarly, in the aversive reactions to the images, the sense of not being able to look at them, of having to flee or withdraw, there is a quality of not just mirroring but malignant mirroring (ZInkin 1983). This describes a toxic relationship between two individuals (usually) who can't bear to be in each other's company, the process suggesting a hatred of the other for representing disowned parts of the self. In this case, one of the figures, the doll, is static and unresponsive but nevertheless seems to trigger a form of malignant mirroring.

As the artist who executed the paintings, there were times I felt overwhelmed by the flood of attributions. One or two members of the group either picked this up or resonated with my surprise, and there followed an interesting discussion about "what is on the artist's mind when he/she paints?" Several people argued that very often, the artist has no conscious intention in producing an artwork, and what people see in the work is their own construction. I agree with this at one level but had myself become increasingly questioning of my motivation for painting the dolls. I was aware of the "objective" reasons associated with my move to a Victorian house and my surge of interest in Victoriana. I was also very conscious of the confluence of my journeys as a psychotherapist and an artist. But many of the viewers' responses triggered an awareness of further, more personal meanings for me, of unconscious reasons for painting the dolls. I describe these in more detail in the next section but want to end my description of this group by highlighting what a rich and stimulating event it was, illustrating the power of visual images to mobilize group reflection and debate. Additionally, the group reinforced the sense not only of individuals' subjective responses but the deeper social constructs that might inform these responses, loosely confirming the categories mentioned previously: the loved doll-child, the monstrous doll-child, and the traumatized doll-child.

The impact of the group discussion is described in an email I received afterwards from a friend/colleague who attended the group:

> What an excellent and memorable discussion your doll paintings inspired. I don't think I have ever been to an art exhibition that has generated such a fascinating, varied and emotional range of responses. My mind has been buzzing with it ever since. Thank you for organizing it and inviting us.
>
> DE

Personal learning

During the weeks of the exhibition, I increasingly became aware that the doll paintings had emerged from some internal pressure of my own that sought an outlet. Much of this, I realise now, concerned unresolved or dissociated aspects of my childhood, such as the early interest in dolls that I think I repressed and, together with this, thoughts about bodies, gender and sexuality. I believe the doll paintings were an attempt to revisit these childhood sites.

There was a theme of the loss of children in my childhood. My mother had two miscarriages and a stillbirth when I was between five and eight years old. I remember being old enough to register the confusion and sadness about her loss. I hardly understood the facts but knew that something untoward and upsetting had happened. More than this, as an adult, I had a powerful fantasy/memory of visiting my mother in a nursing home after one of these failed births, producing in my mind a frightening, lingering image of a mangled foetus. Were the doll paintings an attempt to address and perhaps resolve this memory, perhaps recreating the lost children? Was there a reparative motive behind this work? Or cathartic? Further, as an adult, I have not fathered children myself. This was partly circumstance, partly choice. I had been content with this decision for most of my adult life, but as an older man began to feel twinges of regret, partly to do with a lack of biological continuity, partly the absence of a younger generation who could be by my side as I aged. I sometimes envied friends their children and their grandchildren, the sense of a family unit that would bring comfort and support in the future. Were the dolls symbolically my unborn children, a way of creating my progeny, a symbolic family?

A further association was the loss of friends and family in recent years. In the previous decade or so, I had experienced the loss of a stream of people I loved, including my mother, my sister, a very close male friend and several female friends. With each death, I experienced a wave of shock and sadness, building to an enormous and overwhelming crescendo of loss: a preoccupation with irrevocable change and vanishing time. Were my doll paintings symbols of mourning, a parade of the deceased, of wanting both to revive the dead and say a last goodbye? These reflections put me in touch with more distant and even more catastrophic loss: my father's loss of half his family in war-torn Europe in World War II. My father never spoke about this until much later in life. But I grew up in the shadow of his loss, sensing my father's distant grief but not understanding it, knowing about his murdered parents and brothers and sisters but unable to express what had happened to them. Were the doll images the ghosts of the past, emblems of this massive unspoken loss that demanded recognition and sharing with others? Martha, Genevieve, Natasha, Vicky, Rupert, Luke and all the other dolls, were they proxies for those I had never known, those who lost their lives prematurely and unjustly?

These associations have remained with me since the exhibition ended. It was as if the paintings were an awakening, a reminder, a longing, a wake for all these absent figures in my life. I am reminded of Hanna Segal's observation on the roots of art: "All creation is really a re-creation of a once loved and once whole, but now lost and ruined object, a ruined internal world and self" (Segal 1952, p. 197).

The social unconscious

Moving from the intensely personal to the social, I suggest that what I described above is a history that is shared, albeit in different forms and different contexts, by many others. Most families have suffered trauma and loss. I suggest that the themes elicited by the paintings, in both members of the public who visited and the professional group that met in the studio, are part of a universal history. My work as a psychotherapist and group analyst has put me in touch with this at many levels, and I can see that the exhibition was a visual means of sharing this history with others. My two careers or predominant interests had come together in the exhibition, unknowingly at the start, knowingly in hindsight. Further, while highlighting the individual or personal unconscious responses to the dolls theme, the paintings triggered the social unconscious: shared preoccupations of the past, including hidden fragments of history and repressed or denied memory and knowledge (Hopper and Weinberg 2011, 2016)

A good example is what I described above as the discourse of childhood, a way of grouping and conceptualizing the varied responses to the paintings. The three main categories of response I distinguished – loved, monstrous and abandoned/traumatised – can be seen as reflections of the socially unconscious construction of childhood interacting with personal associations and projections. The consistency of responses within each category suggested a central assumption or belief about childhood. I suggest that these are not arbitrary associations, fortuitously picked up by me, but part of a deeper reservoir of perceptions of childhood, the hidden pool of the social unconscious. Further, as individuals, we may be more sensitive to one aspect of the discourse of childhood than another. Perhaps this comes through our own lived experience, what we have witnessed in others, or what we pick up in common discourse that has most captured our imagination. It is possible that there is a particular valency, in individuals and groups, for certain constructs.

This leads me to highlight once more the intense level of projection onto the images. That these could be so strong, and so strongly defended, even in a psychologically sophisticated audience, raises the question of how our perception is both moulded by and moulds, reinforced by and reinforces, our social constructs. In this interpretation, there is an ongoing interaction between the various discourses of childhood and the way we respond to them. A joint process of introjection and projection occurs: introjection of the social construct and projection of the construct onto a present figure, in this way maintaining the unconscious discourse. Of course, times change and social constructs and conventions change in turn (Elias 1994). What I describe above reflects some core elements of the discourse of childhood at a particular time.

In developing these points, I am going far beyond the immediacy of an exhibition of doll paintings. But it seems to me that it is important to recognize the depth of social representation the images tended to convey, even if only to give weight to the extraordinarily rich discussions that the paintings evoked. I am left with the power of contradiction in the range of responses, perplexing but understandable if viewed as belonging to the same overall discourse of childhood. As one viewer commented, the contrasting images have to live side by side – they inhabit us all. It is challenging for both the developing child to find their way in the contradictory realms of childhood and for adults to appreciate the full complexity and paradox of childhood in their own childhoods and those of children in the present.

Group 2

The second group took place in a very different setting, the American Group Psychotherapy Conference 2020 in New York City. I had been invited to deliver the "Ormont Lecture", a prestigious annual event, in which I presented the theme of the doll paintings and their realisation through feedback and discussion, including the contribution of the Brighton group described above. I gave a PowerPoint presentation to the New York audience showing reproductions of twelve of the original doll paintings. This was accompanied by a narrative describing how I came to the subject and what I had made of it through personal and group reflection. The event was filmed and can be viewed on YouTube in two parts, the lecture https://youtu.be/Bs61crl1jyI and the group/workshop described in what follows https://youtu.be/DeFUKPJhFHY

I followed a workshop structure this time: lecture, small group "demonstration", and large group discussion. The small group was the key intervention, very different from the Brighton group, though equally, if not more, powerful in confirming the impact of the paintings. I set this up as a "fishbowl" group of eight people with myself as facilitator, inviting volunteers from an audience of approximately ninety people. The group ran for an hour, watched by the larger audience. All around the room were positioned, on artist's easels, enlarged reproductions of six of the doll paintings so that these were in full view of all present.

This being a small group probably made it more intimate than the Brighton group, despite the group being observed by a large audience. The dolls theme immediately resonated, creating a close and cohesive group. The discussion was more directly emotional than the previous one, with heartrending stories linked to the dolls of childhood. There were frequent references to the paintings around the room, participants relating in-depth to one or other of the images, their observations of the dolls weaving in and out of their poignant narratives. There was a sense of the dolls of the past merging with the dolls in the room, generating an overall narrative of considerable intensity.

Because of limitations of space, I am reporting this group in less detail than the first but wish to convey the atmosphere of the group. The theme of emotional need in childhood and the way dolls filled this need was prominent in this group.

Briefly, the group started with a woman sharing her intense longing for a doll when she was a child. She had never owned a doll of her own. Her deprivation was linked to a refugee experience in the aftermath of World War II. With her family, she was fleeing a mid-European country for the safer shores of America. They had suffered poverty and hardship in their country, and there was little money for basic provisions, let alone a doll. She had tried to scrape together apple pips as tokens, the only way for her to purchase a doll at the time, but this was a forlorn venture. How many apple pips could a child collect? The apples were not plentiful, but in any case, how many apples could she eat? Eventually, in a stop-over in another city, she was shown a room with toys, including a doll that she was able to choose as her own. She loved this doll deeply. It accompanied her to America, where she had kept it all these years and still cherished it. Her grandchildren now liked to play with the doll, but she was concerned that it would break, that its delicate features and threadbare clothes would be damaged. She tried to keep it safe on a high shelf, yet wanted the children to access it, to share the doll with them. The woman wept through the telling of the story. It prompted another woman to talk about her love of her childhood dolls. In this story, the doll came not from deprivation but from the generosity of a mother who gifted the doll and created a full set of clothes for the doll.

I am focusing on the attachment and love of dolls in this group as it mirrors the maternal theme that emerged in group 1. The stories in the present group similarly illustrated the significance of dolls as transitional objects. In the case of the first woman above, the doll represented the transition from one country to another, something to hold onto in the panic and bewilderment of immigration. Mother exists here symbolically: the mother country, left behind for another country, potentially a new "mother". The dolls, and the paintings alike, served the function of what Volkan (1981) describes as "linking objects".

Although there were other themes in the discussion and some ambivalence both about dolls and the painted renditions of them, the mother-child-doll theme was prominent in this group. The larger audience, watching, was rapt. In the large group discussion, two women, one of whom shared particularly painful recollections of dolls in relation to her parents, communicated a sense of how much they had gained from the presentation. They both said that they had learned more about themselves from this presentation than from many years of psychotherapy. Although I had not intended the presentation as psychotherapeutic, there was little doubt that it created a valuable space for emotional reflection and, in some cases, catharsis.

Conclusion

My painting of the dolls, the exhibition and the garnering of people's responses in both groups were an exciting, moving and revelatory journey. My last question concerns its possible application to psychotherapy. As noted earlier, the presentations had a powerful emotional effect. Artists often create work with the intention of stirring the imagination, evoking the experience of the viewer, but their work is seldom utilized in the structured way described. Yet, there is a rich abundance of artwork that could be drawn on. In principle, any form of therapy that values exploration and appreciates the importance of the symbolic object could make use of this medium. Visual stimuli could be brought into individual psychotherapy, for example, as an adjunct or pathway to uncovering hidden or unconscious memories and fantasies. But I want to highlight the particular value of the group as a medium in this regard. Based on the events I conducted, I would affirm the power of the group to strengthen the experience of visual images through resonance and exchange and to deepen the connection with the emerging themes. The group is fertile ground for the evocation of both personal and social experience, for embracing the wealth of the unconscious realm and for our shared identification as human beings.

Chapter 5

The deserted city

The Deserted City was the second series of paintings I produced, painted in the throes of lockdown. This was in early- to mid-2020, a time when the world seemingly stood still, petrified by the spread of a deadly virus. The paintings in the series were the darkest and most pessimistic of any work I have done. I consciously set out to capture the sense of isolation and fear engendered by the pandemic, no doubt reflecting my own fears and the wish to share with others the growing sense of a beleaguered world. At the same time, I wanted to hold onto something beautiful and hopeful.

The story starts in New York in March 2020, at the very tip of the pandemic invading the city. When I was invited to give the "Ormont Lecture" at the AGPA conference in New York that month, as described in the previous chapter, I decided to bypass the request that I present a well-known theme from my writing, particularly *The Anti-Group* (Nitsun 1996, 2015a). I had given many talks on this theme in the USA and other countries, and I was keen to offer something new. Ironically, the theme of the anti-group, unbeknown to me at the time, was highly relevant to the catastrophe that was about to engulf the world. In various ways, Covid could be seen as an anti-group force, given the massive social disruption it caused, let alone the death and devastation it brought to widespread populations. From another perspective, it could be argued that the pandemic was a reflection – if not a consequence – of existing cultural and political anti-group processes.

As described previously, the lecture I gave in New York, eventually agreed with the conference committee, was on the doll paintings, much as described in Chapter 1. The lecture and the group response following the talk confirmed a sense of something fresh, new and generative unfolding. But it is in this context that I wish to introduce *The Deserted City* as my subsequent theme. My lecture in New York happened in the first week of March, the exact time that the spread of the pandemic suddenly shifted gear, rapidly becoming the overwhelming force that changed our lives forever. Strikingly, I was at a conference of over one thousand people at a hotel in central Manhattan, a huge hotel with throngs of visitors, the city all around teeming with people in typical New York dense density and intensity. Although there was some awareness at the conference that all was not right in the world, that the virus was penetrating Europe and other countries, there

DOI: 10.4324/9781003232230-8

was a peculiar denial of the danger lurking in the midst of the conference. Lecture halls were packed with people sitting in close proximity; there were warm hugs of affection and, on the last night of the conference, a lively dance party, the sweaty crowd of people gyrating in a spirit of end-of-conference abandon. Oblivious to the imminent danger, I too was enjoying New York to the full, dining with friends at restaurants, roaming the art galleries, travelling on packed buses, and on 7th March, my last day in New York, taking the Staten Island Ferry to see the Statue of Liberty and the famous view of Manhattan. I had expected this to be a small ferry with a limited number of people. But it was a busy Sunday, and the huge ferry was crammed with hundreds, if not thousands, of sightseers.

By the time I left for London the week of 8th March, Covid was spreading through New York like wildfire. In a post-conference email network that same week, it emerged that tens, later hundreds, of people who had attended the conference, mainly North Americans, were falling prey to the virus. Many became seriously ill. The virus was now spreading uncontrollably in New York, the hospitals packed to capacity, the mortuaries full, the once busy, noisy streets of the city suddenly abandoned, deserted, as terrified New Yorkers took refuge in lockdown. The same was happening in London, the incidence of Covid rising by the day, eventually overwhelming the UK and triggering the worst health and social crisis in generations.

Quite apart from my own anxieties about infection – I had had a dangerous brush with a virulent killer – I was left with a shocked consciousness of how oblivious the New York conference attendees, myself included, were to the lurking danger. The entire city had been in the grip of denial. This unpreparedness, the initial resistance to accepting a very frightening reality, was repeated in towns and cities across the world.

Trying to make sense of the crisis and the denial festering in its grip, I turned to Ernest Becker's (1975) writing on the denial of death, one of the most powerful existential statements of the last century. Becker argues that our mortality gives rise to a pervasive sense of vulnerability. Attempting to deal with the omnipresent fear, we devise strategies to escape the knowledge of our mortality. The denial of death, Becker believes, is one of the basic drives in people's behaviour and is reflected throughout human culture. In various ways, we inculcate the belief that we are permanent, invulnerable, eternal. But the denial has adverse consequences. It involves a failure to mourn loss and a deep but fragile quest to maintain an impossible illusion. Becker describes the denial as originating in individuals but reflected powerfully in social and cultural groups, seeing religion, for example, as an attempt to manage the anxiety through invocations of the divine, the immortal and the everlasting.

Becker's thesis helped me to understand the denial/dissociation that was so apparent in the New York experience. What is important, as I see it, is the process of *denial-contagion*: the way denial is amplified through the multiplicity of the group process. In the same way, that anxiety can spread across a group through contagion, so denial can be strengthened and intensified by the group.

Usually, this is in order to protect the group, to banish the danger from consciousness, but paradoxically this ends up making the group more vulnerable. A group process of what I have termed "dysfunctional mirroring" (Nitsun 1988) occurs, the group imploding in the grip of survival anxiety. The denial is not morally bad: it is a product of human frailty and fallibility and our need to defend against anxiety, sometimes in deluded ways, resulting in untoward, even tragic, outcomes. Hopper (2003) describes a similar process in his concept of massification.

My experience in New York was a key influence on my producing the series of paintings, *The Deserted City*. I wanted to challenge denial, to confront unflinchingly the reality that was now upon us.

My encounter with Covid

We all have a Covid story to tell. Mine is linked to the New York experience. I was, at the time, due to age and an underlying lung condition, doubly vulnerable. Returning to London, I could see all around me the signs of a gathering storm. Corona was dramatically on the rise. I made an early appointment to consult my respiratory specialist who was shocked at my story, particularly since I had been exposed to the virus in New York. She emphasized that if I contracted Covid, I would be in grave danger, given my underlying lung disorder. She urged me to go straight home, to shield, and to have a Covid test as soon as possible. The latter was impossible in the frenzy of anxiety and scarce supplies at that early time, and I was left for some months not knowing whether I was infected or not. If so, I had only mild symptoms. But later that year, I was able to have an immunity test that was positive, confirming that I had had Covid.

I was by now in full lockdown, transferring my psychotherapeutic practice online and not going out at all. It was in this state, anxious and isolated but with much more time on my hands than usual, that I embarked on the series of paintings that became *The Deserted City*. The paintings all depict cities and towns in Europe. Why Europe? Although my most recent experience of a city outside London had been in New York, what had struck me most on my return to London was the ravages Covid was wreaking in Europe. The early, deeply upsetting descriptions and photographs of urban crisis were coming mainly from Northern Italy, where Covid had struck extremely hard. The entire city of Bergamo and the surrounding environment had succumbed to fear, death and chaos. This shocked me because I loved Italy, had lectured at Bologna University and had spent holidays in these environs. The daily media images of the empty streets and squares in the cities were haunting in their bleakness and despair. This, I decided, was what I was going to paint.

Europe as the site of Covid was significant to me on several levels. Covid struck at about the same time as Brexit was in its final throes, the divorce of the UK from Europe now becoming a reality. I was opposed to Brexit from the start, unwilling to forego the links established. Further, there was a lingering view of

Europe more generally as a sinking ship. This was a picture of a continent in slow decline, the culture of the old world superseded by a brash new world of unknown proportions and unfathomable powers. So, in my mind, the threatened decay of southern Europe went beyond the ravages of Covid. It was as if a valuable old order was being replaced by the vagaries of an unknown future, as if Covid was the harbinger of momentous change. My paintings, I thought, might symbolize a traumatic moment in history.

The paintings

I painted furiously during the months of lockdown. I completed nearly forty paintings on this theme. With all art galleries closed, I decided to show the work online, using the same format as the dolls presentation – the paintings on slides accompanied by a narrative and followed by group discussion. I also included literary references, such as Ernest Becker's writing and Camus's *The Plague* (1947). The first online presentation was to the International Group Analytic Society with an audience of approximately eighty people; the second to the International Association of Group Psychotherapists with a similar size audience.

My focus was on the old quarters of cities and towns rather than the new cities, in line with my observations about European decline. Although the newer cities featured more prominently in the photographs accompanying newspaper and other media reports, particularly hospitals and apartment blocks, it was the old cities that I was most moved by, what they represented in cultural history: their patina of age, the beautiful buildings, the empty streets. These were cities I knew and loved.

The first painting, "View of the Old Town" (Figure 5.1), focuses on a jigsaw of buildings seen from below. These are the old houses and warehouses of a town on the sea, the seafaring past perhaps forgotten with the progress of time. I tried to capture the textures of age, the colours of the past, the higgledy-piggledy buildings tottering valiantly in an attempt to maintain their crumbling dignity. As with all the paintings in this series, the subject was painted on a black background: not so much the light and loveliness of the Mediterranean world: more a stricken world hovering on decay.

The next image, "Town on the City Outskirts" (Figure 5.2), is the largest painting in the series (160 × 120 cm) and, in some ways, the most emblematic. Reproduction here, limited by the width of the page, does not do justice to its size. I had intended a large statement, attempting an immersive image of an embattled town: a modest cluster of vulnerable buildings dominated by a towering sky. I initially painted the sky empty, wanting to convey a sense of the unknown, of infinity. But it looked to me unfinished. It needed something, a symbolic presence, a figure or creature in the sky, an image to complement the existing scene. I then painted a small bird in the distance, perhaps signifying hope. However, I remained dissatisfied, the painting unresolved in my mind. I wanted a bigger, more arresting image. I started now to paint a much larger bird, not being sure of what sort of bird would materialise. I was shocked by what appeared.

Figure 5.1 View of the Old Town
Source: Morris Nitsun 2020, oil, 100 × 60 cm

Figure 5.2 Town on City Outskirts
Source: Morris Nitsun, 2020, 160 × 120 cm

Figure 5.3 Presence in the Sky

Source: Enlarged detail of Figure 5.2

Figure 5.2 shows the finished painting with the much larger bird in the sky. But is it a bird? The image had emerged quickly, suddenly, painted vigorously, and at first glance, I was disturbed by what I saw: a half-bird, half-human spectre hovering in the sky, a much more frightening, ambiguous image than intended. Figure 5.3 is an enlarged detail of the presence in the sky. Is it a bird or an angel? Is it an angel of doom or an angel of mercy? My immediate impulse was to modify the image, to render it more benign. But I realised that it was there for a reason. It symbolized the dark force of Covid hovering over the town. If this was disturbing to viewers, so be it. There was now a dark, sinister, dangerous presence in the world, and my image had unexpectedly tapped into it.

One of the main literary references in my presentation was Camus's *The Plague*, probably the most renowned account in literature of the devastation wreaked by a virus. I was reading the classic for the first time during lockdown, struck by the parallels between the virus that struck the Algerian town of Oran in 1947 in the story and the current more widespread pandemic. One of the main characters in the book is a priest, Paneloux, who, early in the narrative, berates the townspeople for turning away from God, insisting that the plague is a punishment for their disloyalty and wrongdoing. He describes the plague as an evil presence hovering menacingly above the town: a sinister visitation determined to destroy. Seeing the frightening bird-like creature I painted, I made a connection with the visitation in Camus's book. My creature seemed to emanate the same quality of mysterious threat. I decided to leave the image intact.

The theme of home now emerges. Returning to Figure 5.2, "Town on the City Outskirts", a building predominates in the foreground: a worn, weathered building, probably a house, now derelict but once inhabited by people. I see this house as a representation of the importance of the home during lockdown.

People's homes in the long, frightening months of Covid became their refuge, providing shelter and containment from the danger outside. The home provided safety and security. But people's homes also became their prisons. Compelled to stay indoors for prolonged periods, often in inadequate and restricted conditions, people felt increasingly confined, trapped. This polarity epitomizes the claustrophobic-agoraphobic atmosphere that marked the experience of lockdown. People were afraid to go out and retreated into their homes. But then they felt trapped and wanted to break free. We were caught between contradictory pulls. This tension of opposites is reminiscent of the states of mind in severe relational conflict: the fear of being abandoned oscillating with the fear of being engulfed, swallowed up, referred to by Glasser (1979) as the "core complex" At its worst, this produces states of extreme confusion, even disintegration. We know that lockdown took a heavy toll on people's emotional well-being. This agonizing, near-psychotic state of contradictory fears was prevalent for many through the anxious months of lockdown.

I painted a significant number of paintings depicting empty streets in embattled towns. Because of space restrictions, I show only two examples. The first of these is "Empty Town" (Figure 5.4). Note the buildings with their shabby exteriors

Figure 5.4 Empty Town
Source: Morris Nitsun, 2020, oil, 59 × 42

and, in addition, the dark windows and doors. These became a feature of all the paintings. I have a long fascination with the symbolism of windows and doors: as markers of the boundary between inside and outside, architecturally and socially, both fundamental in our relationship with the world. In these paintings, the dark windows suggest confinement and a dread of contact with the outside environment. They are like black holes without the prospect of entry or exit. They reinforce the sense of imprisonment, the claustrophobic atmosphere of lockdown. The doors and windows are characterless in these representations, as if humanity and all that expresses, all life and movement, has vanished, secreted in the hope of safety and protection.

Figure 5.5 is another town scene, emphasising the long, empty street stretching into the distance. Here the buildings retain their colourful exteriors: Tuscan burnt sienna and red and gold ochre are embedded in the ancient walls. The patina of age is intact. But the deserted atmosphere of the town is ominous, and the red flare in the distance is a symbol of danger. No one dares venture into the streets.

The exteriors of the buildings in the paintings shown here retain their colour. But in another set of townscapes, I depicted clusters of buildings where colour has drained away, leaving ghostly white facades, possibly evoking the pallor of death. Figure 5.6, "Ghostly Church", is such a scene, a church dome in the background denoting the presence of religion in the town as a major influence in the life of southern European towns. Yet, where is religion now? Where is God? This crisis of belief is one of the themes of Camus's book. The implacable plague is seen as a force of evil threatening the precious order of ordinary life, the sanctity of nature. This happened similarly in the 21st-century pandemic, fear looming large, faith and hope held in suspension.

Pursuing this theme of belief, the priest in *The Plague* comes back into focus. The novel describes a major and tragic transformation in the man. Having found his congregation deserting the church, largely because of fear of contamination, Paneloux joins a group of volunteers helping with the sick and the dying in the town. A new weariness overcomes him as he encounters the frightening scale of mortality. This deepens when an ill child he has cared for and grown attached to dies. The priest then becomes ill himself, deteriorating rapidly, and he too dies. A mystery surrounds his death. It appears that it is not the virus that killed him: there were none of the usual signs. But what did kill him? Camus suggests that it is the crisis in his own belief. When faced with the horror before him, it is more than he can bear. The child's death is the last straw. The priest, it seems, died of a broken heart.

In the series, I painted two images of churches (not illustrated here), partly in recognition of Paneloux and his agonizing crisis of belief. In the ongoing worldwide pandemic, there are probably many who have struggled with disillusionment and the loss of belief. In the next chapter, *Fragile Nature*, I explore the spiritual dimension in a different, more hopeful way.

There were few figures in this collection. I was predominantly drawn to the architectural landscape, the buildings and the streets, and I initially excluded

Figure 5.5 Empty Street
Source: Morris Nitsun 2020, oil, 59 × 42

Figure 5.6 Ghostly Church
Source: Morris Nitsun 2020, oil, 84 × 59 cm

people, possibly because humans were hidden in their homes, away from view. However, the inescapable fact was that Covid was an intensely human crisis and that the threat to people's lives was at the centre of the gathering storm. I decided to reflect this in my painting. Amongst the figure studies that followed is the couple illustrated in Figure 5.7, "Homeless". The image was taken from a newspaper photograph of a man and a woman on a park bench in an Italian town hit by Covid. There was little accompanying text as if the headline said it all – HOMELESS. I was very struck – and moved – by the image. How awful, it seemed, to be so exposed: how frightening to be without shelter in the midst of a pandemic. This linked, for me, with my previous observations about home and the need for shelter. If home was confining and claustrophobic, how much worse was being without one? How, I wondered, did this couple survive – if they survived at all?

Then came the masks. In the unfolding of the pandemic, there was a point at which everyone started wearing masks. What started off as an encumbrance, a matter of choice – whether to wear or not – increasingly became an intrinsic part of the face: virtually a fixed appendage. I did several paintings of people wearing masks, sometimes a single person, sometimes a group of people and sometimes figures in a crowd, all wearing masks. I included these paintings in the online presentations, but because of spatial limitations, I give only one example here. Figure 5.8, "Man with a Mask", is probably the most arresting of the figure studies in this series.

Figure 5.7 Homeless

Source: Morris Nitsun, 2020, oil, 84 × 59

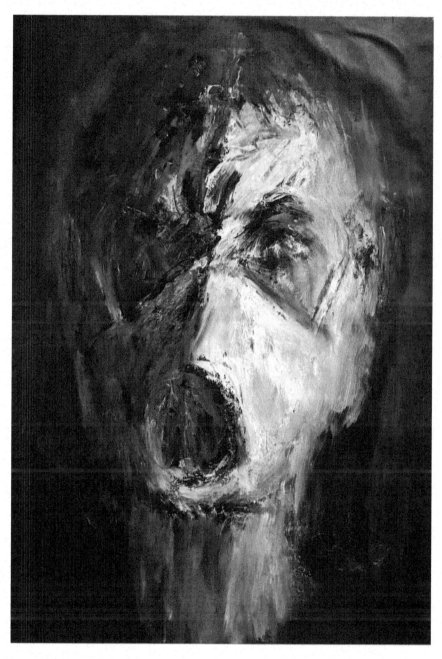

Figure 5.8 Man with a Mask
Source: Morris Nitsun

The painting is based on a newspaper photograph of a doctor surveying a teeming Covid ward in the early stages of the pandemic. What he saw was probably the chaotic, desperate atmosphere of the ward. His expression is one of alarm. His mask has a hard section covering the mouth for extra protection. When I painted this, I realised that I had involuntarily made the man's mouth look like he was shouting or screaming. I was surprised by what I had produced. My immediate impulse was to soften the image, making it less anguished, less shocked. But I decided to keep the initial image. I heeded my unconscious, which seemed to require me to generate an image at its extremes.

A connection from the history of art came to me: Edvard Munch's "Scream". This was not conscious when executing the painting but flooded into awareness on completion. It was a connection that also came readily to others in the discussions. Munch's "Scream" is one of the most famous paintings in art history, an iconic image of dire anxiety and dread. It is usually regarded as emblematic of millennial change: from the 19th to the 20th Century. But it is also an expression of profound existential stress in an imploded environment. There is a telling entry in Munch's own diary (1882), in which he describes the situation in which the scream occurred. He was walking over a bridge when a deep melancholy overwhelmed him. The whole environment seemed to shake suddenly and violently. The sky turned a threatening, bloody red, looming over the fjord and the city. His friends walked on but he stood there transfixed by anxiety. At that moment, he felt a vast infinite scream *through nature*. The screaming man is the voice of something much bigger and deeper than himself: an agonized environment. I highlight this in order to link it to the horror of Covid, which also imparted a sense of an environment gone mad, a breakdown in the natural order of things. Similarly, the man's scream in my painting is not just an individual scream: it is a universal scream.

I included one last painting in the presentation, which strikes a very different, more hopeful note. In the first one or two online presentations of *The Deserted City*, I found that some members of the audience struggled with the dysphoric tone of the paintings and the despairing vision they appeared to convey. Some people said they could hardly bear to look at them. Although I usually do not flinch from confronting the dark side, I was moved to do another painting: a more hopeful work. I painted the scene of an Italian garden in summer (Figure 5.9, "View of the Garden"). In part, I craved this myself as a reminder of what I loved about Italy and these towns in particular: the beauty of the natural environment and the wonderful gardens, whether the magnificent formal Italian gardens or the more modest courtyard gardens. The garden in this painting is more than a garden: it is a symbol of survival and regeneration. There were times during the pandemic, in the long fear-filled months, when we all struggled to hold onto hope. I wanted to end on a hopeful note.

The groups

I presented this series of paintings in several settings, from small, intimate groups of friends and colleagues to large groups, such as the International Group Analytic

Figure 5.9 View of the Garden
Source: Morris Nitsun, 2020, 59 × 84

Society and the International Association of Group Psychotherapists. I followed the by-now well-established online format of paintings, narration and group reflection. In one of the larger events, small breakout discussion groups were set up as part of the zoom event, and members were invited to report back to the large group. In the description that follows, I highlight trends in the discussion across the groups rather than focusing on any one group.

More than any other of my ventures in the overall project, *The Deserted City* divided audiences. While opinions and responses varied across a spectrum, there were those who welcomed and appreciated the presentation and those who were discomfited and disturbed by it, in some cases finding it painful and aversive. There were occasional challenging voices, seemingly questioning the purpose of the presentation. Why paint these dark, disturbing images? Amongst the group that appreciated the presentation, there were statements about the courage it took to produce the paintings and the value of having such a bold, unflinching mirror of the landscape of Covid. In one of the presentations, at a time in the UK when there was a temporary improvement in the daily statistics, with significantly fewer new cases and fewer deaths – in fact, when it looked like the epidemic might be over – a few people commented on the value of having such a vivid reminder of what we had endured. One person commented on how easily we forget. This was in the summer of 2020 in the UK, a warm, relaxed summer when there was a temptation to forget. This participant positively connoted the act of remembering: to guard against denial and complacency. A number of participants spoke of the trauma we had all endured, some having had Covid, others having had close brushes with the virus, still others having lost loved ones and friends. Although this sharing brought participants closer, some people remained uneasy, as if the spectre of suffering and loss was too difficult to countenance. Perhaps there was also a hint of worse to come: the pandemic was about to surge all over again.

Of the group that reacted somewhat negatively to the presentation, it initially seemed there was little that was appealing or sympathetic in the material and quite a lot that was unappealing. A number of people found the dark background of the paintings oppressive and foreboding. The blackened windows and doors were similarly viewed: too sinister and uncompromising. The point that this was a deliberate artistic gesture, an expression of the sense of danger that lurked every-where, reflecting the mood that I had set out to create, seemed to bypass these participants. Almost all the qualities that impressed and moved some participants were the source of discomfort to others.

I was puzzled by the split. How much was it a reflection of aesthetic taste? People vary widely in their standards and criteria of artistic appreciation. Art tends to arouse visceral reactions in people, the same work eliciting strikingly different reactions. This is understandable given the subjectivity that people bring to their appreciation of art, but in this case, there seemed to be an assumption that theirs was *the* way of seeing the work, the right way, not *a* way. I was struck by the tenacity of people's perceptions. Often, as in the feedback about the doll paint-ings, this appeared to be projection rather than perception. People create the world through their own eyes, perceiving life from their own perspective rather than see-ing other perspectives. But were the paintings – and the reminder of the dark days of Covid – too close to home? Some people are keen to confront reality, others not. Some people want to remember: others to forget. How much was the resistance a denial of death and all that goes with it: decay, vulnerability, disintegration? I had spoken earlier in my presentation about the denial of death, highlighting Ernest Becker's profound writing on the subject. But this didn't necessarily make people less likely to deny. In fact, paradoxically, it might have touched a nerve that rein-forced the impulse to deny.

I come back here to "the uncanny", the phenomenon I touched on in relation to the doll paintings. This, deriving from Freud's seminal paper, describes an experi-ence of weirdness, encompassing sensations of fear and fright, stemming from an uncomfortable mix of familiarity and unfamiliarity. It is often a reaction to ambig-uous or confusing stimuli, particularly if there are hints of the sinister. This was how some people reacted to the doll images in the previous chapter. The subject of *The Deserted City* was very different from the dolls, but there was a similar degree of ambiguity in the work. The dark backgrounds, the murky atmosphere, the sense of emptiness and abandonment, and the spectre of death lurking in the shadows all compounded the ambiguity and discomfort. But how much was this a feature of the paintings, and how much did it express the very real sense of an overwhelming and frightening pandemic, a phenomenon that had crept into our lives unbidden and unwanted? We had all been plunged into an extraordinarily weird existence. It was a time when the familiar became unfamiliar, when the streets and towns we knew were denuded, transformed under our eyes, when we retreated into a strange, marginal, isolated existence cut off from others and the world.

I emphasize the uncanny aspect of both the paintings and the reality of the time. But I regard it as necessary to challenge denial. Otherwise, the trauma may be driven underground. Unwitting – or witting – attempts to deny or repress trauma may result in future generations having to pick up the discarded pieces. I suspect that even when memory is kept alive, some aspects of trauma seek an unconscious host, to be lodged away from painful awareness. We can see in this the seeds of a socially unconscious configuration emerging from the trauma of the pandemic (Hopper 2022).

As mentioned earlier, there was a high degree of projection onto the images. Much of this centred on the depictions of windows and doors in the paintings. Whereas some people saw the darkened openings as realistic representations of a shut-down world, others had reactions of fear and horror, describing scenes of forced confinement and suffocation. Doors and windows are powerful symbols: of the boundary between inner and outer, self and other, home and not-home. It is not surprising that these aspects of the paintings commanded such strong, affect-laden attention, as if familiar boundaries had imploded, dissolved, or tightened in response to external threat.

Whereas projection usually operates on an individual basis – coming from individual subjectivity and perceptual bias – it may, of course, also occur at a group level. Group projection, the intensification of attributions by the group as a whole (usually onto another group), can be seen as the basis of all in- and out-group identifications and differentiations, often marked by sharp divisions between good and bad, powerful and powerless, loved and hated (Nitsun 2015a). A very interesting example of a group response occurred when I presented *The Deserted City* paintings to a small group of participants in a European country. This was in the context of a teaching session I did with the group, the presentation coming at the end of the course. I had intended this as a novel way of illustrating more familiar concepts such as the anti-group and authority and leadership. However, the course participants, surprised by the addition of *The Deserted City*, reacted uncomfortably and somewhat critically to the presentation. Unsure of what to make of the paintings, they projected liberally onto the images. Having found the lack of human figures in the deserted streets disquieting, they, one after the other, began emphasizing figures they could see in the paintings, figures inserted into some of the more indistinct, ambiguous patches of paintwork. It seemed to be no coincidence that this was a group in an embattled country with a traumatic past, loss and absence of a pervasive theme in their history. Their responses could be interpreted in various ways, but I felt that it was an assertion of strength over helplessness, of presence over absence, of agency over inadequacy, perhaps life over death. It seems important that projection is not just about unwanted self-attributes extruded into another or persecutory fears displaced. Projection may also reflect the will to assert existence and identity.

The sense of helplessness, and associated fears, that I believe may have been at the basis of this group's responses, was, of course, emblematic of the universal response to the pandemic. Most of us experienced helplessness in facing this destructive threat. The question is of how we handled our anxiety: whether through denial, displacement, projection, or recognition of the anxiety. The responses to *The Deserted City* highlighted these differing modes of defence.

Amongst the many and varied responses to the work, in both groups, one theme elicited a more or less unanimous response. This was in relation to my highlighting the image of home, drawing on the prominent house image in Figure 5.2. My account of the claustrophobic-agoraphobic tension arising from lockdown, reflecting the conflicting pulls of safety-confinement and freedom-danger, struck a chord with many people. The ambivalent significance of home during the pandemic was actively taken up: the sense of being trapped inside but terrified of the outside. The image of the simple dwelling in an Italian town, protective but confining, became a powerful, shared symbol.

The chat

In several of the Zoom presentations of *The Deserted City*, there was a chat facility that was very well used by participants. I was until then unfamiliar with this function, still being relatively new to Zoom, and was pleasantly surprised, indeed overwhelmed, by the large number of messages. Moreover, these were very affirmative, often deeply appreciative messages. Of course, not everyone did send a chat message, and there is a question about what was *not* said as opposed to what was said. However, the following were examples of the feedback:

> "Very powerful"
> "Compelling presentation and paintings"
> "Very striking images"
> "Wonderfully atmospheric"
> "Very moving"
> "Memorable – I will be haunted by some of the images"
> "Terrific paintings"; "immensely moving – what a time we have been through"
> "A darkly brilliant vision"
> "Much more than I expected – very grateful"
> "Great insights"
> "Remarkable combination of story and paintings"
> "I loved being in the discussion"

Reflection

Insofar as my approach represents a heuristic inquiry, *The Deserted City* was a highly productive theme. Starting with my own preoccupation with Covid and the profound meaning this had to me personally, I chose to extend this outward to others in the way described by Moustakas (1990). For some time, I felt that I had perhaps imposed too dysphoric a vision on others, that I was bringing "too much reality" to bear – at a time of a frightening reality. But, increasingly, I sensed that the impact of the paintings and the narrative was such that people could express a range of reactions, particularly necessary at a time of dread and confusion. If there was an element of denial – about vulnerability and death – that too was understandable as a way of managing fear.

Freud (1919), writing about the uncanny, stated that what people seek in art is beauty, not the weird, unfamiliar, or disturbing. Perhaps this presentation showed that the two may go together: beauty *and* the uncanny, the familiar *and* the unfamiliar, the intact *and* the damaged. Also, although this series dealt with an immediate environmental threat, it touched on universal themes of protection and survival at personal and social levels. Further, I suggest that the archetypal equivalents of these experiences, the earth mother and the universal father, in both their containing and rejecting versions, are symbolically present. The next chapter, dealing with the natural environment, picks up on the themes of containment and renewal. The personal journey I experienced in this initiative brings to mind Picassos's (2021) statement, 'Every act of creation is first of all an act of destruction'. In the midst of the pandemic, the pervasive dark, I had found a glimpse of light.

Chapter 6

Fragile nature

Throughout the pandemic and in the dark months of lockdown, I, like many people, took solace in nature. I had the advantage of living in a very green part of north London, surrounded by woods. My house backs onto Queen's Wood and is a two-minute walk from Highgate Wood, both ancient woods with a rich history of topographical and social change. The woods create a unique atmosphere in this quiet London suburb and offer a refuge from the pressures and noise of the city. The series of paintings titled *Fragile Nature* was the third of my series, immediately following *The Deserted City* and offered a different, gentler vision of life under lockdown. More than that, the paintings are a celebration of the woods, the fragility and tenacity of nature: a meditation on life's transience.

My renewed relationship with nature and the opportunity to transform the experience into painting was essential not only in helping me to survive lockdown, but in gaining something immeasurably valuable in the process.

Most of the paintings were done in summer and early autumn 2020, when there was a brief, hopeful respite from the virus. The incidence of Covid temporarily stalled, only to be followed by a surge that took the country into its second lockdown. But the lull was a time for contemplation, for reflection, in a way that persisted through the bleak months to come.

I presented *Fragile Nature* more frequently than any of the other series, recognizing the resurgent interest in nature that was one of the unexpected fruits of lockdown, coupled with the longing for a way of understanding the catastrophe that had befallen the world. In my own case, the additional time afforded by lockdown meant that I could spend hours exploring the nearby woods and the secret, verdant pathways of north London. I had lived in this area for over thirty years, my house nestled between woods, and I had come to take the green environment for granted. Busy with work, commuting weekdays to central London, preoccupied with the minutiae of everyday life, I was spending less time in nature as the years passed by. Now, I had the opportunity and impetus to renew contact with the riches on my doorstep. I realised that the visual impact of the woods was translatable into paint and that there was the potential for a series of paintings that would, hopefully, embody the mood of this exceptional time.

DOI: 10.4324/9781003232230-9

Although my excursion into nature brought stimulation and solace, it was against a background of loss. I lived in a city transfixed by the fear of contagion, the incidence of illness and death rising and falling unpredictably in waves, my own anxiety exacerbated by my underlying vulnerability. This universal anxiety was the background, at times foreground, to other losses I had suffered in recent years: the loss of loved ones and close friends, sometimes in rapid succession, allowing little time to grieve, yet with an accumulating sense of implacable, overwhelming change. My own loss of youth, more poignant than ever in the face of a new and growing danger to survival, added to the picture. This is why, for me, and I suspect for many others, refuge in nature was so meaningful, not just for its containing beauty, but for the promise of resilience in the face of fragility. We are all fragile and yet tenacious, often extraordinarily so. And we are all part of something bigger that, when acknowledged, adds to understanding and acceptance.

In this chapter, I follow my usual sequence of the background to the paintings, the presentation itself in words and images, the group responses, and reflections on the process of inquiry and what it tells us. I also offer fragments of poetry (not my own) that mirror some of the visual images.

The paintings take the form of a journey through the woods, the discovery of nature being the overriding theme: the trees and leaves, the theatre of light and shade, all part of the accompanying spectacle. But there is also an encounter with the wildlife in the woods and the people who frequent the woods, completing the circle of nature, animal life and the human presence: a world within a world.

Painting nature

The first image, "Autumn Leaves" (Figure 6.1), is a simple composition of leaves in autumnal colours, painted in oils but with real dried leaves added in fragments to create more texture. This was typical of this series of paintings: a burning inclination to experiment with different techniques and textures, no doubt in response to the myriad textures of nature. I used collage, leaves, glue, glass, oil paint, marble dust and various glazes to achieve my effects. I tried here to capture the essence of autumn, an explosion of rich brown-reds and golds, but with a sense of beauty crumbling away.

This became a theme as the paintings progressed – beauty and decay in continuing interplay, the possibility of renewal embedded in the process. In Figure 6.1, the leaves are crumbling, dead or dying, but they may also be exploding – life in the germ of decay. This theme, the dialectic of creation and destruction, has been an essential aspect of my writing on group process (Nitsun 1996, 2006, 2015a) and is mirrored here in the evocation of nature: the underlying struggle that unites human destiny with the natural world.

"Light in the Woods" (Figure 6.2) was one of the first paintings I did in the series. It followed a pattern of execution that became typical of the paintings in this series. Starting as a representational image of the woods, trees and sky shown in semi-photographic realism, it morphed into a more abstract, intuitive painting.

Figure 6.1 Autumn Leaves

Source: Morris Nitsun 2020, oil and collage, 59 × 42 cm

I realised as this happened that I wanted to convey something of the spiritual connection I felt with the woods. The yellowish light in the central lower part of the painting is both the real light in the woods and the light of awareness, essence and spiritual awakening. As I roamed the woods by day, I often experienced that combination: a burst of sunlight as a message of hope and transcendence.

Walks during lockdown brought me back and back again to this vision: the light in the darkness. It was a way not only of experiencing nature but of symbolically facing the pandemic and the fear of death.

Figure 6.3, "Woodland Triptych (Transforming Woods)", is a large painting in three parts. Like the previous painting, it emerged during a struggle to portray the woods accurately, then realising that the image was too tight, too constraining, too "objective". I allowed myself to experiment, to play, to turn the painting upside down and from side to side, to rub over and blur the image. From this emerged a very different painting: ambiguous, near-abstract, offering the *atmosphere* of the woods rather than an accurate depiction. Here, the woods shimmer in a haze, with trees, sky and water merging into one.

Paintings of this kind were truer to the felt, subjective sense of union with nature I experienced than any literal depiction of the world around me. As the paintings emerged, I was gratified to see the immersive quality they conveyed.

Figure 6.2 Light in the Woods

Source: Morris Nitsun, 2020, oil, 90 × 60

Figure 6.3 Woodland Triptych (Transforming Woods)
Source: Morris Nitsun 2020, oil, 90 × 42 cm

As a painter, I don't follow a particular school of tradition for painting, possibly because of being largely self-taught – in spite of some instruction both in South Africa and London – but this series of paintings struck me as close to the spirit of French Impressionism. Those artists, particularly Monet, Pissarro and Berthe Morisot, strove to capture a moment in time, particularly the movement of light in a landscape or seascape. My paintings end up being more abstract than that of the French Impressionists and, in this sense, may be closer to the Expressionists who followed the Impressionist movement and added a new vigour and drama to painting, taking further risks with the subject matter and painting technique. As Expressionism goes, my work has sometimes been compared to that of Chaim Soutine, a bolder, more expressive, more emotional artist and part of the later tradition. This is a flattering comparison – Soutine is one of my favourite artists. But the link is truer perhaps of my more figurative work, such as the doll paintings (Chapter 4) and the subjects of *Four Women* (Chapter 8). However, it is possibly relevant to the nature paintings as well, insofar as they seek to express something of the strength and turbulence of nature and not only its fragility.

These considerations sometimes took me along mystical paths, my meditation on nature opening up questions about a deeper, mysterious essence in nature, about phenomena that either defied linear analysis or invited a different order of understanding. One question that struck me was what happened to nature's decay, to the way in which the abundance of spring and summer, the palatial forest of trees with their brilliant canopies of leaves, collapsed into the fields of autumn and the wastelands of winter. Where did all the leaves, once bright and beautiful, go? Questions of this sort are often reflected in poetry that explores nature's mysteries. W S Merwin's (2007) well-known poem "To a leaf falling in winter" describes the imaginary passage of weathered, decayed leaves drawn back to their source – to the trees that produced them. A similar idea came to me after I had struggled with the painting in Figure 6.4, "A Pool of Leaves". I had turned the canvas in different ways and settled finally for an image that was other than what I intended. The painting shows a loose carpet of leaves, or even a pool of water with floating leaves, lying at the foot of a tree, the roots of the tree evident at the top and to the side of the painting. Ordinarily, the leaves would crown the tree rather than be below. But the leaves, as in Merwin's poem, look as if they may be gravitating back towards the tree from which they came.

There is magical realism in this image, the vision one of reconciliation and synthesis in nature as part of an ongoing process, as opposed to the "logical" constraints of time and space. This was very much my experience of the woods: a sense of dissolving boundaries in time and place, a vision of the ultimate connectedness of all things. This was not just a philosophical standpoint: I experienced a oneness in the world and felt at one with the world.

Several of these themes come together in "Buddha in the Woods" (Figure 6.5). This illustrates the figure of a young Buddha sitting under a shrub ablaze with autumn leaves, akin to the mythical tree of enlightenment. The image reflects

Figure 6.4 A Pool of Leaves

Source: Morris Nitsun 2020, oil, 84 × 59 cm

my interest in Buddhist philosophy. All the themes that I was struggling with in the paintings are represented by the Buddha – the interconnectedness of all things, the impermanence at the heart of life, and the possibility of transformation through an awareness of our place in the life cycle. These potentials in Buddhist teaching are set against the suffering of people caught in vicious cycles of desire, attachment and illusion. This philosophy was exactly what I was trying to grasp in the face of Covid: seeing the pandemic not just as a catastrophe but as an intensification of the process that makes us mortal, inevitably and intelligently so. In the group presentations, I describe Buddha as my guide, mentor, friend, accompanying me through my journey into the interior of the woods. I have reservations about the extent to which we, as human beings, can detach rather than attach in the way Buddha suggests, but I am comfortable with the idea that we can attach in a way that recognises both our strength and the frailty. This is one of nature's lessons.

In the next painting, "A Walk in the Woods" (Figure 6.6), I tried to convey the experience of treading through the woods, as I did for many an hour. A largely abstracted image, attempting to convey an experience rather than a realistic representation, the painting shows the path (one of many) on which I would walk and the mounds of leaves on the side of the path. In the narrative, I describe my sense

Figure 6.5 Buddha in the Woods

Source: Morris Nitsun, 2020, oil, 59 × 84 cm

Figure 6.6 A Walk in the Woods

Source: Morris Nitsun, 2020, oil, 59 × 84 cm

of the leafy carpet growing day by day during autumn, the carpet getting denser and thicker as more and more leaves fall to the ground, the layers gradually crumbling to dust. This became an emblematic experience for me, walking and seeing the mounting spectacle of the leaves – and then their disappearance. The pile of leaves highlighted the significance of each separate leaf, a creation itself that lives and dies, in a way telescoping the entire drama of birth and death in a single leaf: the universe in a leaf

I am reminded of Robert Frost's (1923) famous poem, "Nothing gold can stay", which celebrates the splendour of a single leaf, bathed in green and gold, yet destined to sink into decay.

Animals in the woods

The woods are a haven for animal life of the smaller species. The animals are usually seen in glimpses, as if there is a whole secret life in the woods that emerges sporadically into view. They come and they go, these residents of the woods. There are many bird species, often heard in intense recitals of bird song, particularly at the start and end of the day, and usually seen in flashes of feathers and flight. Squirrels are numerous, scurrying up trees, from branch to branch, sometimes stopping to size up the world or eating a nut or an acorn. I painted many of these animals – birds, squirrels, a fox, a bat – but because of space limitations, I am showing here only an owl and the fox.

The owl ("Owl", Figure 6.7) particularly interests me because of its mixed associations. I love the hooting of owls. At night, from my bedroom high above the woods, I can hear them, the clear, sharp toot-toot carrying across the woods, strangely familiar and comforting. On the other hand, they are predators, rapacious when it comes to insects, mice and other small creatures. A member of one of my groups recalled seeing a mouse trembling as an owl was about to swoop down. I mention this here so as to highlight that not all is fair and just in the universe of the woods. Most of the wildlife prey on other wildlife. This is why I have also included the fox ("Fox", Figure 6.8), stealthily emerging from the undergrowth of the woods. I haven't seen many foxes in the woods, but they are frequent visitors to the back-gardens and streets of my neighbourhood, and I'm told that they prowl the woods at night.

Danger in the woods is by no means confined to the wildlife. There is an increasing awareness of the struggle for survival amongst the plant species: the battle for space, particularly amongst trees, but more generally, the whole ecology bristling with activity and challenge of one sort or another. Additionally, there is the looming threat of climate change. Although this has seemingly not affected the local woods as yet, there is the question of what will happen in time to all our natural habitats. The woods are unlikely to remain unscathed. The dramatic improvement in air quality during lockdown brought with it a sudden, welcome influx of wildlife, birds, bees, butterflies and all else, attesting to the insidious impact of air pollution. The exhilarating change during lockdown was evident in the woods, the

Figure 6.7 Owl
Source: Morris Nitsun, 2020, oil, 59 × 42 cm

lush greenery now a setting for renewal and revitalization. This was one of the few reassuring aspects of lockdown: the air purified and new life emerging.

Human figures

Although the plant and animal life of the woods were the predominant themes of my paintings, there is a significant human presence in the woods. The woods are a magnet for people seeking communion with nature, apart from the opportunity to exercise body and mind. Many people, especially during lockdown, found their way to the woods, people of all ages and stages, singly, in couples and in groups: children, adults and older people. I include two paintings I did of people. Both show two individuals in a relationship of some sort as they encounter the woods.

"Man and Boy" (Figure 6.9) depicts an adult man holding a child in his arms. It captures a scene I witnessed one wet, muddy day in Highgate Wood. I saw the small boy walking beside his father, struggling to keep up, trudging through the mud in his little wellies. He looked up at his father and pleaded, "Pick me

Figure 6.8 Fox
Source: Morris Nitsun 2020, oil, 59 × 42 cm

up. Please pick me up". The man responded affectionately but teasingly, "I can't pick you up because you're so filthy". "Please daddy", said the boy. The man then bent down and picked the boy up, holding him aloft, as in the painting. For a moment, they stood still as if resting or contemplating the woods, looking, listening. It was a moment of stillness, of containment. In that moment, I had an insight into what nature might mean to us at a deeper level. In the same way that the man held the boy in his arms, so nature contains us. Rather like a parent who puts his or her arms around a child, nature embraces us with its wisdom and generosity.

The second painting of people, "Couple in the Woods" (Figure 6.10), shows an elderly couple walking together. The image is ambiguous. Some viewers of the painting have difficulty perceiving the couple, not unusually seeing it as a horse from the back. However, when the figures are pointed out to them, they are usually able to recognise the couple. It shows a figure, a man, supporting another, probably a woman, who is leaning against him. The painting conveys an image of age and fragility: the woman is the weaker of the two, possibly tired or ill.

Figure 6.9 Man and Boy

Source: Morris Nitsun 2020, oil, 84 × 59 cm

Figure 6.10 Couple in the Woods
Source: Morris Nitsun 2020, oil, 76 × 59 cm

This is a couple I had seen previously in the woods, noticing the slow, hesitant way they walked, their mutual dependence. They conveyed to me a parallel sense of human fragility and the fragility of nature, the transience of human life and the transience of the natural order. But nature is also strong, its tenacity and continuity enduring through decades and centuries. Witness the vast trees that have stood there for hundreds of years, the landscapes that have endured through centuries. This may give us reassurance as humans, the reassurance of survival, if not in our limited life spans, then beyond us, beyond our lives. The couple in the painting return regularly to the woods. They must want the exercise, to breathe the woodland air. They probably find solace in the woods. Perhaps their mutual dependence mirrors our complex dependence on the natural world: conversely, the woods' dependence on us: for care, attention and appreciation.

There are benches situated at points throughout the woods. They offer a resting place, an opportunity for quiet contemplation. Most of them have been donated and bear the names of a deceased loved one or friend. In pre-Covid days when I went to the woods, I tended to take the benches for granted, striding past them without much thought. This changed during lockdown. With more time to wander – and wonder – I stopped and looked. I became interested in the benches, how they came to be there, and what stories lay behind the inscriptions. I was particularly struck by one that had a brass plaque containing a memorial message:

> In loving memory of John Gunter (1938–2016) who is dearly missed by his family. He loved these peaceful woods and its beautiful trees which inspired his theatre designs.

I was intrigued by the message, also noticing bunches of fresh flowers attached to both sides of the bench. Not knowing the name John Gunter, I went home, googled him and found out that he was a very distinguished UK theatre designer. He had designed productions at the National Theatre and other prestigious venues and had won numerous awards. I later found out that his widow, Micheline Gunter, lived in the neighbourhood. Through a mutual friend, I was able to invite Micheline to a presentation of *Fragile Nature*, the event I held for my neighbourhood community. She was delighted to come, a warm presence who had once been a member of the New York City Ballet. She participated in the discussion and, when asked about the flowers on the bench, explained that her daughters brought the flowers, particularly at key times such as John's birthday. Incidents like this – meeting Micheline and hearing her story – strengthened my contact with the local community. The woods became a hub, a place where the encounter with nature and the human encounter came together, and I strove to reflect this in the paintings.

The benches that appear at intervals in the woods, almost always bearing a dedication to a deceased loved one, became a symbol for me on these walks in the woods: a symbol of the modest, easily ignored, or forgotten gestures we make for those who have passed. My walks often evoked thoughts about loss, not just the inevitability of loss but the way we encounter and process loss. Very possibly, my musings were a response to the frequent news and images of people ill and dying from Covid, often tragic accounts of how people died alone, fears of contamination and strict rules about contact keeping relatives and friends apart. I thought of the various rituals accompanying death, religious and humanist rituals, all trying to make meaning of the finality of the loss, with their different beliefs, hopes and illusions. There was something about the benches in the woods that seemed particularly meaningful: a real testament to the past, a message of the love of nature, a wish to position loss in the arms of nature, and a gesture of generosity to the many others who would walk and love these woods and who would one day want to be similarly reconciled with nature.

The final reference to a poem highlights the cyclical nature of the seasons in a way that affirms both change and continuity. However fragile nature might be, leaves disintegrating, tiny and immense changes occurring all the time, the rhythm of the seasons remains predictable: spring, summer, autumn, winter; year in and year out. The seasons, at least for the present, are indestructible.

The poem is P B Shelley's "Ode to the Western Wind" that ends with these famous lines:

O Wind,
If Winter comes, can Spring be far behind?

The simple words in Shelley's question convey a resonant message of continuity.

The groups

This was probably the most popular of my presentations, repeated in various contexts, including a group in Brighton mainly comprised of artists, my neighbourhood group in London and two large professional/psychotherapeutic groups. It was also the most unifying of my presentations. Participants identified immediately with the theme, the images and narrative evoking strong resonances, as if there was a readiness amongst the audiences for a presentation about nature. They welcomed the immersion in the woodland environment and the hopeful message of nature's resilience and continuity. Mish, the partner of the late theatre designer mentioned earlier, described the presentation as a "love song to the woods". She felt deeply touched that I had included her husband in the narrative, saying that he too would have been touched as he was so attached to the woods.

Since there was much consistency in the main themes from group to group, I am concentrating on the responses of my predominantly neighbourhood group (36 people) as they were particularly engaged with the presentation. They mostly live in close proximity to the woods, so the theme was of immediate interest. One participant emphasized how connected she felt to the group: she was from outside the neighbourhood but felt privileged to be included and sensed the cohesiveness of the group. She regarded this as especially meaningful during the lonely days of lockdown, when she and others felt very disconnected. She felt great poignancy in the theme of growth and decay. She loved the symbolism of the humble leaf as a fragment of nature that, in its brief existence, reflects the macrocosm of nature.

Several people felt that the opportunity to consider loss in this context was particularly meaningful. A woman shared the news that a beloved aunt had recently died, and the presentation provided an unexpected way of connecting with her loss. The mirror of nature, she said, was soothing, comforting. Another woman commented that the loss of connectedness during Covid was not just a product of the pandemic and lockdown. In her view, it might be the other way round: the pandemic might not have happened, or not on such an overwhelming scale, had people been more connected to nature. A further participant felt that the presentation, and the coming together with others, gave her an overall perspective on the times we live in: we were together appreciating the beauty before us, but in the face of the "terrible uncertainty" about the future, be it still in the grip of a pandemic or a radically altered post-Covid world.

In another group, a woman described going with a friend a day earlier to a mutual friend's funeral in an ancient city cemetery. The friend's death was sudden and shocking, and there was an atmosphere of painful disbelief at the funeral. Afterwards, she and her accompanying friend, trying to leave the cemetery, got lost. Panicking initially, they decided instead to take their time wandering around the cemetery and its beautiful grounds. They eventually found their way out and had no regrets, having spent valuable time on the grounds. It had brought them closer to each other as they had shared a deepened appreciation of the life-cycle and the inevitability of death. The woman was struck by the parallels between her experience and the *Fragile Nature* presentation. She was moved by the coincidence and spoke with great feeling about it.

Several people described unique or precious experiences they had had in the woods. A man spoke about the unexpectedly warm contact he could feel with strangers in the woods, compared to the brusque indifference of people passing in the street. He mentioned a recent experience (still in lockdown) of being in the woods on a bright spring day. It had been raining for some time, and although the woods were muddy and in parts difficult to traverse, he had a wonderful sense of renewal. The birdsong was clamorous. The sun shone through trees and shrubs, creating brilliant shafts of light. The woods shimmered. Nature was alive. He decided to take a seat on a bench to drink in the atmosphere, and he sat there for some time. A group of three older people walked past him. One of them struggled to walk, awkwardly using poles. The other two seemed concerned about her. In a moment, the threesome and the man on the bench caught each other's eye and there was a sense of heightened contact. The passers-by stopped. One of them said, "This is lovely, isn't it? It's sunny and bright and nature is all around us. What more could we want?" They all agreed. The woman with the walking sticks looked up and smiled. They stayed like this, in deep, silent, grateful contact, for some minutes. Then the little group walked on and the man never saw them again. But he had a sense of profound connection. He described it as a transcendent moment: a simple shared truth about existence and the link between being in nature and being human that transcended illness and suffering.

Perhaps one of the great lessons of the pandemic is that reconnecting with nature is a way of also connecting with other humans. We share a love of nature, and through this, we discover our common humanity.

There was much resonance and warmth in the groups, and the discussions tended to highlight this: the pleasure of participating with others in an online presentation of this kind. The comments were highly affirmative. One woman emphasized the value of an online event given the ease and safety with which people could join, considering the restrictions on movement outside the home. Another described how in art galleries and museums, she sometimes longed for more discussion with other viewers – and here she had exactly that. Several people encouraged me not only to hold more presentations of this sort online but to do so in the real world of galleries once they reopened. One man, an artist himself who met regularly in an artists' group to discuss each other's work, commented on how much more psychological this discussion was, and usefully so, bringing art and psychological reflection together in a novel way. He said that in many years of experience in art discourse, he had never felt the value of cross-fertilization he felt here. Some of the remarks were complimentary to me as presenter, a woman commenting how my narration enhanced the presentation. She quoted words I had uttered that had an alliterative or onomatopoeic ring, for example, "transience and transcendence", and felt that they fitted with the rhythm and sounds of nature. People similarly responded strongly to the poetry, appreciating the heightened meaning the poems offered. In one group, two different people spontaneously shared poems themselves, one reciting the poem by heart, the other quickly look-ing up a poem online and reading it out to the group. Both poems highlighted a sense of wonder and awe at nature, with a longing to embed the awareness in daily life. There was an eagerness in this group to participate and contribute that I have seldom seen before.

There was much interest in my technique and approach to painting. Several people were intrigued by my experimenting with different techniques and textures and enjoyed the freedom I expressed in moving the paintings around to get the right composition, also allowing the painting to emerge from the blur of paint-work rather than setting out with a strict vision in mind and sticking to it. This applied particularly to "Light in the Woods" (Figure 6.2) and "Woodland Trip-tych" (Figure 6.3), where viewers felt that I had transmuted the obvious, realistic images of nature into something more mysterious and mystical. Since many of the paintings were on a black background, in line with previous series, there were comments about the effectiveness or limitations of this. One person observed the light in the paintings taking on an added luminosity as a consequence of emanat-ing from a dark background. Another felt that the dark background of my paint-ings signified the danger in nature. She referred to my highlighting the struggle in nature for survival, the continuing battle amongst species to grow and thrive. She also referred to large-scale natural disasters, like earthquakes and hurricanes, and their destructive power. We should not forget these, she suggested: the violence at the heart of nature.

Reflection

There was a last contribution that differed from the others. A man described getting lost in the woods. This was in nearby Queen's Wood, a particularly rambling, hilly wood with wild, overgrown areas bordering on the winding pathways. At first perplexed by his disorientation, the man began to experience surprise and excitement at discovering not just unknown parts of the woods but perceiving the surrounding area from different vantage points. He suddenly realised that he was looking at the backs of houses that were familiar to him but not from this angle. Then, another residential area appeared that he did not know, or barely knew, but was delighted to discover. This kept happening, as if seeing the world through fresh eyes, a visitor to his own well-known universe, realising that everything we experience is perspectival, that there is no fixed point. I identified strongly with this man's experience. More than that, I felt gratified that the sense of no fixed point, of the world seen from different perspectives, of the potential for ongoing discovery, was an insight that emerged from my presentation.

Themes such as the aforementioned had moved away from the immediate preoccupation with the pandemic, but this in part was the value of this presentation: not only the respite from anxious concern but the sense of a whole world out there, waiting to be discovered and rediscovered.

Chapter 7

Dancers

Introduction

Dancers was the second series of paintings I completed, starting in the latter half of 2019, pre-Covid, and ending in 2020 in the midst of lockdown. I had attempted paintings on this theme in previous years, but little had materialised: the paintings lacked vitality. Both the strength of physical movement and the intensity of emotional expression that I wanted to convey were missing. Once I started the new series, the paintings flowed more easily, images emerging in close succession, the paintings viscerally alive and real. I felt that I was achieving my aim: to capture the experience of the dance; the precision of movement, particularly in the ballet; the strength and agility of the body; and the psychological expressiveness of the dance. It was as if a long-suspended impulse in my own development had finally broken free. The theme of dancing had held a poignant significance for me since childhood: the story I presented in tandem with the paintings was that of a child – myself – who wanted to be a dancer.

This chapter includes more autobiographical material than others, given the personal relevance of the subject. Poetry is also used to highlight themes. The selection of paintings mainly illustrates classical ballet and Spanish dancing, depicting both sexes but with a preponderance of females. Some figures are shown full-length, others focus on the torso, and still others are close-ups of faces. There are also back views of dancers, usually in a moment of strain or rest. My aim was to capture the figure in its changing moods, the thrill of dancing contrasted with moments of quiet, of contemplation. Beautiful and exciting as the dancers may seem to the viewer, dance is exacting, often exhausting, and the body goes through agonies of wear and tear. It is a competitive environment, too, with many aspiring dancers clamouring for the limelight in a tough, often ruthless world.

Although the focus is on dancers and dancing, the series touches on a universal issue: the challenge of that precious but vulnerable possession, our bodies. In dancing, we see the body at its extremes, muscularly taut, brilliantly co-ordinated, intensely engaged. Most of us never come anywhere near this perfection, struggling with bodily imperfection and awkwardness. But the body holds our personal

DOI: 10.4324/9781003232230-10

histories, our secret longings. The presentation, while inviting responses to the paintings themselves, is aimed at opening up a discourse about the body. We each have a body history, usually private, complicated and hidden rather than shared with others.

The body as a subject of inquiry and concern was intensified by lockdown during the pandemic. There was, first of all, the threat posed by Covid, a deadly virus that brought the spectre of death close to home, intensifying our awareness of body vulnerability. At the same time, severe restrictions on movement outside the home threw people back onto their bodies. Many attempted to cope by increased physical activity, going for walks wherever possible and adopting fitness regimes at home, all reinforced by an explosion of online courses. Dance classes of various sorts were part of the momentum, with some people discovering a love of dance for the first time. It was as if people realised how much they had taken their bodies for granted, how much pleasure and pride were to be discovered in a more active relationship with the body. That there was more time than usual during lockdown to engage with the body facilitated the discovery. This was one of the useful outcomes of the pandemic: an enhanced body awareness, though sobering that it required a pandemic to remind us of the complex asset of the body. How long-lasting the realisation will be remains to be seen, given cultural and psychological contradictions in the appreciation of the body, and hence, the tendency to secrete the bodily self.

The psychology of the body

Western views of the significance of the body were to a large extent influenced by the Cartesian split between body and mind, giving primacy to the mind as the seat of an existing self. "I think therefore I am": Descartes' famous dictum relegated the body to a secondary place in the experience of the world. Later philosophers, notably Merleau-Ponty (1962), challenged this assumption, not only questioning the split, but developing the notion of embodiment, with an emphasis on the crucial role the body plays in human development and, further, the inextricable link between mind and body. The body, once we recognize its significance, is the medium through which we relate to the world, the site of the senses, and where the emotions are felt in the complex interactions we have with others. In dance, the body comes into its fullest being.

For all its joys, the body is also the site of anxiety and shame. It changes as we grow older, at first with the youthful surge of growth, getting bigger and more powerful, later with the shock of ageing and decline. Eventually, we have no choice but to confront our mortality. The inevitability of death is a shadow hovering over the body all our lives, making death, and the vulnerable, deteriorating body, a source of nagging existential anxiety. The denial of death becomes an illusory way of coping with the unthinkable (Becker 1975). Our bodily functions, the evidence of a living body, are part of our corporeality, our animal selves, often a source of shame rather than pleasure.

Culture plays a huge role in influencing attitudes towards the body, in particular the "culture of narcissism" (Lasch 1987), with its demands for youth and beauty. The striving for bodily perfection is a never-ceasing feature of a world that promises eternal youth, the cessation of ageing and triumph over death. The discrepancy between the fantasy ideal and the actuality of bodily ordinariness and imperfection is, for some, too hard to bear, exacerbated by social media in which the young, especially, are rendered slaves to impossible standards of physical beauty. Culture is important also in influencing attitudes to dance. Gender, class, status and identity all interweave in the story of who becomes a dancer and who not: the dancing body does not metaphorically dance alone. The dance expresses cultural myths and constraints in every movement of the dance.

The emphasis on psychological trauma in psychotherapy in the last few decades increasingly identifies the body as the site of trauma: "The body keeps the score" (Van der Kolk 1990). The anxious, traumatized body might appear to be the opposite of the dancing body. Yet, it is important not to idealize the experience of dancing. In its spontaneous forms, dancing is usually fun, liberating. But dancing professionally, as in classical ballet and other formal dance forms, produces stresses and tensions of its own. Not only is the dance physically exacting and the training exhausting, but, as noted, the competition for success, identity, renown, even survival in a tough environment leaves some in states of painful failure and disappointment. The life of a ballerina, its highs and crushing lows, is vividly portrayed in a recent autobiography by Georgina Pazcoguin (2021), a dancer with the New York City Ballet.

I highlight the body under duress so as to introduce my paintings in a light that reflects the full experience of dancing, its elegance and vitality, as well as its rigour, its excitement and its suffering. I emphasize the theme as a lead into our personal stories of the body, a site of personal struggle and cultural imprint, whether in dance or the many forms of the expressive body.

The paintings

Ballet dancers

The first painting (Figure 7.1) and several others depict the classical ballet: a figure captured in momentary movement. My work follows a traditional line of ballet paintings, including Degas' depiction of dance in 19th-century Paris. Yet, the theme is surprisingly infrequent in art history, given the traditional, time-honoured investment in ballet. Degas' work is notable for its paradoxical aspects: showing the beauty of the dancers yet hinting at the harsh reality in which women and young girls were exploited and often cruelly sexualized (Greer 2009). Degas' figures are noted for the unusual angles from which they are viewed and the way the picture plane is truncated as if in a contemporary photograph. Considered daring at the time he painted, the scrambled perspectives may reflect something of the complexity and contradiction in the dancers' lives. The dancer I painted

Figure 7.1 Ballerina in Pink Tutu
Source: Morris Nitsun, 2020, oil, 74 × 65 cm

in Figure 7.1 is similarly viewed from an angle and occupies only a section of the painting. She expresses the exuberance of dance, the flurry of movement and texture captured in the vigorous brushwork, but the dark background suggests a hidden, anxious, indeterminate environment. She holds her pose for a moment, but in that pose, what sort of world is reflected?

Figure 7.2, "Ballerina in Movement", similarly shows a dancer against a dark background, the grey-black shadow outlining her figure with the same sense of lurking uncertainty or anxiety. The lightness of the ballet is etched against a darker force, the threat – of loss, disenchantment, death – sometimes played out in the story of the dance, a foil for the glittering light of the dancers and the studied grace of their movements.

In the online presentation, I interjected the show of paintings with fragments of my biography.

Memoir 1

I was entranced by dance in childhood. My natural tendency was to express myself through dance rather than sports. As a boy in 1940's/1950's South Africa, growing up in a small, white-dominated town, a huge Dutch Reformed church looming over the town, putting the fear of God into anyone who challenged the strict Calvinist doctrine, this was more than unusual. Gender roles were defined as absolutes: boys are boys, girls are girls. No ifs and buts, no in-betweens. My sister (four years older) danced. This was not only acceptable but actively encouraged. She attended ballet classes in a nearby town and came home filled with the spirit of the ballet: the magical, shimmering costumes, the ballet shoes, and the spirited movements, from little pirouettes to daring leaps into the sky. I loved to imitate her, usually practising movements secretly in my bedroom.

I also took opportunities to dance publicly. My older brother and sister once put on a concert in the tiny local town hall. I remember barely two handfuls of people in the audience, but to a child this was an event of great moment. I (age eight) persuaded the others to let me dance and my dance, I remember, was a form of contemporary ballet with free-flowing movements, accompanied by a long orange-red silk scarf, the thump of dramatic music on an old 40's gramophone in the background, and me prancing around the little stage. I do not remember the audience reaction, other than perhaps a ripple of polite, embarrassed clapping, but I think of that performance as my swan song. I stopped dancing. I was becoming increasingly aware that my interests were regarded as odd, feminine and to be repressed rather than expressed: the fear of being called sissy. My conventional parents were bewildered bystanders. I don't remember any explicit prohibition, but they were puzzled by this wayward son. When asked by others, in front of my parents, what I wanted to be when I grew up, I boldly announced, "a ballet dancer or a dress designer". My parents flinched.

Figure 7.2 Ballerina in Movement
Source: Morris Nitsun 2020, oil, 65 × 50 cm

I have divided the figures in the paintings into female and male. Although by today's standards, this might be a backward move, I did so in order to highlight the gender split that I believe not only inhibited me as a child but may be a reason for many people's struggles with their natural impulses to move and dance. Male and female, and their social inscriptions, figure strongly in people's attitudes to bodily expression. That moment's hesitation, the body suspended in motion, is not just personal: it reflects the penetration of powerful cultural constraints, including gender constraints.

Similarly to Degas, several of my paintings show the figure not so much dancing as bending, crouching, or in some other, possibly awkward, movement (see Figure 7.3, Ballerina Bending). I have always been fascinated by the bending figure, possibly something to do with gravity and the body's need to go back to the earth, to touch it, feel it: to reunite with our common, ancestral ground, to go back to our mammalian trope to scuttle forth on all fours. This offsets the opposite impulse, to reach upwards, to touch the sky. I believe that as humans, we are very much suspended between earth and sky, that we need both: the upward surge and the downward reach, feet on the ground, head in the heavens. This is partly why dance fascinates me. It is as if the dancing figure is finding its centre in the vertices of above and below. He/she is simultaneously romancing a place on earth and a dream of transcendence. The dance epitomizes our humanity in its power, grace and fragility, its relationship to something bigger and higher.

Poem I

There is a well-known poem by the American writer Emily Dickinson, "I cannot dance upon my toes", that conveys a longing to dance that cannot be realised. It ties up with my own attraction to dance as a child and the difficulty I had sharing this interest. In the poem, Dickinson not only expresses a longing to dance: she suggests how passionate she would be if only she could. She would have to be taught, though, she confides. As with most artistic expression, so much depends on support and encouragement. Untutored, Dickinson can only write about her restrained passion, muse on it. This ties up with my concept of the "artist's matrix" in Chapter 3, where I suggest that recognition and feedback are major components of an artist's creativity, whether in word, image or movement.

Memoir 2

The poem by Emily Dickinson not only reflects my youthful attraction to dance. It reminds me of my fascination with the dancer's footwork and the feat of balancing on toes. Figure 7.4 is a painting of the ballet pumps. The pumps intrigued me as a child. One day I decided to try on my older sister's ballet shoes. They were too big for me and I remember the embarrassing moment when, wearing the shoes, I took a leap in the air and the shoes went flying across the room. I was too small for the shoes.

Figure 7.3 Ballerina Bending
Source: Morris Nitsun 2020, oil, 80 × 60 cm

Figure 7.4 Ballet Shoes
Source: Morris Nitsun, 2020, oil, 40 × 50 cm

There is great passion in dance. Dancers are usually intense about their art, driven to extremes by their hunger for the performance, for pitting their bodies against the odds of exhaustion and injury. The narrative of dance, "the story", often expresses this passion. Think of Giselle, Swan Lake, The Firebird and many more: brilliant evocations of passion at its limits. I did not attempt in the paintings to illustrate any particular ballet but to show figures in states of intense concentration. Figure 7.5, Reverie, is an attempt to convey some of the complex feelings of the dancer. Here, we see only her head atop an elongated neck, which I had painted deliberately to symbolize the dancer's possibly troubled relationship with her body. Of all my dancer paintings, this tends to elicit the greatest ambivalence and range of associations: she is dreaming of the dance; she is in pain, hurt, frustrated; she is in an anguished relationship; her passion is spent. The figure's elongated neck triggers much comment. Some find it a powerful, provocative feature. Others find it odd, distorted and disturbing.

Then come the afterwards or in-between times, in between the acts or after the performance, when the dancer is alone or seeks solitude. It may be a moment of

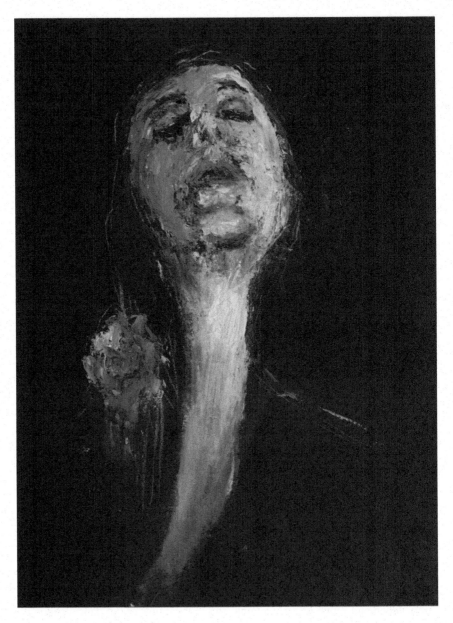

Figure 7.5 Reverie

Source: Morris Nitsun, 2020, oil, 84 × 59 cm

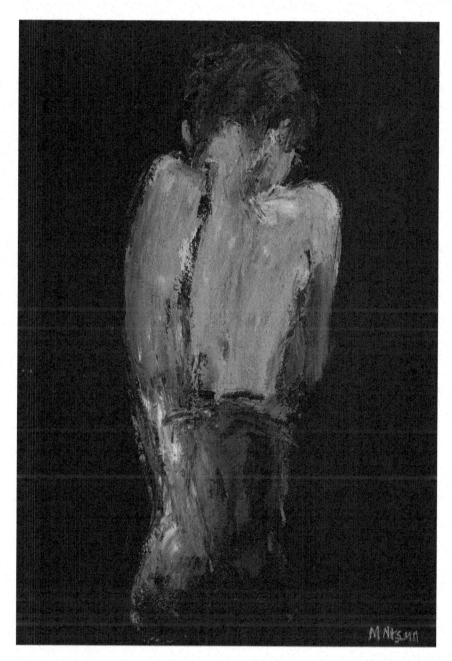

Figure 7.6 Young Dancer
Source: Morris Nitsun, 2020, oil, 59 × 42 cm

quiet reflection. Or the dancer retreats, possibly in pain, struggling to carry on. Away from the others, from the crowd, from the music, the dancer can breathe and allow her feelings to surface.

Figure 7.6, "Young Dancer", shows such a moment. I painted several figures in back view as this tends to offer a more intimate glimpse of the figure, more intimate than from the front. It is as if we are witnessing a private moment, looking over the dancer's shoulder. Dancing seriously is an endurance test, with injured and damaged joints and limbs par for the course. "Young Dancer" suggests a girl's vulnerability, her sense that she has taken on more than she can manage, her doubts about herself. Does she have the talent? Does she want to go on? This painting attracted much interest, with a number of people saying it was their favourite of all the dancer paintings, the most memorable. It was also one of the paintings that were chosen by the dance group I mention later in the chapter: the image inspired a poignant dance sequence by an individual in contact with the rest of the group.

Painting the dancers was cathartic for me. Not only was I able to produce the images, expressing a long-standing interest in the dancing body, but exploring the many facets of dancing enabled me to work through some of my unresolved feelings about a youthful ambition.

Spanish dancers

And now for the Spanish dancers. This is where passion comes to the fore. The delicacy of classical ballet gives way to the fiery burst of flamenco. Usually accompanied by guitar music and haunting song, Flamenco declares unbridled passion, the atmosphere of the dance mounting, arms and hands in a frenzy of movement, feet clicking sharply together. The Spanish writer Federico Garcia Lorca (1933) describes a musical sequence in which the dancer may fall into a *duende*, an intensely focused, trancelike state of transcendent emotion. Also called "*los sonidos negros*", these are "the dark sounds" that invade the performer's body. This state is enhanced by rhythmic hand-clapping and loud interjections from the audience and fellow performers. This has been described by some flamenco dancers as a form of prayer. In the duende, the belief goes: the dancer communicates not only with an audience, but with God.

Poem 2

A poem by Rainer Maria Rilke (1918) vividly captures the atmosphere. Note the emphasis on the body and movement and the intense imagery of fire, flames and serpents, capturing the animalistic aspect of a dance that is yet powerfully co-ordinated.

The Spanish dancer

As a lit match first flickers in the hands
Before it flames, and darts out from all sides

Bright, twitching tongues, so, ringed by growing bands
Of spectators – she, quivering, glowing stands
Poised tensely for the dance – then forward glides

And suddenly becomes a flaming torch.
Her bright hair flames, her burning glances scorch,
And with a daring art at her command
Her whole robe blazes like a fire-brand
From which is stretched each naked arm, awake,
Gleaming and rattling like a frightened snake.

And then, as though the fire fainter grows,
She gathers up the flame – again it glows,
As with proud gesture and imperious air
She flings it to the earth; and it lies there
Furiously flickering and crackling still –
Then haughtily victorious, but with sweet
Swift smile of greeting, she puts forth her will
And stamps the flames out with her small firm feet.

Figure 7.7, "Flamenco Dancer, Female", shows a woman in typical flamenco attire, her red skirt billowing around her. She is in sharp, jagged movement but turns sideways to look at her audience, haughty, challenging, her manner filled with the pride and the passion of the dance. Spanish dancers are wonderful images to paint: the rich colours and textures of the costumes; the expressiveness of the figure; the sense of music throbbing; the unseen audience enraptured, shouting, clapping. I wanted the painting to convey the full atmosphere without depicting the whole scene. This is dance at full throttle, yet, as the quote from Lorca suggests, there is a spiritual dimension in the dance, the woman's expression in the painting possibly one of existential assertion: "I am here! Death beckons at the end of it all but right now I am present, alive, my body awake with the sensation of living".

The figure in the next painting (Figure 7.8, "Spanish Dancer Turning") similarly turns to look, either at another person or at an audience. Her gaze is enigmatic. She could be judging the response of the audience, uncertain of the impact of her dance, or it could be a seductive glance, a come-hither invitation to closeness or intimacy. Yet, she could also be sad, conveying a sense of loss or disappointment. Rather like my paintings in the dolls' series, the dancers generally triggered a wide variety of responses, the ambiguity of their faces and expressions inviting many projections. In each of the dancers, we see, through the paintings, a history, an inner world of experience and an outer world of admiration or denigration. This leaves it to the viewer to respond in their own way to the painting, to select what is meaningful to them. We all dance in this in-between world of meanings, and I attempt to explore this vicariously through dancers' intense relationship with self and other.

Figure 7.7 Flamenco Dancer, Female
Source: Morris Nitsun, 2020, oil, 59 × 42 cm

Figure 7.8 Spanish Dancer Turning
Source: Morris Nitsun, 2020, oil, 59 × 42

Male dancers

Introducing the male dancers, I return to my personal experience, going back to childhood.

Memoir 3

The consequence of suppressing my early interest in dancing was not only the loss of dance itself but possibly the loss to bodily vitality. Disinclined to compensate with sports, I believe I began to lose touch with my body. Sports became an unwelcome challenge. I felt inadequate, inept when it came to most boys' activities. Gym at school was a nightmare. What I regret is that no one seemed to notice or care, no one took me by the hand, reassured me, tried to instil confidence, or show me how. I associate this with my difficult, distant relationship with my father. He was the opposite to me: active, physically confident, daring other men to arm wrestle or race him to a finishing post. But instead of identifying with him, I drew away. As I grew into adolescence, I felt physically alone, my inhibition further complicated by puberty, my body changing in unwelcome, ungainly ways, my voice breaking. Instead of adolescence being a time of physical expression, of experiment, of sex, I virtually became a boy without a body. I excelled at school, had friends, discovered a strong interest in art, but bodily I was mute, alone.

The first of the male paintings (Figure 7.9) continues the Spanish dancing theme and is a flamenco dancer caught in a moment of intense engagement with the dance. What is striking is his masculinity. This is a man with a strong face, strong gestures, strong commitment to the dance. What it signifies for me is the realisation I came to in later years that dance is as much a masculine activity as a feminine one. I had for some time assumed that only *queers, poofs or fairies*, to use the pejorative terms of the time, became professional dancers. I had bought into the stereotype. This was why I turned away from dance. It might be true that male dancers are likely to be more sensitive and aesthetically minded than most other men, and professional dance is attractive to gay men, but the generalisation belies the complex range of masculinity and forms of male dancing. Certainly, male Spanish dancers appear to be virile but are likely to be sensitive, feeling, suffering men. Even if there are gay men amongst them, they are probably indistinguishable from the rest – and, in any case, what does it matter in the creative fervour of the dance?

Memoir 4

I had a late flourishing. It's not as if I remained dormant, physically or expressively. In fact, I did dance, more as part of the club scene of the 80's and 90's than anything more formal or artistic, but enjoyable and freeing, nonetheless. I also joined the Five Rhythms dance movement, a particularly liberating experience. Then, as the century turned, possibly buoyed up by the spirit of newness and promise, I started fitness training. I acquired a personal trainer,

Figure 7.9 Flamenco Dancer, Male
Source: Morris Nitsun, 2020, 65 × 50 cm

a young man who visited me at home for training sessions. In time, I had further trainers but the first one, Paul, made the most impact on me. In spite of our coming from totally different backgrounds – he was an "Essex lad" and I was a north London Jewish psychologist-artist – we had an excellent rapport.

We chatted easily, joked, laughed, and what had always seemed exacting and arduous – the exercise – was suddenly fun, stimulating, enlivening. That he was straight and had a girlfriend and I was gay with a partner helped to deal with issues of attraction and closeness and, if anything, we achieved the warmest intimacy.

Figure 7.10 shows the head and torso of a male dancer in a striking pose, deeply absorbed in the dance. The perspective from above and the diagonal of his arm and hand pointing downwards seem to invite attention to his inner experience. But his face is turned inwards, concealing his emotions – enjoyment, pain, fear? The dance may be the culmination of a journey, decades coming together in a moment of intense presence: life embodied in a dance.

Couples

I realised in the course of painting that I had concentrated on dancers in solo performances, singling out a figure from the rest. This reflects my interest in the dancer's inner, subjective experience. But, of course, dancing usually takes place with others. I was drawn now to couples, couples dancing in partnership, expressing the intimacy of two people dancing together. Here the dance brings people into close physical contact, arousing not so much the intense self-absorption of the solitary dancer but the creativity of the dancing pair, the awareness of the other's movement, the sensual feel of the other. The few paintings in this series focused on ballroom dancing, a universally popular dance form, very different from ballet or flamenco.

Ballroom dancing is a way of people achieving a degree of intimacy and closeness within a prescribed form. But the painting illustrated here (Figure 7.11) is different. It shows the tentative movement of two figures towards each other.

This painting, the last in the series, "Black and White Dancers" (Figure 7.11), depicts two men dancing or about to dance. I was unsure of how to treat the subject but was struck by what emerged. Male dancing in couples is now much more prevalent than in the past, the acceptance of gender and sexual fluidity part of present-day culture, as is the normalisation of male-male relationships in general. But the internalised rejection of same-sex partnerships over decades runs deep and is not easily dispelled. The two men in the painting are drawn to each other, but there is uncertainty in their tentative encounter. In addition to the same-sex theme, the painting depicts a white male and a black male coupling, adding the racial dimension and, with it, further tension and uncertainty.

Memoir 5

The racial difference in the painting takes me back to my childhood in South Africa. I grew up in a small South African town steeped in the rigors of apartheid, my contact with black people limited. The painting evokes a question

Figure 7.10 Male Dancer, Torso
Source: Morris Nitsun 2020, 59 × 42 cm

Figure 7.11 Black and White Dancers

Source: Morris Nitsun, 2020, oil, 90 × 60 cm

about what was lost in such a separation. What did I project onto black men and what was lost to me? Did I regard the black man as male in some stereotyped way: aggressive, sexual, potentially dangerous? I ask this, wondering whether my early estrangement from my body was a function of the projection onto the other of a violent masculinity. In these terms, the painting is not only about physical or sexual closeness as it is about opposites coming together, about the possibility of re-integration. I am reminded of the Jungian concept of *coniunctio*, the marriage of opposites (Jung 1956). This might be a vision of what it means to have a body that is fully realised: not just for me, but for us all. I suggest it is in the embrace of opposites, the capacity to integrate self and other; the weak and the strong, the ugly and the beautiful, the vulnerable and the powerful, that we may integrate. In that way, the dance is a marriage of opposites.

Groups

The online group

I undertook presentations with two different groups. The first took place online on 24th April 2021 with thirty-five people. Aware that this was probably the most personal of my presentations thus far, and since this was an initial try-out, I decided to invite only friends or close colleagues, people who knew me and something of my struggles and with whom I felt comfortable. The result was an intimate, sensitively appreciative audience.

The interconnecting strands of autobiography and painting were immediately grasped by the audience, the group responding to the wholeness of the presentation as well as to details. There were many perceptive comments about individual paintings and aspects of the images. Of all the paintings in my various series, the dancers were probably the most popular, the most admired and enjoyed, with frequent comments such as "beautiful", "moving", "compelling", "exciting", even "thrilling". The combination of appreciation and serious regard for my personal story, weaving in and out of the presentation, created a particularly engaged online atmosphere.

Amongst the links people made between the dancers and my personal story, there was a strong emphasis on the theme of restraint and freedom. One participant commented that virtually every painting conveyed the image of a spirit struggling to break free. This person highlighted the parallel with my early development, as I narrated it, from childhood onwards. The image of a free spirit trying to get out was very meaningful to me, and I was touched by the way this was observed and communicated in the group. It also stimulated more general group discussion about control and repression vs freedom of expression, a theme many could identify with.

The theme of control and restraint in the portrayal of the dancers was linked in the discussion to the demand for discipline and rigour in the training of dancers. The group produced vivid descriptions of the physical and mental demands on those who chose dance as a profession, the extraordinary wear and tear of training and performance, and the limited chances of success in the fiercely competitive environment. These considerations became strongly linked in people's minds to gender differences. Girls and women in the ballet were seen as especially subject to these pressures. I had described boyhood wishful fantasies of becoming a dancer, with a note of regret about my lack of opportunity, but it was observed that females, often at a very young age, are forced to go to ballet school, often against their will. This could lead to years of subjection, with consequent physical and emotional injury. One group participant, a psychotherapist who lives and practises in New York, mentioned her work with ballet dancers. The toll it took on them was cruelly evident. She described a woman, a former prima ballerina, prematurely confined to a wheelchair, disfigured, incapacitated.

Possibly because of the preponderance of women in the audience, much attention was given to the body shape of the ballerinas in the paintings. Many saw them as strikingly thin. One or two perceived them as anorectic: so thin, so bony, a woman suggested, that it was difficult to believe they could actually dance. A doctor member of the audience commented that some of the figures looked as if they belonged in a hospital rather than on the stage. Several commented that the male dancers, by contrast, appeared strong, robust, powerful. The male dancers were also seen as having more freedom of choice, to dance or not to dance, unlike the women who might be shunted into the profession at an early age. While knowing that I had portrayed some of the female dancers as skinny, I regarded this to a large extent as an occupational requirement, or hazard, and was unaware myself of the marked difference in the paintings between the male and female dancers' appearance. Once this was pointed out with some consistency, I realised that it must be significant. Since I was the painter, the difference must be my creation. Reflecting further, I got in touch with my own long-standing anxieties about women's fragility, having had a depressed mother and a frequently ill sister whom I saw changing from a sturdy young woman to a thin, ailing chronic patient. My father and brother, by contrast, were fit and healthy for most of their lives. This real-life difference had undoubtedly affected me, influencing my relationships with men and women in complex ways. The surprise was that these attributions had imperceptibly crept into the paintings of dancers and that it took a group audience to see that. I realised that, while dealing consciously with one subject, I was unconsciously exploring another troubling subject in the paintings.

It is insights of this sort that made the discussion challenging and meaningful to me personally, demonstrating how a group's response to an artist's productions can illuminate not only the artwork but the artist's psychology. The audience itself became aware of this unfolding process. One participant described it as a creative loop in which the art stimulated the group's associations, and these, in turn, provoked the artist's awareness. In this presentation, there was a particularly creative loop.

Another meaningful theme highlighted the similarity between painting and dancing. An art therapist in the audience initiated the theme. As creative arts, both painting and dancing involve physical exertion and symbolic expression. Both stimulate the senses, for the exponent and the audience, and both result in the creation of a new form. This was a useful insight. The group's capacity to play with this idea helped me to recognise the overlapping energies in my own creative initiatives.

In summary, this was a very gratifying event for both the audience and presenter. Many people requested further similar events, emphasizing, apart from the significance of the subject matter and the narrative accompaniment, the pleasure of being in such an open, expressive group – and wanting to meet again. The quality of discussion was frequently commented on. Given the impact of the event, it is useful to consider the nature of the relationship between the group and myself. As presenter, I had multiple inputs. I was the facilitator, narrator, artist, biographer and educator, in that I presented both an art-historical background and a psychological perspective on the material. This is very different from the role I am accustomed to as a group analytic psychotherapist, in which I conform much more to a standard process. This was one of the revelations of the project for me: the surprise and joy of finding a new way of facilitating a group. In a sense, this parallels the theme of restraint and freedom inherent in the paintings. Through undertaking this project, I was able to venture from the zone of comfort and familiarity and discover a new way of being a group conductor. At the same time, I was the beneficiary of insights that struck a deep, personal chord. The new way of facilitating a group had unexpected benefits: I could both give and receive.

The dance group

The second group in this series was an altogether different group – a dance and movement group organized to improvise to my paintings of dancers. It took place in real, physical space – momentous itself after lockdown – and was one of the most exciting events that came out of this entire project. The group is called SpiralArts, an innovative dance theatre company with a multi-talented membership, including musicians, singers, movement specialists, and even an ex-circus performer. The director of the group had attended my online presentation of the paintings, was inspired and, together with a close friend of mine, suggested arranging an event focused on my painting, using the images as stimuli for dancing in an exploration of the visual, musical and dance arts coming together. I welcomed the opportunity, and the event took place in September 2021. Twelve people attended, ten women and two men, apart from myself, all with their considerable talents, bringing alive the imagery and spirit of the paintings.

The experience benefited from a wonderful venue – a spacious, light-filled penthouse studio atop a green haven of trees, with extensive and commanding views of London. There was ample space to move and breathe, to dance alone or with others.

I began by describing the background to the paintings, drawing on the autobiographical history described earlier. This was a condensed version of the narrative, focusing on my love of dancing as a child, my thwarted aspirations, and how, at a much later stage of life, this was expressed in the current series of paintings. In discussion with the director, I had decided to show only five key paintings, with the idea of concentrating the dance on each work in turn. These are all paintings illustrated previously in the chapter. I introduced each image, describing the significance of the painting, what it represented and how I had used oil painting techniques to express the image. This was the stimulus for the dance. The director, who led the event, invited one person to start by responding to an aspect of the painting that struck her/him and embodying that in a dance. She then invited anyone who felt moved to join in, encouraging the whole group, in turn, to join as the impulse took them. The group was highly responsive, the movement and dance flowing effortlessly, spontaneously, playfully. A musician accompanied the movement on simple percussive instruments and drums, producing a deeply sonorous background, sensitively attuned to the spirit of the dance. She and two other singers also vocalized to the dance: non-verbal sounds, varying between guttural low and eerily high, sudden shouts, calling, moaning, then lingering, amplified by other voices in turn. There was a tremendous synergy in the group, the different movements and sounds building to climactic moments of beauty and intensity.

Rather than describing each of the five dances in turn, I am focusing on one image to illustrate the process as it occurred. The painting is called "Young Dancer", Figure 7.6 in the chapter, and shows a young woman, possibly still a girl, with her back to the viewer. It is as if we are looking over her shoulder into her personal space, away from the dance. Her back dominates the picture, the line of her spine pronounced. The image conveys vulnerability, retreat, possibly shame. This was one of the people's favourite paintings in the series, evoking strong associations. The woman who came forward to take the floor at the start of the dance said the image touched her deeply. She was a contemporary dancer, trained in ballet, now branching out into further aspects of movement and dance. She expressed an empathic link with the girl in the painting. She started her dance bent, half-crouching, moving slowly, almost painfully, her back in full view. She moved her arms around her breasts in a cradling fashion, as if she was holding something, protecting it. The rest of the group was very quiet, rapt, watching, a singer's plaintive voice in the background. After a while, a man joined the dancer, moving behind her, his open hands hovering on her back as if wanting to touch, to soothe, to reassure. Then another man joined, this time in front and to the side of her, similarly with open hands, mirroring her movement as if to track or support her. Others in the group slowly, tentatively joined the three figures, taking up complementary positions, moving in gentle, sympathetic ways, the atmosphere one of compassion and care, all circling around the first dancer.

The dance was followed, as with each of the five dances, by a group reflection. There was initially a hushed silence, then people began to share feelings and associations. My own association was of a baby. I saw the dancer's arms as cradling a baby, at least something very young, very vulnerable. The group was in tune with the association, recognizing their strong inclination to protect, to hold, to contain. The image of mother and child, which seemed symbolically present in several of my other series of paintings, felt embodied within the dancer's movements. I recognise in this my own subjective association, if not projection, but it ties up with a developing theme in this book: the mother-child relationship embedded in the search that inspired this project.

This is just one example of an afternoon filled with sensitive moments, the dancing coming together with the paintings to create an exceptional event. I had started the day not knowing what to expect. This was very new territory. I was worried that it would fail, that it was a risky, unthought-out experiment, that it would end in confusion and disarray. The opposite happened. It came together with remarkable ease, as if it was intuitively the right thing to do, leaving the group and myself feeling surprised, exhilarated, touched. The musician in the group wrote soon afterwards, describing it as "a very moving afternoon".

Reflection

The dancer paintings were a major shift from the dark pessimism and gloom of the Deserted City – and the pall of the pandemic – to a lighter, more human, more animated universe. Yet, I was keen to convey in the paintings something of the dark side of dancing as well, the stress, disappointment and exhaustion that is the other side of the dance. These contrasting aspects of the dance were fully embraced by the audience. The live dance group's response in the second, "real" event confirmed this impression, taking the project into an altogether new, experimental zone, transferring the spirit of the paintings into a very alive experience, seemingly for all. Overall, the dancers' theme and its reception in the two different groups was a step closer to what I experienced as a transformational journey, the origins of hope and disillusionment in early experience transmuted through painting and an empathic audience.

Chapter 8

Four women

Introduction

There are four women in the title of this presentation, but it mainly concerns one woman – my mother. I've included the three other women as points of reference or contrast. It is difficult to be objective about one's mother: such a deep and complex relationship. I hoped that by positioning my mother with the three other very different women, I would get closer to the essence of her. By the end of this series, I felt that, to some extent, I had achieved this. I sensed not only that I had a deeper understanding of her and her influence on me, but I could also see more clearly, more fully, the overall purpose of the project that informs this book. I could see it now symbolically, in part at least, as an attempt to revisit the mother-child relationship, in both a generic sense – all our mothers – and a specific personal sense – my mother.

The twelve paintings in this series I consider to be amongst the most powerful figurative paintings I have produced. However, the paintings depend on a narrative to fully communicate their message, requiring a more substantial text than any other chapter in this book. The narrative concerns women who were/are towering figures in 20th-century cultural history. There is one exception – my mother, who was the opposite, an ordinary woman unknown to people other than her immediate family and, even then, only dimly so, since she was quiet, retiring and somewhat unknowable. Also, since she died twenty-five years ago, the memory of her has faded. It is partly this, the forgetting of a loved one, swept aside in the waves of time, that has prompted this inquiry, hoping not just to salvage the fragments of her life but to do justice to her as a person. Her name was Bessie Nitsun (nee Joffe). She was born in Lithuania in 1908, emigrated to South Africa in 1920 and died in 1996 at age 88.

I have put her alongside three famous, extraordinary women who established very strong identities and made major contributions to humanity: Rosa Parks, Mother Teresa and Jan Morris. If this seems incongruous, there is a reason for it. My mother was of a generation of women who entered the modern age but lacked the opportunities and support to make something of their lives outside the family home and their roles as wives and mothers. She was an anxious, complex, often

DOI: 10.4324/9781003232230-11

depressed woman who was in some ways consumed by the pressures and tensions of family life. Yet, she had a keen interest in medicine and general health, read widely in this sphere, and taught herself to practise one or two alternative therapies, though in her usual self-effacing way. She was shy, quiet, and made few claims for herself. I always felt that she could have made much more of her life. She could have been a doctor, a healer. She had a sensitive appreciation of nature and beauty, managed a sprawling Johannesburg garden, and furnished the family home with old-fashioned flair. In some ways, I associate my artistic talents with her. At first puzzled by my painting – it was not part of her tradition, coming from an orthodox Jewish family in an Eastern European village – she grew increasingly appreciative of it, particularly in her last years when she would study my work for some time, asking questions, making comments. She loved my use of colour. She began to appreciate the importance of composition and texture, and she responded eagerly to the new work I painted. We had always had a fond relationship, but in those final years, when I saw something awaken in her, this deepened.

I have put my mother together with three powerful women in this presentation in order to substantiate her more fully as a person and to initiate an inquiry. There is a question, perhaps naive: how is it that the three other women were able to find and fulfil themselves, at least as we know publicly, when my mother was so limited in her horizons, so restrained in her ambitions, so unhappily resigned to her position in life? I ask these questions knowing that we cannot easily compare lives, that what happens to each of us is puzzling, an enigma. But possibly, the juxtaposition of these lives will yield insights. No doubt, my mother's life reflected her own biographical history, genetic influences and social constraints, all of which contributed to who she was. However, my presentation through painted images and biographical narrative aims to explore her struggle in a different way and, more widely, to address the question of female identity: how different women find their way in the cultural maelstrom. These four women in particular interest me. I give weight to the socio-historical context of their lives, to the time and place they lived and to the predominant challenges of the day. Erik Erikson (1959) said that birth is a moment in history, in a highly specific time and place, and in that moment, we become who we are. What forces in society attracted these women, what stirred them, and what enabled them to find a voice – or not?

There is a further aspect to my inquiry – the search for myself. Since childhood, I felt more identified with the women in the family, my mother and older sister, than with the men. I felt a particular kinship with Bess, my mother. As the youngest child, I was sometimes told that I was her favourite. I felt very close to her and sensed, rightly or wrongly, that I understood and appreciated her more than most. Further, I felt that who I became in life was profoundly associated with her, not just in the broad way that links family biologically and historically, but in a very specific way: the development of my creativity from childhood until the present time. I believe this happened through the vision she had of me. She once said, "You will grow up to do important things. You will be a teacher, a leader. I think you will also make things that many people will see". That she observed something in me, even if exaggerated, a potential that others did not see, is important: that she intuited early talents and resources that set me on a creative pathway. However, I wonder also whether it was her *wish* for me to succeed, to express myself fully, to create, that drove me, and, further, that it reflected the part of her that could not be fulfilled, that was trapped in the role she adopted as wife and mother, and that she transferred onto me. I see it not so much as her living vicariously through me but as a gesture of generosity and love. This included her unexpressed wish to be a healer and, very possibly, her own untutored artistic potential. If so, I owe her a lot. Although disappointed herself, she must have provided a setting in our early relationship that equipped me with the drive to make something worthwhile of my life.

In large part, this series of paintings, *Four Women*, is a tribute to her: a tribute and thanks for what she gave me. By recognising her contribution in this way, I hope to give something back to her. In Christopher Bollas' (1987) terms, I believe she had the function of a transformational object, someone who early on holds a key to one's development. The "idiom" (Bollas 2019) she established in our relationship provided the ground for my later excursions into psychology and the arts. In the work of this chapter, I wish to reciprocate: perhaps to be *her* transformational object.

I am aware that I am entering sensitive territory when addressing women's identity. Here I am, a man, setting out to explore women's identity, at a time of heightened awareness of women's place in society, of their oppression, often by men. My agenda, however, is complicated by my own struggles with identity, not only the familiar artist-psychologist struggle that underlies this book, but the deeper issues about who and what I am as a man. I am familiar with the male and female parts of myself, yet these parts remain open to interrogation. In my closeness to my mother, I believe there was a strong identification with her femaleness, including her oppression, but I also sensed her male side and was puzzled by this. Then, too, what was/is female and what male? So, in searching for her identity in this presentation, I am also searching for myself. And by grouping her with three highly differentiated women, I hope to open an inquiry into gender and identity that may have a wider relevance to both men and women.

The heuristic of this inquiry again starts with me, focusing on my love of my mother, my questions about her life, and my search for insight into my own identity. Through painting and narrative, I hope to stimulate an expanded awareness that illuminates the hidden side of ourselves, our creative origins in our relationships and our quest for who we are.

Why these three women?

Many women, despite constraints, have made profound contributions to society. Why, then, the three women I have chosen – Rosa Parks, Mother Teresa and Jan Morris? The truth is that the idea of these women came to me spontaneously, with little forethought. It is as if, as cultural icons, they simply presented themselves. I am here, they said. Once they appeared in my mind, I knew that they were relevant to my inquiry. I decided to trust my intuition, to make these women the focus and to go no further other than including my mother, and to look for themes that both united and differentiated the women.

Also, without realising this at the time, I chose women who lived at broadly the same time in history: Bess (1908–1996); Rosa (1913–2005); Teresa (1910–1997) and Jan (1926–2020). They had very similar lifespans, dying at comparable ages (Bess 88, Rosa 92, Teresa 87, and Jan 94). Possibly I chose them unconsciously to heighten the comparison, to look at the different ways they all inhabited the same world. I produced three or four paintings for each woman linked to different stages of their lives: youth, middle age and old age. I followed their developmental journey to see how they were formed, and how they formed themselves, through time. The paintings provide a narrative frame for each, following a sequential pathway from early beginnings to major achievements to decline and death. The three women other than my mother all took bold steps in the worlds they inhabited, actively expressing who they were, what they believed in. In their own ways, they changed history. My mother took a bold step in getting married – a complicated commitment that was as problematic as it was fulfilling.

Bess (1908–1996)

My mother came with her family to South Africa in 1920, fleeing pogroms against the Jews in the town of Panevezys in north-eastern Lithuania. They had previously spent harsh years on the edge of Siberia, spuriously exiled there by the Russians as spies for the Germans. They knew hunger in those years and the death of a child, the youngest daughter, in the frozen Siberian landscape. Later, they emigrated to South Africa. Depictions of Bess as a twelve-year-old girl in Potgietersrust in the then Transvaal suggest a bright, pretty, chubby child who adjusted well to the new country. She fell in love with my father, Joe, in her late teens. He had similar origins in Lithuania and had emigrated to South Africa in the hope of a freer life and greater opportunities. However, he had a reputation as a dandy, a ladies' man, and had not yet succeeded in establishing himself in Johannesburg, where they met. Her parents bitterly opposed the marriage. They did not want their eligible daughter marrying a ne'er do well, as they saw him, and Bess was torn between her family and him. Her letters to him from this period, which I have in my possession, reveal her desperation. She felt terribly trapped. But she decides to leave her parents and marry him.

They elope in dramatic circumstances, and Bess goes to live with Joe in the rural Cape province, where he has opened a small business. They eventually settle in the farming town of De Doorns ("The Thorns" in Dutch). Her parents agree to give them a formal wedding and they return to Johannesburg for the event. By now, though, there is a rent in her relationship with her family, particularly her mother, a rent that will never be fully repaired.

Figure 8.1 is based on her wedding photograph. She is a beautiful bride, bedecked in a delicate white dress with a veil flowing from a slender floral tiara. She holds

Figure 8.1 Bess, as Bride

Source: Morris Nitsun 2021, oil, 120 × 80 cm

a bunch of white lilies. She is the picture of a bride of the 1920's. But there is a sadness. She stands rather stiffly, pensively, as if in suspended animation. What has she done to create such division? A marriage is meant to bring people together, not drive them apart. What does this mean for the future?

The problems came in the first year or two of marriage. Joe was a philanderer. He had casual affairs from early on, leaving Bess feeling isolated and abandoned in the small, rural town. They were the only Jews in the area. The thousands of miles from her parents in Johannesburg accentuated both her physical and emotional separation. She gave birth to three children in these circumstances, largely unsupported, and had two miscarriages and a still-born child that left her drained and vulnerable. Bitterness crept into the marriage; Bess, aware of the sacrifices she had made to marry my father, felt deeply let down. Joe, resentful of her family's rejection and sensing her estrangement, withdrew.

I was often confused by them as marital partners. As much as there was a painful emotional rent, they at times also seemed happy and still in love. My mother was an active support in my father's business and enjoyed the agency this gave her. Joe often commented on how able and hard-working she was. She thrived in a situation in which she had challenge and responsibility. But Joe could not restrain his wilder impulses and had one or two long-lasting affairs that poisoned the marriage. I remember the increasing periods of tension between them erupting into open hostility. The pattern of withdrawal continued, and the marriage at times looked like the empty husk of a once full, brave relationship.

If emotionally the marriage was failing, they achieved notable business success, having commissioned in the late 1930's a magnificent art-deco building that became the home of the "De Doorns Bazaar". The success of the business was at further personal cost to them, though, through the strain of managing a growing enterprise without sufficient support, and in the early 1950's, my father decided to sell the business. They then embarked on the trip of a lifetime. – a voyage to Europe on one of the great ocean liners of the day, the Queen Mary. A new vista beckoned.

Figure 8.2 shows my mother in Trafalgar Square during the European tour. The painting is based on a photo of her standing amidst the pigeons, holding one in her hand. There was something about her gesture and the symbolism of the bird that stirred me. In the painting, I exaggerate and enlarge the bird, trying to express something about the prospect of flight. My association is not so much of my mother literally wanting to fly from her marriage. It is more generally about her freedom, or lack of it, to find herself. She came alive during that European trip, in letters to me describing places as "exciting" and "romantic". I sensed a new energy in her, a freedom from constraint. My parents seemed to get on well on that trip, the stimulus of a bountiful world probably drawing them closer. But, additionally, something else seemed to awaken in Bess, as if anticipating the possibility of wider horizons.

The promise did not materialise. The business was sold and we moved as a family to Johannesburg. Joe had been invited to join Bess' brothers in their growing wholesale business in the booming city. This was, seemingly, both a business proposal and

Figure 8.2 Bess, with Bird
Source: Morris Nitsun, 2021, oil, 120 ×80

a gesture of goodwill: the hope that there could be a reconciliation and, above all, that Bess could be close once more to her family. The opposite happened. There were further, more acrimonious divisions and Bess was more than ever trapped in the hostile link between Joe and her family. I sensed her despair, and from that time onwards, her depression deepened. In her withdrawal, she turned to a continuing interest – medicine and health in general. She read books and articles, quoting new research findings and expert opinions. As she grew older, her knowledge and wisdom deepened. She was particularly attracted to natural remedies and taught herself reflexology and shiatsu. She sometimes tentatively practised these skills on family members.

As she grew older, everything seemed to worsen. My older brother and I both emigrated from SA, I to London, he to the USA. The family house emptied out. Bess became psychosomatically ill, prone to a variety of debilitating auto-immune diseases. While there was probably a physical basis to her problems, she was, at the same time, I believe, a mother in mourning. Her two sons had left the country. Unlike other mothers in this position, she made no protest, lodged no complaint, cried few tears, from what I remember. There was a resigned stoicism in her response that I felt hid her pain. She seemed to become emotionally paralyzed.

I returned to South Africa on an annual basis for many years, mainly to see my family. Bess was always overjoyed to see me, and there usually followed a brief period of warm reunion in the house. But I soon sensed her loneliness and estrangement from my father. Increasingly frail, she had a serious fall in her late eighties, which was the beginning of a slow decline. She could no longer walk. She took to her bed, often reading medical publications and listening to health-focused broadcasts on an old, battered radio. She died of stomach complications following surgery at a Johannesburg hospital. By that time, my father had moved to a retirement home, was no longer driving or mobile, and my sister, struggling with her own family problems, developed an acute eye infection that made her unable to visit my mother in the hospital. Bess was very alone in a small hospital room in those last few weeks. I had been to Johannesburg to see her and spent many hours at her side, but had returned to London shortly before she passed. I gathered that she died on her own.

Figure 8.3 shows her as an older woman. The painting hardly conveys the depth of sadness I felt in her – and for her. Instead, her expression seems to be a mix of anger and suspicion. On completing the work, my initial impulse was to modify the expression, making it softer, sadder, less angry. But, on reflection, I realised that I had probably unconsciously evoked an important aspect of her: her anger about betrayal, about an unsympathetic family of origin, and the sense of what, for her at times, felt like an empty life sacrifice.

Through all the years I knew Bess – I was fifty-three when she died – I felt a kinship with her. It may be that she turned to me from early on for the closeness that was missing in her marriage and that I responded out of my own needs as a child, sensing her need. That this complicated my childhood emotional development, not necessarily in a positive way, almost goes without saying. I suspect that I was subject to the same pressures that Alice Miller (1983) describes in "the drama of the gifted child", the child who is so finely tuned to the needs of a parent that their own development suffers. However, like the gifted child, I almost certainly gained in the process. As described earlier, I believe that my mother's confidence in me, her interest in my talents and my future, whether or not a projection of her own frustrated longings, provided the experience of a transformational object – and, further, that the wider project culminating in this book is an attempt to re-find that object for myself – and, belatedly, for her.

If there are hints of the complicated woman Bess was, I need to highlight aspects of her that I disliked. She could be stubborn, intransigent, sharply dismissing views that differed from hers, and she was prone to self-martyrdom. Not that she lacked cause for complaint, but she could indulge her misery in a bitter, self-demeaning way. My biggest difficulty with her, though, was her racial prejudice, specifically towards the black population. Although she displayed the denigration of blacks that was endemic in white apartheid South Africa, it was her treatment of the black domestic servants in the family home that upset me most. She was suspicious, demanding, critical and querulous in her relationship to them. Since I mainly had very good relationships with the black "staff" and was appalled by the dehumanization of blacks, I strongly disliked this aspect of my mother and frequently challenged her. I am not sure that this achieved anything. She was very hurt by my accusations, and my challenges became part of a repeated, pointless cycle of blame and self-justification.

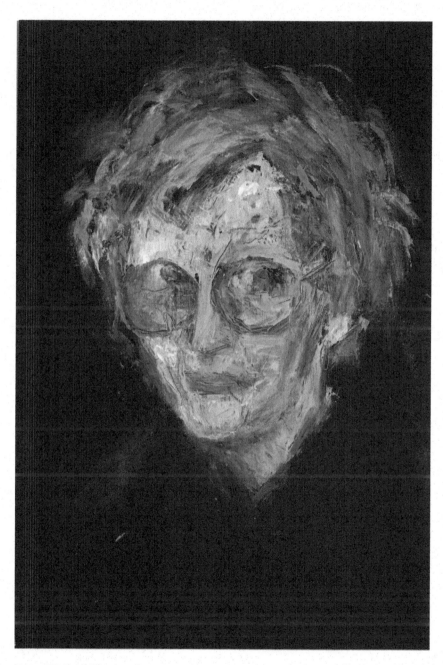

Figure 8.3 Bess, Older
Source: Morris Nitsun 2021, oil, 90 × 62

It is not difficult to explain this aspect of Bess in terms of the norms of a society organized by racial discrimination. She reflected the world around her, white and black cruelly divided. Further, it was almost certainly her own sense of inferiority and disempowerment that was projected unknowingly onto blacks, especially black women, as I recall. And even deeper in her background was her own traumatic history of forced dislocation and deprivation. Experiences such as these make some people more sensitive to the suffering of others, but they can also compound prejudice and rupture humanity.

I highlight Bess' problems in this area as a segue into the next section, focusing on a black woman, Rosa Parks, who exemplified strength and power in the fight for racial equality and, through this, realised herself as a woman.

Before moving on, however, I wish to share an actual photograph of my parents (see Figure 8.4). This came to me by surprise. Not a photo in my possession, it was sent by a cousin in Melbourne who discovered it in his own collection and thought I might want to see it. This happened serendipitously as I was preparing the slides for the presentation. Here they are, Bess and Joe, in their early 80's. There is a further note of serendipity. In the background of the photograph, on the wall behind my parents, barely visible, hangs my very first oil painting, painted in South Africa in 1961, when I was 18.

Figure 8.5 is a reproduction of this early painting, showing an elderly couple, probably Russian, preparing a meal together. There is a remarkable parallel here:

Figure 8.4 Bess and Joe

Source: Morris Nitsun, 2021, Photograph by Joel Nathan, 3.5 × 11 cm

Figure 8.5 Preparing a Meal
Source: Morris Nitsun, 1960, 60 × 44 cm

my parents, with their Eastern European background mirrored in the couple in the
painting, as if the worlds of the past and the present have come together. My own
evolution as an artist has also seemingly come full circle, beginning with the first
painting and culminating in my present initiative – all revealed in a photograph
that came out of the blue.

Rosa Parks

Rosa Louise McCauley Parks (February 4, 1913 – October 24, 2005) was a black American activist who played a pivotal role in the early civil rights movement, leading to desegregation in the American south and inspiring similar changes across the world. The United States Congress honoured her as "the first lady of civil rights" and "the mother of the freedom movement". In 2000, Time Magazine voted her as one of the 20 most iconic figures of the twentieth century.

The key incident, although she worked tirelessly for civil rights throughout her life, was her refusal to vacate her seat for a white passenger in a segregated bus in the town of Montgomery (Parks 1992). At the time in the mid-1950's, buses were strictly segregated, with specific rows of seats designated "coloured". Although the division between black and white seats was strictly maintained, a black passenger might be asked to stand up and allow a white passenger to sit if the "white" section was already filled. On this occasion, Parks rejected the bus driver's order to move. She was arrested for disorderly conduct in violating Alabama segregation laws, triggering a widespread bus boycott by the black residents of Montgomery for over a year. Dozens of public buses stood unused for months, severely damaging the bus company's finances. Eventually, the US Supreme Court repealed the law requiring segregation on buses, ruling that it was unconstitutional.

Figure 8.6 is based on a famous photograph showing Rosa on the same bus on which the incident occurred. The picture, also showing a white male, was taken

Figure 8.6 Rosa Parks in the Bus

Source: Morris Nitsun 2021, oil, 100 × 70 cm

subsequently as part of the publicizing of the event. This was an unusual scene for me to paint, given that all the other paintings in this series are portraits, but I was struck by the image and wanted to capture it in painterly form. I was interested in the scene having been staged after the event, a constructed tableau, as if enshrining a seminal moment in history. My painting serves as a further reminder. Perhaps this says something about the making of a legend and the use of visual images to convey symbolic events of cultural significance: the way the visual image itself gains an iconic status. There are many photographs of Rosa through the decades, mostly focusing on the period of her protest, but providing a visual narrative of her life and this significant period in 20th-century history.

Figure 8.7 is a depiction of another famous photograph – Rosa's arrest. It shows her holding the placard with her police arrest number. I painted several versions, finding it difficult not just to get a sufficient likeness to Rosa but to strike the right note of the arrest. The other versions I painted made her look smarter and more poised than she was, even oddly glamorous. I wondered why the problem. Had I wanted in some way to aggrandize her, possibly to deny the grim reality, the humiliation, of her arrest? Did I want the paintings to convey something of her defiance? But is this, too, a reflection of what happens to iconic figures in history: their image manipulated again and again, their "ordinary" humanity subsumed by an idealized legend?

Rosa's life was like this: fame and humiliation oscillating in dialectic tension. She was widely honoured in subsequent decades but suffered badly for the act that brought her fame. She was fired from her job as a seamstress in a departmental store, and her husband, Raymond Parks (who was a strong support), also lost his job. In both cases, it was almost certainly a punishment for the bus protest. Rosa continued to receive death threats over the years.

In subsequent years, Rosa continued to contribute actively to the civil rights movement, taking a stand on many issues of education, employment and housing. She had links with all the important figures of the movement, including Martin Luther King, and she strongly supported the Selma-to-Montgomery marches that, in the face of police violence, further progressed the struggle. As her fame spread, many public buildings, railway stations, roads and parks were named after her, statues and busts commissioned, commemorative events and days instituted across different states in the USA. She received honorary doctorates from at least twenty universities and many highly prestigious awards, including the Presidential Medal of Freedom.

Figure 8.8 shows Rosa as an old lady. Photographs of this period depict a refined, even gracious woman, well dressed, grey hair neatly tied back, tastefully bedecked with jewellery and the occasional decorative flower. She was obviously proud of her appearance and dressed for the occasion. But, as she grew older, life was by no means easy. She suffered major personal losses in later years, with the early death of her husband and her only brother. Her own health waned. Donating the bulk of her earnings through talks and public appearances to black rights causes and charities, and incapable through illness and the day-to-day life burdens

Figure 8.7 Rosa Parks, Arrested

Source: Morris Nitsun 2021, oil, 90 × 62 cm

Figure 8.8 Rosa Parks, Old

Source: Morris Nitsun 2021, oil, 84 × 59 cm

of managing her financial affairs, she was unable to keep up payments on her apartment in Detroit and was served an eviction notice in 2002. Although the notice was rescinded in the face of protests, she continued to live alone in very modest surroundings. She died in 2005, at age 92. She and her husband never had children and she outlived her only sibling. Her coffin was flown to Montgomery, and in the procession that followed, thousands of people lined the streets, cheering, clapping and sending up balloons. The coffin was transported to Washington DC in a bus similar to the one in which she made her protest. She was the first woman to lie in honour in the Rotunda of the Capitol in Washington. An estimated 50,000 people viewed the casket.

Rosa Parks' life and achievements stand in marked contrast to that of my mother, Bess. The contrast is almost too marked, too glaring, to draw. But I wanted to include Rosa at this point in the narrative to compare the lives of the two women, to highlight the courage of a woman fighting against considerable odds, as Rosa did in segregated America of the early 20th Century. But I also wanted to reconstruct and repair the image of the denigrated black woman that I associated with apartheid South Africa and with Bess' intolerance towards the domestic "helps". There are further parallels and differences. My mother came from a background of considerable oppression, from a small shtetl community pitted against violence and victimization. Her family was fragmented following unwarranted exile to Siberia, where they nearly starved and saw a small child frozen to death. Although South Africa seemingly offered a safe haven, this was also an oppressive environment, impossible to oppose in any way. The Jews in South Africa felt very vulnerable. There was a lurking sense that if they set a foot wrong, the target of hatred and oppression might swing from the blacks to them. Bess and Rosa are like reverse mirror images: two women struggling to survive, to find themselves in an embattled world, but reflecting opposite sides of the political spectrum: one woman changing history, another lost in history.

Perhaps the key focus of this comparison, though implicit in much that has been said, is the role of women. Rosa and Bess inhabited the same world, a world in which women had diminished power (they lived at approximately the same time, Rosa a few years later). Yet, one can see Rosa's achievement as an achievement for women's rights as much as for civil rights. Without acting from a feminist platform, she struck a powerful blow for women's freedom. What sort of woman was she up close? Much as she is renowned for her act of assertion, she was described as a gentle woman. A quote from a male activist who knew her describes her as "so quiet, serene – just a very special person." I am not sure where this leads in terms of understanding Bess, except perhaps the insight that gentleness and power are not mutually exclusive. Bess, mostly gentle in her bearing, quiet and self-effacing, probably had far greater potential for assertion and self-expression than she was able to realise, her harsh stand towards blacks a displacement of hostility rather than real assertiveness.

Coincidentally, the inscription on my mother's tomb in Westpark Jewish cemetery, Johannesburg, reads "A Woman of Valour." The inscription, taken from the 31st chapter of the Book of Proverbs, epitomizes a woman of substance. This woman is a nurturer, but in another sense, she is also a warrior, a fighter at heart.

She fights not only for her personal world and those she loves, but also for the world around her. At first glance, apart from Bess' courage in defying her family and claiming a life of her own, the epithet does not immediately seem to fit her. It more readily fits a woman like Rosa. Yet, the inscription was chosen, unhesitatingly, by me, my father, brother, and sister, as if we knew something about Bess that was unrecognised, something about the courage it took to be her, to brave the rejection of her family and the disappointment in my father, to adjust to life in dusty small-town South Africa, to raise three children in near social isolation.

Mother Teresa

Probably the most controversial of the women included in this chapter, Mother Teresa gained international fame for her humanitarian work in the 20th century, won the Nobel Peace Prize in 1973 and was canonized in 2016, twenty-one years after her death. Few women have achieved this level of recognition. At the same time, she bitterly divided opinion. She was both revered and despised.

She was born Mary Teresa Bojaxhiu in 1910 to an Albanian family in Macedonia. She lived there for eighteen years, moved to Ireland to pursue a religious calling and then to India, where she lived most of her life and established her lifelong project of combatting poverty, disease and destitution. Leaving her family and her hometown, she apparently never saw them again, foregoing the secular world for a lifetime of devotion and duty. Taking her solemn vows as a nun in 1937 and increasingly aware of a calling to serve the poor and the abandoned, she, in 1950, founded the "Missionaries of Charity", a Roman Catholic enterprise that in 2012 had become a worldwide organization with over 4500 nuns in 133 countries. Members take vows of chastity, poverty and obedience and also profess a fourth vow – to give "wholehearted free service to the poorest of the poor". Mother Teresa headed the organization with enormous zeal, famously setting out to serve humanity in a white sari with a blue border, her trademark attire.

Like Rosa Parks, she was photographed innumerable times, the figure of a haggard nun in her sari with its blue band becoming one of the iconic images of the 20th century. The painting in Figure 8.9 is based on one of these images, showing Teresa in a typically supplicant pose, her face expressing both her spiritual devotion and the pain of suffering that became her life-long preoccupation. Almost all the photographs of her, particularly the many portraits, show the same visage, the combination of piety and suffering.

Looking back on Teresa's life, when she was young Teresa and not yet Mother Teresa, there is a photograph (not illustrated) of her aged about nineteen with two young women friends. There are few photographs from this period before her religious conversion, and those that exist reflect her life as an "ordinary" girl/young woman in a seemingly ordinary family in Europe. This poses the question of how she went from an ordinary life to an extraordinary one, how some people achieve monumental life change while most never even imagine or consider the possibility. I mused on Teresa's two friends in the photograph, knowing nothing about them, but wondering what choices they made, how they differed from Teresa and

Figure 8.9 Mother Teresa

Source: Morris Nitsun 2021, oil, 84 × 59 cm

how all three women were poised on the brink of adulthood, about to become more fully who they were: to encounter their destinies. This continues the theme I posed at the start of the chapter: how my mother Bess found – or didn't – herself and how this compares with other women.

There are many photographs of Teresa ministering to the sick and the destitute, often holding a small, wasted child in her arms or bending down to comfort a weak elderly person. Figure 8.10 is a typical example taken from one of these photographs. Teresa looks to one side, the child to the other. Although the overall impression is one of Teresa's compassion, the lack of visual contact between Teresa and the child may or may not point to some disjunction, some lack of contact, an issue that is hinted at in some of the criticism of Teresa. These scenes were obviously posed, no doubt to promote the work of her mission, to use as persuasive material for fund-raising, but probably also to strengthen the considerable worldwide literature, in books, papers and pamphlets, that was being fed to millions. Teresa once said although her heart belonged to Christ, she as a person belonged to the world. Through the many pictures of her, in a caring relationship with the needy, in solemn prayer, meeting crowds and dignitaries throughout the world, receiving honours and awards, she indeed belonged to the world – and, seemingly, the world to her.

Teresa frequently proclaimed her religious devotion, often emphasizing that her love of Christ was her overriding priority, if anything more than her programme to help the poor: an admission that tallied with some of the criticism that later came her way. But she also made clear what an uphill struggle it was to realise her

Figure 8.10 Mother Teresa and Child
Source: Morris Nitsun 2021, oil, 120 × 80 cm

mission, to gather resources to meet the overwhelming needs of people, desperate adults and children who existed on the poorest margins of society. Teresa wrote in her diary that her first years were fraught with difficulty. With no income, she begged for food and supplies and experienced doubt, loneliness and the temptation to return to the comfort of convent life. Increasingly, however, she attracted the attention and support of Indian officials, including the Prime Minister, and her efforts at fund-raising internationally began to pay off.

Like Rosa Parks, Teresa was the recipient of multiple awards and honours, notably the Nobel Peace Prize, but the most exceptional posthumous honour was her canonization in 2016. Commentators point out that she was moving inexorably in this direction, that she was increasingly regarded as transcendent: a holy woman. The process of canonisation required the documentation of a miracle resulting from the intervention of the prospective saint. When this was achieved on two occasions, in both of which Teresa was deemed to have cured a serious or intractable illness, the road was clear. She was canonized by Pope Francis in St Peter's Square in the Vatican City in 2016. Not only was the authenticity of the miracles questioned by a range of people, relatives of the "cured" as well as medical authorities, but her work and her bearing became the target of criticism. Some of this came from Indian authorities, who challenged her for promoting a "cult of suffering", exaggerating work done by her mission and misusing funds and privileges at her disposal. Medical opinion criticized her reluctance to use effective medicines, accusing her of indulging suffering rather than seeking to cure it. One of her most outspoken critics was the English writer and anti-theist Christopher Hitchens (1995), who claimed that Mother Teresa was not a friend of the poor. She was a friend of *poverty*. She regarded suffering as a gift from God. Hitchens also accused her of hypocrisy for choosing medical treatment for her own heart condition while eschewing that for others. There were further criticisms of her vocal stand, based on the sanctity of motherhood and the family, against both contraception and abortion. Most of the criticisms were refuted by Teresa's many supporters, but the rumours of misappropriation and mishandling did not go away.

It is difficult to judge the validity of the criticisms, but there are indications of moral rectitude in some of the doubts that Teresa herself expressed. She stated that she experienced considerable struggle and pain in her religious beliefs, including doubts about the existence of God and worry about her lack of faith. This suggested an honesty of spirit that may counteract the accusations of moral turpitude. But Hitchens regarded this with suspicion, emphasizing that Teresa admitted that she wasn't working to alleviate poverty: she was striving to expand the number of Catholics. She was a proselytizer. He quotes her as saying, "I'm not a social worker. I don't do it for this reason. I do it for Christ. I do it for the church." Whatever her own personal spiritual doubts, she remained unswervingly true to her cause, but this was not as simple as it may have appeared to the world: her main mission was to stay faithful to God and to spread his word.

Figure 8.11 is a painting of Teresa as an old woman. Again, there are many photographs of her praying or in a religious reverie of some sort, but I wanted to

Figure 8.11 Mother Teresa, Old

Source: Morris Nitsun 2021, oil, 84 × 59

convey in the image something of the anguish she may have felt as she neared the end of her life. Was this the anguish of religious doubt, the anguish of contemplating the suffering around her, or that of finding herself the target of devastating criticism?

The emerging picture is of an extraordinary but complex woman whose motivation remains ambiguous. It is useful nevertheless to look at her in the light of the main theme of this chapter: the way the four women steered their lives. The overriding impression is of a woman who forsook conventional family life, marital union and childbearing to follow a path of intense spiritual commitment and service to many thousands of the sick and disadvantaged. She was a "bride of Christ", not of mortal man, and her children were not born of her loins but the multitude of the needy. This is different from the three other women in this series, all of whom married and had children, including Jan Morris.

Jan Morris

Jan Morris was born *James* Humphrey Morris in October 1926. She is probably the most unusual and extraordinary woman in this series, starting life as a male, living as a man well into adulthood, marrying as a man, and undergoing pioneering gender reassignment in the 1970's when *James* became *Jan*. And what a life! Before becoming a woman, she was already a celebrated writer, journalist, reporter, continuing to write right up until her death in 2020, highly regarded as a historian and immersive travel writer. One of the most extraordinary and touching aspects of her life was her marriage to Elizabeth Tuckniss, which lasted fifty-two years. This started pre-transition and endured through and beyond gender transition, right up until her death, producing four children and nine grandchildren. This has all the elements of a remarkable love story.

Early in her career as a journalist, she, then James, was the only newspaper correspondent accompanying Edmund Hilary and Sherpa Tenzing on their famous conquest of Everest in 1953. She was the first to break the news (in code) to the world, the triumph coinciding with the coronation of Queen Elizabeth II. To the outside world, at that time, James Morris seemed to enjoy an exemplary life as a man. He had already, aged 17, joined the British Army during World War II, serving as an intelligence officer in Palestine and embracing what he described as the "military virtues of courage, dash, loyalty, self-discipline". For all his appearances, however, James was secretly deeply troubled by the conviction that he was a woman. In her best-selling book, *Conundrum* (Jan Morris 1974), Jan describes in detail the misery of her sexual uncertainty as a man. She recalls how age four, she had an epiphany as she sat under her mother's piano. She realised that "she had been born into the wrong body and should really be a girl". She describes this as her first memory and one that clung to her. *Conundrum* goes on to describe the years of doubt and anxiety that culminated in a ten-year transition period, the hormone regime that accompanied the transition, the shock and incredulity of many around her, the uncertain outcome of surgery, and the hostility that greeted her once the reassignment was complete. Yet, *Conundrum* is not an angry book. It has a lightness of touch, flashes of irony and humour, and presages the full, happy, creative life that was to come.

Figure 8.12, "James Morris", is based on one of the few photographs of Jan as a man. The photographs are very much of a man: handsome, well-groomed, exuding a certain confidence and charm. The photos of the time also place James in typically masculine settings – holding radio equipment in preparation for the Everest ascent, leading an expedition, and generally conveying the sense of a man at one with himself. James was an attractive man and, in *Conundrum*, describes the problem he had fending off the advances of both males and females. I decided to base a painting on a 1955 photograph of "the man" as it seemed to exemplify these qualities and also to highlight how remarkable and successful the subsequent transformation was from male to female.

The story of her marriage is similarly remarkable. Jan met Elizabeth, a tea planter's daughter, in 1949. There was an instant attraction that would last a lifetime. Still mired in the confusion about his gender and sexuality, living in a "remote and eerie capsule", Morris describes in *Conundrum* the powerful impact of the relationship. He found himself enjoying:

> one particular love of an intensity so different from all the rest, on a plane of experience so mysterious, and of a texture so rich, that it overrode from the start all my sexual ambiguities and acted like a key to the latch of my conundrum.

Children were born, Morris wrote, not out of duty but out of love. "In performing the sexual act with Elizabeth, I felt I was consummating a trust, with luck giving ourselves the incomparable gift of children". The marriage "had no right to work, yet it worked like a dream, living testimony, one might say, of the power of mind over matter – or love in its purest sense over everything else" (Morris 1974).

Figure 8.13 is a portrait of Jan post-surgery. She looks happy, friendly, engaging, even ebullient. I was struck on completing the painting by the quality of the ebullience. The photographs in the period following the operation generally do show a happy woman, smiling, enjoying life. But the quality of zest is not quite as marked as in my painting. I wondered why I had produced a somewhat exaggerated image. It stands in contrast to the confusion, anxiety and suffering Jan must have endured through the years of slow, painful transition and the uncertain outcome of the surgery. The operation was undoubtedly a success, but I wonder about the euphoria. Was it genuine euphoria, expressing liberation from the oppression of living a lie, of being estranged from what she felt was her true self, her natural gender? Or was there a quality of manic denial? I hesitate to use a psychological explanation but wonder about the hidden cost of the overall venture and whether her remarkable adjustment and unassailable confidence concealed her deeper doubts.

Figure 8.12 James Morris

Source: Morris Nitsun 2021, oil, 90 × 60 cm

Figure 8.13 Jan Morris (Post-surgery)

Source: Morris Nitsun, 2021, oil, 120 × 80 cm

Elizabeth stood by James/Jan through the long and difficult years of transition, supportive throughout. They were forced to get divorced, however, because a British surgeon refused to operate if they remained married. Although Jan subsequently was operated on by a surgeon in Morocco, they decided anyway to divorce in the face of the then powerful injunction against two women being married. But in 2008, they took a momentous decision: they forged a civil partnership. Newspaper articles describe a small, low-key ceremony in the Welsh village in which they lived all their married lives. It was witnessed by a local couple who invited them home for a cup of tea. They continued a happy life together, not without domestic differences and squabbles, but ever committed. The children visited often, as did the nine grandchildren. In a newspaper interview soon after the civil union, Elizabeth describes the tremendous bond they still enjoyed. Jan was coming home from abroad in a few days' time. Elizabeth describes how much she was looking forward to seeing Jan. She adds, warmly, quizzically, how much they were still in love.

Jan Morris died at age 94 at a hospital near her Welsh village. She and Elizabeth had had a headstone erected for their burial plot in the village. The inscription reads: "Here lie two friends, at the end of one life".

Figure 8.14 is a portrait of Jan towards the end of her life. Of the many paintings I produced in the overall project, this painting elicited the most varied and contradictory feedback of all, akin to the doll paintings (Chapter 4) but with even greater variation. What the painting seemed to have in common with the dolls is a high level of ambiguity. With the doll paintings, however, I was conscious of creating ambiguity, whereas with the painting of Jan, I chose a photographic image from the last year of her life that struck me as very positive: an expression of a fulfilling, rewarding life, a joyful statement about old age – and I was keen to embody this in the painting. On completing the painting, I was reasonably satisfied that I had achieved this. I was surprised then by the hugely conflicting feedback. One group of people expressed a strong dislike of the painting, seeing Jan as mad, deranged, distraught, suffering, some linking it to what they saw as the wild, uncontrolled state of her hair. This did not altogether surprise me as I was aware of exaggerating the unruliness of her hair. But I did this with a view to dramatizing the image, emphasizing a mop of hair that had seen and made history, the crowning glory of a remarkable life. One person was particularly upset about what she felt was a misrepresentation of Jan. "I've read the book", she said, "and Jan Morris was happy, not unhappy. She had a successful life, and she was happy at the end". I was struck by the strength and conviction in this observation, almost as if I had transgressed in some way or violated Jan's legacy. I felt a twinge of doubt, even guilt, about misrepresenting Jan. However – and here lies the contradiction – several people saw the painted image in exactly the positive light I had intended. They saw fulfilment and satisfaction in a happy, smiling face. "A life well lived", one person said, "you can see it in her eyes". Another described the painted Jan as "smiling mischievously, a twinkle in her eyes. You've really caught that".

Figure 8.14 Jan Morris, Old
Source: Morris Nitsun 2021, oil, 120 × 80 cm

Pondering the contradictory nature of the feedback, I considered that these might be projections in much the way that the earlier series of doll paintings triggered projections (Chapter 4). Allowing for at least a degree of ambiguity in the image – my painting technique might have created that – I realised that the reactions to Jan's face might say more about the perceiver than the painting. People who resisted the image were probably projecting their own fears, doubts, unhappiness and anxiety about ageing. Conversely, the enjoyment of the image might express the good life experienced or hoped for in a wishful way. However, I began to wonder, as with the dolls, whether the varied responses might also be tuning into something more fundamental in the narrative of Jan's life, perhaps something intangible, something complex. This might lie in the deep contrasts of her life: true happiness and success mixed with real suffering and confusion, the triumph of the will against continuing tensions and lingering doubts. What I learned more and more in my presentations was the way in which people's feedback, when put together as a totality, reflected the wholeness of a subject, with the many shades of self that make up a paradoxical whole. The contradictions, then, are not contradictions as such, but the pieces of a complicated puzzle. Jan was probably all these things: bold, brave, happy, fulfilled, but also anxious, confused, embattled.

Drawing back for the moment from these ambiguities, there remains the inspiring story of a woman who dared to seek her true self, undertaking what few people had at the time and making the most of a long, fruitful life.

The group discussion

In line with the previous presentations, I was keen to share *Four Women* with a group, anticipating with interest what others would make of this dense, highly personal material. Partly because of its personal nature, I was, by the time of writing, able to show it to only one group, a small group of close friends who were aware of my project and whom I felt I could trust with the sensitive material. This group had attended most if not all my previous presentations and knew of the book I was writing. I had shared many aspects of the project with most of them and found them engaged and encouraging.

In August 2021, I gave the zoom presentation of *Four Women* to the group. The response was very positive, participants stimulated, struck, moved by the theme, the paintings and the narrative. One member emailed me afterwards, summing up her reaction with the words –

> Wonderful. I enjoyed this immensely and thought the paintings wonderful – although I am of the group that found the grey-haired Jan Morris painting rather grotesque! I loved the tormented Mother Teresa – it reminded me of "The Scream". I was also very moved by your mother as a young bride.
>
> SP

This was typical of people's responses – heartfelt, deeply identified, yet free to express likes and dislikes. There were numerous references to the individual women, also searching for connections between the four women. The overriding theme, they agreed, was one of courage. They could all recognize the courage it took the three women, Rosa, Teresa and Jan, to fulfil their missions, but they also emphasized my mother Bess's courage. She might not have achieved worldly ambitions, but it took courage for her to oppose her parents' objections to her marriage, to elope, and to give up the comforts of a family home: then, to take up life in a small rural outpost, to stand by my father through thick and thin, to survive foetal loss and remain a loving mother. I found this understanding of Bess reassuring and edifying. She may not have been able to fulfil dreams of a more creative life, but she showed courage in being herself, in making the best of her life – and she made my life possible. I was touched by the compassion the story evoked in the group.

This perspective of Bess prompted a lively discussion about the one life we all have, how we make sense of it, how we come to terms with it. The sense of a "little life", the fact that we are all a proverbial drop in the ocean of humanity, a grain of sand in the massive shoals of time, a tiny fragment in an unfathomable universe, was pitted against a sense that we are all heroes. We are heroes in coping with the many obstacles, shocks and disappointments life throws up, in dealing with the decline of ageing, of inevitable loss and grief, of facing mortality. I was very gratified that this presentation had stimulated a discussion of this depth. I was glad that the issues of the four women, my mother in particular, took on such universal significance. Above all, I felt that Bess had been seen. She had been recognized, understood, appreciated. The story of her life had brought people, albeit in a relatively small group, closer together, had offered points of identification and empathy. The sense that she could have made more of her life remained, but I could see this more in perspective: she had lived a courageous life. She was "a woman of valour".

The issues that both linked and differentiated the four women could be interpreted in the light of Bollas' (1989) distinction between fate and destiny. In these terms, fate connotes an outcome that is predetermined, a future fundamentally outside the individual's control, the subject dependent on the vagaries of chance. Destiny, although similar, has a greater sense of calling, spurring action and initiative, creating a sense of purpose: we go to meet our destiny. Although Bess was active in deciding to get married against her parents' wishes, she might have felt a loss of agency and control in the rest of her life, in a sense surrendering to fate, possibly even as a punishment for her defiance. Rosa, Teresa and Jan, on the other hand, seemed to follow their destinies, actively pursuing a sense of identity and a place in society – and history.

While knowing that the paintings and the presentation did not retrospectively transform Bess' life – how could they in reality? – that she was known and appreciated through the paintings and the narrative felt like reward enough. Further, my striving to get closer to her, to resuscitate the bond of old, to give thanks was evident not only in the presentation of this theme. It grew powerfully in my mind as the motive for my entire project.

Comment

Four Women brought to a close my complex undertaking on canvas, ending on a more personal, emotive note than anything I expected at the outset. The challenge of bringing together my psychological and artistic interests had stimulated an open-ended inquiry, with little sense of where I was headed, but I now realised the deeper personal reasons for embarking on this journey, not simply as an attempt to reconcile two somewhat divergent vocational interests but as a means of exploring the existential issues of a lifetime. This is the value of a heuristic inquiry: the willingness to suspend judgment, to maintain an open mind, to allow the process to find its way.

Part 3

Reflection and review

Part 3 is an evaluation of the overall project, attempting to stand back, where possible, and take an "objective" view of this exploratory venture. What can I, we, learn from the journey?

Chapter 9 revisits the major painting themes, attempting an analysis of the sequence of presentations as a totality. It suggests an implicit, deeply personal purpose that became clearer with the completion of the fifth and last series of paintings.

Chapter 10 evaluates the project as a heuristic inquiry, highlighting key findings with suggestions for the further application of the method, implications for psychotherapeutic practice and for the active use of art as an exploratory medium.

DOI: 10.4324/9781003232230-12

Chapter 9

A deeper view

In Part 2 of the book, a detailed exploration of the five paintings series, a hypothesis gradually emerged. These were not five arbitrary themes, as I had supposed. They were themes of universal significance, as well as different ways of exploring personal development, with particular relevance to my stage in life and some dilemmas of the past that sought resolution. I attempt in this chapter to pull these threads together. Further, and unexpectedly, a previously marginalised theme – "the missing link" – comes to the fore.

Through the months of painting, emboldened by the pandemic and the unexpected time generated by lockdown, I had to make decisions about what themes to pursue and how to imbue them with relevance to both the present and the past. Although the world of Covid and lockdown was intensely present, the personal reasons for embarking on the project gradually became apparent. At a late stage of life, having struggled to reconcile my interests as a psychologist/psychotherapist and artist, I seemed to be finding a way to bring them together, to forge a synthesis that offered something original and new. This development stimulated all that came in its wake. Age had sparked a strong interest in revisiting my personal history, trying to give shape and meaning to my life, to acknowledge the opportunities that marked my development, as well as the losses and disappointments. Only aspects of this were clear, factual, "objective", in the sense of knowing for sure what had happened and why, what it meant at a deeper existential level. My years of personal analysis, in individual and group formats, had penetrated much of this, yet also left areas barely touched or understood, leaving me with a paradoxical sense of understanding and not understanding. Part of this search inevitably involved others, the people who inhabited my world, the key figures who helped to make me who I am, who both inspired hopes and challenged them. Within this matrix, my creative efforts loomed large: to follow the vision that swirled through the dreams and actions of a lifetime.

Time was a key consideration. On the one hand, there was the extra time afforded by lockdown, with little sense of how long this would last, the possibility looming of ever-extended time: an infinity of time. On the other hand, there was the sense of time running out, of dwindling years, of encroaching mortality, sharpened by the fears of Covid and the vulnerability of ageing and underlying health concerns.

DOI: 10.4324/9781003232230-13

In this contradictory time-space, it felt important to use time productively, to strengthen the search, to aim high.

The painting project I embarked on therefore had multiple levels of inquiry: a heightened awareness of the troubled world in parallel with the preoccupations of ageing, overlain by the considerable challenge of putting this all into paint, producing a body of work of substance and making something visually arresting and meaningful to others. When this became the basis for group presentations, both in real space and online, another level of complexity was introduced. The material had to be organized, the paintings reproduced, a narrative composed, at the same time as inviting and facilitating an online group process that could provide recognition and feedback. Multiple inputs, multiple outputs, yet gradually acquiring a direction, a purpose, that increasingly helped to bring together the disparate elements of life and art into something of a coherent whole.

Much seemed to reside in my choice of subjects. I had, for the most part, chosen subjects spontaneously, not thinking beyond the immediate impulse, the sense of what was urgent or important at a particular time. Lifelong interests in familiar, comfortable subjects, painted in a well-tried way and admired by those who knew my work, had yielded now to a different, risker impulse. I followed my instincts, producing five series of paintings, each on a different theme: *Dolls and Demons*, *The Deserted City*, *Fragile Nature*, *Dancers*, *Four Women*. This happened so forcefully, without enough time to assimilate the weight of what I had produced, that I tended to think there was little overall coherence. I could see the point of each of the separate themes, but not a meaning to the overall body of work. Yet, by the time I completed the last series, *Four Women*, a new understanding began to emerge.

I realised that much as I was preoccupied with the vicissitudes of the pandemic and keen to reflect this in my painting, the hidden purpose was a much more personal one: a search for the mother, both the symbolic, universal mother and the real mother – my mother. This initially seemed oddly predictable: so blatantly psychological, so rooted in a psychoanalytic mindset, that I was surprised and hesitant to pursue it further. Is this what it's all about? Does it, must it, always go back to mother? Does this cancel out all the rest, the preoccupation with the pandemic, the blight on cities, the search for nature? Does it rule out the other important people in my life, including my father, siblings and friends of many years, all of whom have stories to tell and about whom I have stories to tell? Most of these people have now passed, but I feel a bond of loyalty and love to them and would like to honour them, each in their unique way. However, I felt that this time, in this context, I needed a predominant focus. The maternal theme was important at a personal level, but there was also the symbolic connection with Covid. The pandemic was an environmental phenomenon, an attack on mother earth, on earth's children. It reflected a world gone awry, imperilled by climate change, consumerism, splitting, destructive leadership: as if an environmental mother had been attacked and now lay distraught, damaged. My paintings, I realised, were an attempt to represent this complex coincidence of the deeply personal and the deeply environmental.

The significance of the maternal theme came to the fore in *Four Women*. In Chapter 8, I described how my mother was the key figure of the four: how my attempt to understand her and symbolically repair aspects of her life was the key consideration. However, I now realised – with some surprise – that the search started not with this series but at the very beginning of the project – with the doll paintings. In Chapter 4, I highlighted the significance of dolls in childhood: the child's relationship to the doll and its place in psychological development. I explored this in a general way in terms of the discourse of childhood. Although the theme resonated with people at several levels and triggered wide-ranging discussions about family history and loss, I could now see something additional: the symbolic attempt to revive my relationship with my mother, to bring her alive through memory, painting and narrative.

New perspectives on the dolls unfolded when seen this way. These meanings are not entirely clear, given the pointed symbolism of dolls and the remoteness in time from my actual relationship with my mother. However, I wondered whether it is linked to her depression. Do the dolls reflect something frozen in the past? Did Bess freeze in response to hurt and disappointment? Did she have to play the role of a wife and mother when inwardly she felt estranged from her marriage, her family, herself? Did she feel like a doll, unreal, unseen? Was I in some way also a doll, a child who could not be fully alive in this frozen matrix? And was my painting dolls-as-children a way of unfreezing the past, of animating lost figures? Additionally, the paintings of my mother in the last series are based on photographs. Photographs are, of course, not real: they are flat, one-dimensional images of the past. By painting the images, I am trying to bring them alive. But then I am in the realm of the "uncanny valley" (see Chapter 4), the in-between state of what's real and not real, and the uneasy but potentially generative process of staying with the ambiguity, the disquiet.

Another aspect of my mother merits comment – something not mentioned before. She placed great emphasis on appearance. Although a beautiful woman herself, or maybe because of that, she was very concerned about how her children looked. She was almost obsessed with my sister's appearance, wanting her to look her very best, perhaps understandable through the feminine identification with a daughter. However, she similarly took note of my appearance, watching how I walked, what I wore, frequently commenting, advising, urging. My sister and I once discussed this and agreed that it was excessive. It made us both over-conscious of our appearance, over-sensitive to the approval of others. The emphasis should have been on how we felt inwardly, not on how we looked outwardly to others. In a sense, my mother treated us as dolls.

Although I was critical of my mother for this tendency, I now, looking back, see it in the perspective of her own struggle as a person. Coming to South Africa as an immigrant, poor, unhoused, largely uneducated, she, like many immigrants, was concerned about fitting in, being accepted in a new community. She wanted this more than anything for her children, perhaps also hoping, as with other immigrants, to find acceptance herself through them, wanting respectability, acceptance.

Added to this was the disappointment and unhappiness in her marriage. She must have felt shame: shame about failure, about an unfaithful husband, about being less than a perfect family, about not being cherished and loved by her own family. Did she have to dress us up as dolls to prove that we were respectable, loveable?

The pity about this, apart from the anguish she must have felt, was the way it concealed her better, more complex interests. I mentioned in Chapter 8 her strong interest in medicine and health. Had she had the confidence, the encouragement, to pursue these interests, she may have been less worried about appearances, about fitting in. But mired in her unhappiness, in a restrictive, conventional community, there were no outlets, no opportunities beyond her own private, almost secret, investigation of what makes us healthy and strong. Further, and in spite of her interest in outward appearances, I believe that there was something very positive in our relationship, something intrinsically good. That I grew up with a sense of wonder about the world, a great enjoyment of the environment, a delight in beauty was, I believe, in large part thanks to her. She related to me from the sensitive, artistic side of herself. She believed in me. I have referred to her as a transformational object.

Seen in this way, each one of my painting themes emerges as an aspect of the search for her, of gauging her emotional state, of looking at ways to repair and restore. Or is the quest not for her, in the narrower, more personal sense, but a search for the archetypal mother, all our mothers? *The Deserted City* is very much about a depressed, devastated environment: a sense of abandonment, loneliness, fear inhabits the empty streets. A response to the pandemic breaking in the beautiful towns of Northern Italy, the paintings are an attempt to capture the mood of an embattled world. Within this, humans are lost, imprisoned in their own homes. Symbolically, this is the tragedy of the environmental mother, the overarching mother who contains and holds us safe, and by association, the personal mother, the mother of our childhoods. But where is mother? Is she alive? Is she dead? Has she been damaged beyond repair?

Fragile Nature as a theme brings a glimmer of hope. Painted at a time when the first lockdown eased and there was the hope of recovery, the work celebrated my reconnection with nature, in particular the woods where I live in North London. Illustrating the cycle of birth and death in nature, it positioned our own vulnerability as humans within the frame of nature's vicissitudes. Everything decays, withers, dies, but from the remains, new life springs. For many people during the pandemic, the rediscovery of nature was deeply reassuring, life-giving. It was a reminder of continuity, of survival. Symbolically, it was a hedge against the threat of the virus, reminding us of our own strength, our resilience. In one of the paintings, an elderly couple cling to each other, the frail woman leaning on the man. In another, a man holds his little son in his arms, the two of them in a moment of reverie captivated by the woods around them, the rich greenery, the birdsong, the glints of sunlight through the trees. Reflecting on the last painting, I drew a parallel between the father's containing of the child and the sense of nature containing them. I spoke about "nature's arms", like the arms of a parent: Mother Nature. Mother is here again: silent, unspoken, holding.

Dancers is a further step towards redemption, the reclaiming of an alive mother. The dancers are full of life: they move, they emote, they express their bodily vitality. Interestingly, although viewers commented on the sense of movement in the paintings, I struggled to express bodily movement in paint. It is easier to capture movement in line drawings than paint. Once paint is applied, especially thick, layered paint, it tends to fix the image. The impression of movement weakens. Although this is mainly a technical problem, I wonder whether it also reflected the challenge of animating a half-alive figure, of my struggling to emerge from the gloom of the pandemic, symbolically the depressed mother. This is probably why I also painted dancers in states of exhaustion, pain and despair. This reflects the reality of many dancers' lives, the struggle to survive against the odds, but was it unconsciously a recognition of mother's fragility, the sometimes thin line between life and death?

The last series, *Four Women*, deals directly with my mother, no longer the symbolic mother: the real Bess. Now, having explored the psychic equivalents in the wider environment, I locate her with other women, actual women, no longer alive but once alive in the fullest ways, innovating, rebelling, challenging, offering something of immense value to the world. I believe I did so in order to substantiate my mother, to give her the recognition she deserved, to highlight her undiscovered talents, to celebrate the potential she hardly fulfilled. I do this both unselfishly, to honour her place in womanhood, to rank her amongst the best, but also selfishly, since my search for her is also my search for myself. Finding her means finding myself.

Although I have focused on the personal mother, I am hopeful that the analysis will resonate with others, that the struggle of my mother, her strengths and shortcomings, will be more widely relevant. Of course, not all personal mothers are the same – they come in all shapes and sizes – but we share a universal mother, the archetypal mother. The challenges of our time, highlighted by the ravages of the pandemic and climate change, have made us all too aware of our dependence on the environmental mother. We are all individuals in this ineffable, turbulent, unpredictable world, and what we gather for ourselves is the creative texture of our lives.

The missing link – black dolls

Finally, a theme that was implicit in the text but undeveloped in its own right comes to light. It is telling that this is so late: the theme is racial difference and, by implication, racism. Paradoxically, it takes me back to the very beginning of the project: the dolls.

Readers may have noticed in chapter 4, in the description of the doll paintings, that there were no black dolls. There were dolls from various other cultures: Victorian English dolls, French, German and Russian dolls, and so on, but they were all white dolls. I was aware, though dimly, of the existence of black dolls but made no effort to include these in the series. It was only at the

New York presentation of the doll paintings in 2020, described in chapter 4, that this was noticed and commented on. A white woman in the audience stood up and made a firm point about the absence of black dolls, challenging me on the grounds of my being a white ex-South African. I was rather taken aback but felt, and said, that it was an important omission.

The group discussion in that meeting drifted away from the theme, but the absence of black dolls lingered in my mind well after the conference ended and after I had given further online presentations on the doll paintings. I began to research black dolls, and as with dolls of European cultures, there was a considerable diversity, although I could find few if any Victorian black dolls, which was the main focus of the series. Nevertheless, I decided to paint images based on my findings and I produced several black doll paintings.

Until now, the theme was entirely missing from my presentations, other than the comment from the New York audience. Now that I had painted a series of black dolls, there was a question about how to include them at this late stage, when the presentations had taken place, without this seeming like tokenism, an afterthought. How to address the omission, and how do I explain the social and biographical processes that produced this unusual and, yet not altogether surprising, situation? My solution was to highlight the problem here, near the end of the book, in the context of what deeper discoveries lay behind the more explicit, shared themes. These themes touch on both structural issues about society and our personal responsibility as individuals. I felt that this was where the missing black dolls belonged.

Unable to include all the black dolls I painted because of publishing constraints, I selected the painting illustrated in Figure 9.1, Catherine holding her own doll, Marcie. I chose this because, as two figures, they establish a link with the first image in the book, the photograph of a Victorian child holding a small doll of her own (Figure 4.1), as well as the painting in my original exhibition of doll paintings, "Laura and Teddy" (Figure 4.2), in which a girl clutches a teddy bear. In this way, Catherine and Marcie complete a circle that starts at the beginning of the book and ends here. Symbolically, each of these pairs highlights the reversibility of the doll-child-mother relationship that has been a leitmotif in the narrative of these paintings.

There is little doubt that the omission of black dolls in my project parallels the marginalisation of black people in the apartheid South Africa in which I grew up. Apartheid was all about the invisibility of blacks. Although blacks far outnumbered the white population, there was every attempt to marginalise them, to erase them, to drive them into the townships, to radically control their freedom of movement. Probably because of their numbers, there was a fear of not just being overwhelmed but of being attacked, punished, a fear of brutal retaliation: the bloody revolution that was dreaded and that nearly materialised.

It was in this context that I, as a child, adolescent, and young adult, felt no alternative but to conform. I was already struggling with two oppressive forms of difference: being Jewish and being gay, both of which put me in a vulnerable

Figure 9.1 Catherine and Marcie
Source: Morris Nitsun 2021, oil, 84 × 59

position. There were lurking fears that the apartheid government, if it shifted its pernicious focus away from the blacks, would readily scapegoat other groups. The anxiety about gayness was compounded by the dictates of a very conventional Jewish community, itself anxious to avoid difference and deflect hostile attention. As described in Chapter 8, where I explore my relationship with my mother, I made clear my strong dislike of the prejudiced view of blacks she adopted and the arguments that threatened our otherwise close relationship. Looking back, I remember how shocked I was by what I saw, the humiliation of blacks, their confinement in poor quarters at the back of luxurious white homes, their cramped and often poorer existence in the vast, shabby townships on the fringes of the city. This is what I mostly saw as a child, in the safe confines of comfortable white suburbia.

What was also denied, in the domestic setting of white families and black servants, was the important role the blacks played in white children's upbringing. This applied particularly to the black women who not unusually acted as mother surrogates. Warm, attuned, spontaneous and playful, they were often better mothers than the white mothers. I recall these black "mothers", one or two in particular, with great affection. I remember periods of painful conflict about where I belonged, where my attachment lay, with white or black. Even as a child, I wondered why there was so little recognition of these relationships in our lives – including its significance for the black "mothers" themselves since they almost certainly felt attached to the white children they fed, nurtured, cared for, and then handed back to the often remote white parents. There is an added poignancy in the separation of black women from their own children. Working in the cities for months on end, they rarely saw their children, who sometimes lived hundreds of miles away in rural locations. Possibly this is why these women had so much to give the white children: they were mothers with thwarted love. They had love to give, and mostly, they gave generously, unstintingly.

Returning to Figure 9.1, the image of Catherine and her baby doll harks back to the theme of the apartheid black mothers' separation from their own children and their compensatory relationship to white children in their care. But this time it's different. Catherine-as-mother is not a surrogate: she has her own baby, Marcie. I decided to include this painting precisely for this reason. It symbolically repairs the damaged relationship of the black mother and her own children while at the same time fully recognising the generosity of these mothers' care for their white children.

Perhaps the ultimate sadness is that so few black people, or indeed the black community as a whole, were "mothered" in the sense of being respected, understood, appreciated, cared for. As a people, they were unhoused, unparented. The doll paintings initiated an inquiry into the nature of mothering that comes full circle in this theme. The omission of dolls of colour both concealed and revealed the significance of the black mother in my past and that of many others.

This project was ultimately a journey of discovery. Allowing the heuristic inquiry to unfold, what was revealed in the end was more than the sum of the parts and much more than I ever expected at the outset. The combined approach

of painting and narrative, of art and psychology, starting off on impulse and continuing in an experimental way, proved to be of much significance, not just as a
project but as an insight into the deeper recesses of creativity, the link between
our early relationships and the mainsprings of our creativity: a mirror that reflects
the disturbing, damaged aspects of life and, at the same time, the urge to live, to
thrive, to create.

Chapter 10

Concluding thoughts

When I began the project underlying this book and for some time into the project, I had no plan in mind, no thesis to accomplish, no overarching framework for the meaning of my initiative. I was simply following an intuitive line of inquiry, allowing ideas and impulses to develop spontaneously, to give form in paintings to some of my conscious and half-conscious preoccupations, and to invite groups of people to participate in the inquiry. It was only later in the project, as my approach became more structured and the groups became more planned and organized, that I realised I was on a pathway of inquiry. I could recognize a direction of travel. This led to my adopting a phenomenological framework of inquiry, in line with the heuristic approach of Moustakas and Sela-Smith, as the most appropriate way of evaluating and communicating what I was doing, an approach that allowed me a loose conceptual frame, leaving me free to improvise and experiment.

I at first hesitated to employ as seemingly arcane a method/term as "heuristic". Most people, I suspect, are unsure what heuristic means. However, it is relatively easily defined as a phenomenological inquiry based on self-discovery that is extended to others with the aim of building and "thickening" the inquiry in such a way that a body of knowledge or insights emerges. Although it is recognized as a qualitative research method, the heuristic approach is immersive and exploratory in a way that is not altogether different from psychotherapeutic inquiry – and very different from typical quantitative and most qualitative research approaches. This was part of its attraction, as was its emphasis on a significant personal concern or preoccupation as the starting point of the research. This struck home with me as I had experienced my art-psychology project as a major, exciting but in some ways puzzling initiative, if only because of its sudden and intense momentum.

I did not follow some of the standard processes adopted in a heuristic investigation, such as interviewing participants. Instead, I regarded the group feedback as an emergent and valuable source of information, more in line with in-depth qualitative inquiry than the sometimes rigid format of interviewing. Having described in detail the painting series and group responses in previous chapters, I sum up here the main findings in this concluding chapter.

DOI: 10.4324/9781003232230-14

"I can be both!"

Harking back to the title of Chapter 1, "Can I be both?", the main finding was that I could indeed be both an artist and psychotherapist. Of course, this was hardly surprising, given that it is what I had been doing all my adult life, but the internalization of early constraints and proscriptions was such that I had, to a large extent, created a divided world and a divided self. It required the deep immersion in my art, the production of almost two hundred paintings in eighteen months, together with the organizing and delivery of some twenty presentations, mainly online, to create the conditions for a full, final, incontrovertible conclusion that I was – and am – both. Not only that, but the combination of the two interests/talents generated a configuration of visual and verbal communication that appeared to be stimulating and inspiring to others and deeply satisfying, exhilarating, if at times exhausting, to myself. It awakened insights into some of the seminal moments and influences in my personal development, ultimately producing a body of painting, narrative and insight that I regard as transformational.

Although we all differ, I suggest that the division between "selves" (psychologist, artist, etc.) that I grappled with is an expression of the human condition. As some thinkers have argued, it may be that we are all, at heart, fragmented beings, struggling to find an elusive wholeness in a confusing world. Other writers suggest there is an experience of wholeness to begin with, born in the throes of union with mother, only to lose this in time and to yearn for most of our lives to rediscover that wholeness. Still other writers argue against the illusion of wholeness and the problems of fostering a false belief in wholeness, suggesting that this belief might provide the basis of a totalitarian mentality (Deleuze and Guattari 1987). The experience with my project suggests to me that wholeness is not a God-given condition of existence: neither is it totally elusive. It can be gained or regained, I consider, not through the grace of God, but through our efforts to creatively achieve wholeness, even if fragile and temporary, and that we can enlist the help of others, as I did, in finding that wholeness. Possibly, the starting point, as suggested in the heuristic approach, is to find one's passion, to be as clear as possible about what is of significance to oneself. This is not easy, given the many distractions in the ethos of self and other in an overwhelming world. It requires courage: to recognize oneself and to follow through.

I do not want to give the impression of a blissful state of wholeness – that is indeed an illusion – but to suggest that even touching the whole for a moment, like a hand on an elusive, mysterious grail, is possible. What I discovered through the project was a way of putting aspects of my life together, not just art and psychology, but lost passages of time, rites of passage, faded memories, hidden dreams that were now formed through words and images into a more coherent whole than I had previously known. That this required the courage to share difficult developmental issues in a group space with others is true, but the benefits of doing so, through group resonance and affirmation, were more than evident. This requires resilience in the face of exposure, facing vulnerability, at times wanting to turn away, to deny, to repress. But in my experience, the engagement with others helps through the impasse. The group's support is like a compassionate friend.

I believe strongly that it is the combination of approaches, visual and verbal, that made the aforementioned possible: that one method alone would not have been as effective. Language alone is limited in its reach. While language can, of course, and does, facilitate communication, it can also create a split in the experience of self. Experiences that cannot be verbalized are "driven underground" and disconnected from the aware self (Sela-Smith 2002). This is where I believe my paintings had impact, not only in their content but in the access they gave to different modes of awareness. Ultimately, the real strength came in the interaction of the visual and the verbal, each stimulating the other as if in a dialogue between expressive modes, opening up vistas that might otherwise have remained hidden. The same can be said for the confluence of psychotherapeutic wisdom and artistic inquiry. The two approaches, which in some aspects of my life I had tried to keep apart, were the connecting point at which awareness unfolded.

While I approached the inquiry through painting and narrative and drew on the wisdom of a group audience, similar, as well as different, methods could be employed to facilitate others' inquiry. Most people, I believe, have under-utilized talents and skills that are in danger of atrophy in later life through sheer lack of use, coupled with a growing apathy and sense of bleak resignation. I am appealing to people's agency at all ages, but particularly in advanced years when agency so often suffers. This perspective touches on Erik Erikson's (1959) formulation of the challenges of the two last phases of life – generativity vs stagnation (late middle age) and integrity vs despair (old age). I am grateful that, through an active life stance, I was largely able to maintain generativity in the middle years. I now faced the later-life challenge of integrity vs despair. In Eriksen's terms, integrity refers to a sense of wholeness and purpose in evaluating one's life. The present initiative was, in large measure, an attempt to achieve integrity, to try and put the fragments of the puzzle together. In various ways, it put integrity within reach.

Self-and-other discovery

I have highlighted the unexpectedly personal journey the project became for me, culminating in the heightened awareness of the transformational aspect of my relationship with my mother and the quest to reciprocate, to give her something transformational in return, albeit posthumously. I went as far as to suggest that this, symbolically, was the motive power behind the project. Even the bringing together of my psychological and artistic interests could be seen as an attempt at synthesis that is more than the exercise or integration of two interests: it may symbolize a restorative, reparative search in the matrix of mother and child, both my maternal matrix and that of others. That this happened in later life is also significant, both as a personal, developmental review and as the hope of unifying aspects of my mother's life, of transforming some of her painful emotional struggles and, in an imaginary but heartfelt way, giving her another chance.

Realising what I gained from the project, the depth of self-discovery leaves me with some concern about a seemingly selfish, self-satisfied outcome. To some extent, this feeling is assuaged by the knowledge that participants, particularly in the group presentations, gained something of value for themselves, be it the stimulus of an exhibition, the membership of a reflective group, or the insight they gained into aspects of their own experience. Beyond that, though, is the suggestion that the experiment could be repeated, that the method is available to others to explore, whether using their own or others' art, or indeed undertaking a phenomenological inquiry that has different components. This is relevant at any age, but I have highlighted the particular value for older people, who may be struggling with the meaning of their lives, struggling to integrate the threads of existence, struggling to arrive at integrity rather than succumbing to despair.

The method I have developed has a variety of potential applications in education and therapeutic settings, utilizing the approach in whichever way is congruent with the aims of the setting. There are also further possible applications in the arts, illustrated vividly by the success of the dance event organised in response to my dancer paintings. This opened exciting vistas of the visual and movement arts coming together and is currently the focus of a joint plan with the dance group to develop this further. My own painting has been central to all the endeavours in this project, but there are many artists whose work could be used in similar ways and who might welcome entry into a theatre of the arts.

The paintings

Given the number of factors to consider in the project, there is (and was) a danger of overlooking the most important component: the paintings. Additionally, because this book is mainly a verbal account of what happened, albeit with illustrations, the visual aspect is reduced in immediacy. Yet, from a personal perspective, this was the most extraordinary period of artistic initiative I have known. In approximately eighteen months, I produced more paintings than I had done in a typical five-year period, my subject matter transformed, my approach to painting invigorated, my colour palette altered, and the experience of painting acquired a greater intensity than ever before. I was seeing my painting as part of a wider project than art for art's sake, and this had a strongly motivating effect. I painted now, not with a vague sense of the meaning of my work or a nebulous plan to exhibit paintings in a gallery at some future point, but with a clear intention to show my work to groups of people and bring the work closer to them.

As mentioned before, there was a radical shift in subject matter in my work during the period of inquiry. Although I was pleased to have transitioned to more challenging and ambiguous subject matter, I was anxious about the new work, its value and its reception by others. Also, the online format, generative as it was, meant that people saw visual reproductions rather than the "real thing". This has advantages and disadvantages. The advantage is the greater accessibility of the work: more people can see it than if it were on a gallery wall in some inaccessible place. The problem, as pointed out by the philosopher Walter Benjamin (1935), is that the painting, when reproduced *en masse*, loses its "aura", its uniqueness as a work of art. Possibly because of this, I sometimes experienced the paintings as somewhat lost in the overall process, not helped by my moving rather quickly from one slide to another, aware of the time constraints in each presentation. I sometimes felt that the paintings were marginalised in an ambitious project with competing inputs. However, many people spoke enthusiastically about the work, remembering the images well into the discussion and commenting on the overall quality of the work. People also bought paintings. Selling was not particularly on my mind, having assumed that because of the greater "seriousness" of the subject, I was sacrificing the chances of commercial success. However, there were sales following the presentations. Some series sold distinctly better than others. The paintings in *Fragile Nature* were the best-selling work, reflecting the appeal of themes of nature and the reassuring message about the life-cycle. *The Deserted City* series was least in demand for sales. This is not surprising, given that it holds up a mirror to the pandemic and portrays a distinctly bleak vision. Many of these paintings were described as powerful and moving, with the caveat, "It's great but not sure I'd like to see it hanging on my wall". One participant commented positively: "The paintings don't just speak: they sing". Another said that the painting "Town on the City Outskirts" (Figure 5.2), the revised version with the menacing birdlike creature portraying a grim vision of the pandemic, was one of the most powerful paintings she had ever seen.

My plan, assuming the reopening of galleries, still unclear at the time of writing, is to exhibit an overall collection, possibly with a series of group events, aiming at the convergence of word, image, and interactive live group exchange. Experiments, such as the dance theatre group's participation in a live event based on my dancer paintings, also have great potential. It remains to be seen how the transfer back to physical exhibitions and group presentations will compare with the mainly online presentations: a further step in the heuristic inquiry. What balance of actual exhibitions and online events will materialise? Many artists are struggling with the same issue now: how to position their work in a post-Covid world in which the virtual has assumed as much if not more cogency and accessibility than the real world.

The artist's matrix

While my predominant interest in the online exhibition was showing my own work, my experience has implications for other artists. Many, if not most, artists suffer from a lack of sufficient visibility and recognition. This is probably true of practitioners across the arts but may be especially relevant to visual artists who, by definition, rely on their work being seen in order to give it meaning. Social media now provides infinite possibilities of exposure but in such a dense firmament of images and accelerated modes of feedback that an artist might end up feeling as isolated as ever. My experience of involving groups directly in the viewing of my work offers a precedent to other artists who might welcome the immediacy and richness of feedback. This might apply whether online or in a real-world setting. The diversity of opinion and feedback, and the imaginative potential of people freely associating to visual stimuli, can only, in my view, strengthen the context in which the artist shows his/her work. Hence, my formulating and giving weight to the concept of the artist's matrix.

The bringing together of art and narrative in the group space is akin to what Winnicott (1953) calls a transitional or potential space in which a new process is generated, linking participants in a shared creative process. This is much more than viewing paintings as objects on a wall. It gives an entirely different context in which a wealth of personal, social and cultural phenomena come into play. Play is a useful way of describing the process. Winnicott (1974) highlighted the overlap of two play spaces in psychotherapy. My presentations stimulated the overlap of the "play spaces" of a large number of people. A member of the audience in one of my presentations commented on the value of technology in affording opportunities of this kind, a surprising observation, in her view, given the sometimes alienating effect of technology. Others noted the fortuitous, if not paradoxical, way in which Covid had brought something valuable to the fore, suggesting that what was most oppressive in lockdown – the restrictions on freedom of movement – opened up new, creative possibilities. Assuming a return to a more "normal" world of communications post-pandemic, there will be the option of arranging similar group events in real space or continuing the online opportunity, both with their advantages. Whatever happens, I am suggesting a significant widening of the artist's matrix in a way that may alter how art is viewed, not just as a compensation for stifled traditional exhibitions, but as a new, enhanced field of dialogue.

The group process

The value of the group as an active agent, rather than a passive audience, is implicit in much of what I have said and is a core requirement of a new visual matrix. I come to this via my group analytic knowledge and experience, which predisposes me to see the potential of the group format. At one level, its value resides in the simple fact of bringing people together. A member of the audience, a colleague who had been present at several of my presentations in the UK and abroad, commented on how much they had brought people together in a spirit of curiosity and appreciation. This was especially important in the dark days of Covid when people were stuck in isolated bubbles and felt cut off from the world. That the presentations touched on universal concerns facilitated closeness and mutual identification.

This was combined with the creativity of the group, the imaginative leaps that people were able to make, and the ongoing processes of resonance, amplification and exchange that are the hallmarks of the group analytic process (Schlapobersky 2016). The freely associative process of the group evoked not only conscious areas of experience but unconscious associations that were seminal. It was through the groups' associations that my own awareness expanded, and half-forgotten, dissociated or denied past experience became available to me. This is what I referred to previously as the creative matrix: the creative power of the group. This has great, unrealised potential, I believe, for artists seeking more of a dialogue with an audience. The point, though, is that the group was not so much an audience as a *partner* in the inquiry, adding greatly to the heuristic exploration, which is the framework of my approach.

What people brought to the group from their own lives is what is known group analytically as the *foundation matrix* (Hopper and Weinberg 2016). This is the common pool of experience and history that defines group culture at a given point in time. During the time of Covid, the foundation matrix was impregnated with fears of disease, death and disorder, exposing the elements of crisis and catastrophe that have dogged humanity across the ages. This is partly what gave my groups so much cohesion: we were all in it together. It's also why my choice of themes resonated. By participating in the event, the groups themselves changed, if only for a limited time, gaining in depth of awareness and emerging with greater insight and possibly hope. The many affirmative messages, texts, emails and chats from people after my presentations confirmed the sense of participants having felt enriched, enlightened, moved. Group analytically, this would reflect the *dynamic matrix*, the matrix that changes over a period of time. Usually, this refers to the broad strokes of history, the large-scale events that change nations and history, but it can happen in smaller ways, as in psychotherapy groups and other growthful events, such as the presentations I describe. Small, strengthening changes of the matrix are valuable at a time when there is so much uncertain, unwelcome, destabilizing change in the world around us: when the foundation matrix is shaken to its roots.

The group provides a fruitful combination of what is known group-analytically as the vertical and the horizontal axis (Berman and Avrahami 2022). The vertical axis refers to the relationship of group to conductor. It is hierarchical in character in so far as the conductor is the authority who composes and facilitates the group. The horizontal axis refers to the relationship of group members to each other and to the group as a whole. In group analytic therapy, this is seen as a figure-ground relationship, the vertical and the horizontal axes operating reciprocally in a state of flux and reversal. In Chapter 3, I linked this to Deleuze and Guattari's (1987) concept of the tree (a metaphor for the vertical) and the rhizome (the horizontal). This shifting vertical-horizontal axis was a key, energising feature of my group presentations.

The Anti-Group? No study of mine would be complete without reference to the anti-group, given my long involvement with the concept (Nitsun 1991, 1996, 2015a). The overwhelming impression is how little anti-group was apparent in these events. Everything I have said in the earlier observations of the group process confirms the sense of well-functioning, cohesive groups closely attuned to the subject at hand and appreciative of this opportunity. Although this affirms the presence of the "pro-group", there are caveats. The groups were highly structured, with an overarching theme of shared significance and a clear role for group members should they choose to engage. They were also offered, free, an opportunity to view an online art exhibition and the narrative that went with it. These are very different from the usual conditions of the anti-group – absence of structure, lack of focus, ambiguous goals, problematic leadership (Nitsun 1996). So, the anti-group was probably pre-empted, contained by a stable, focused, functional group process. This has implications for group analytic psychotherapy, the context in which my original observations of the anti-group were made. Although the notion of a free, largely unstructured group space, with little if any direction, has considerable value in group psychotherapy, with the potential to evoke the full gamut of emotional experience, this must be weighed against the potential for unearthing explosive projections and interpersonal conflict that can be difficult to manage and may have a less than favourable outcome.

It is significant that most of the groups took place online during the pandemic. The threat of contact and contagion, necessitating isolation from others, almost certainly strengthened motivation to attend these group events, a safe way of meeting others. This was also a period of considerable political and social unrest, particularly in the USA, but also worldwide. In the UK, there was the marked tension and splitting occasioned by Brexit. The wider environment was saturated with large-scale anti-group processes, fear driving people into opposing groups, creating mistrust and division. The groups in this project offered a safe, reflective, even intimate space, with considerable holding through structured presentations on themes of universal import.

Memoir

Sharing aspects of my life narrative in the presentations was an essential part of the project. It highlights the significance of a memoir. Whether art is best viewed independently, separate from the artist and his/her life, is debatable, even allowing for the unarguable influence of the person of the artist on their work. Yet, in many gallery viewings, this is exactly what happens. There may be information about the artist, catalogues, reviews, snippets of news, but essentially the artwork and the producer are in separate domains. I have never before had the kind of opportunity to make myself as visible as an artist as I did in the online exhibitions. I can only affirm the value of so doing. This includes not just the technical information about the paintings and the thinking behind each series, but myself as a person in a historical dimension. Weaving together the narrative of my own life through the prism of the paintings appeared to be part of the glue that helped bring together the disparate elements of the presentations. In presentations of this sort, sometimes requiring concentration over an extended period, people generally appreciate the personal: stories and anecdotes that animate the narrative and help to create a bond of trust with the audience. But, beyond that is the added meaning memoir gives to the work: understanding the painting in context rather than as an isolated work of art. And for oneself, the presenter, seeing the jigsaw of one's life reflected in the group mirror, is both affirming and humbling.

There has been a renewed interest in recent years in writing and narrative in psychotherapy (Nitsun 2019; Weegman 2019; Weisel-Barth 2020; Golinelli 2021). "The story is all" appears to be the maxim. In part, this may be linked to debates about truth and post-truth in present-day culture, the struggle to capture truth in the flux of information and disinformation. We are faced nowadays with narrative truths, narrative fictions and narrative hybrids that interconnect truth and fiction. In my own case, I was keen to tell my story as it happened, with minimum embellishment. This might have been meaningful at any age, but it gained added poignancy as a late-life inquiry, being able to unearth and share lost or forgotten aspects of the past. As highlighted earlier, it helped to approach what Eric Erikson described as the challenge of the last stage of identity formation: *integrity vs despair*.

There is a further aspect of this phenomenon that plays a part. This is the idea of performance and/or performativity. The act of sharing a life narrative in addition to the overall requirements of group presentations of this kind, such as making direct contact with an audience of varying sizes, facilitating the group, guiding viewers through the paintings, and dealing with questions, probes and interpretations, involves a measure of performance. I wanted the presentations to be engaging and touching in some way – entertaining, perhaps – rather than dry, academic and impersonal. In Chapter 3, I debated whether this was a form of performance art, the subject of a chapter in my previous book, *Beyond the Anti-Group* (Nitsun 2015b). It is worth considering this as one of the elements that breathed life into the presentations. In as much as I was the artist, the psychologist and the group conductor, I was also a performer. Perhaps when opening the doors to hybrid art events of this sort, the process lends itself to a range of creative inputs. The role of performance is part of this.

Psychological learning

While not setting out to make this primarily a psychological study, I inevitably observed psychological processes and was stimulated to make inferences. Indeed, many are shared in previous chapters. Aspects that bear comment here concern the power of perceptual processes and the way they reflect both the positive and negative attributions we give to others, in turn influencing our social behaviour. This applies particularly to the many instances of projection I witnessed in people's responses to the paintings. The most compelling were the strikingly varied perceptions of the doll images, where there were massive projections, often presented as absolute and inconvertible, as if the image was one thing and one thing only: fixed and unassailable. The deserted city paintings elicited similar, though not as pronounced projection, and projection came up again in response to the *Four Women* paintings, notably Jan Morris and the painting of her as an old woman: these responses are all described in detail in Chapters 4–9. Having been interested in the projective process for many years and having used projective techniques routinely in my earlier career, I was astonished at the levels of projection, often from psychologically sophisticated people.

In Chapter 4, I interpreted the projections onto the dolls and, by association, children as reflections of the discourse of childhood: the deeper constructs underlying our view of children. But the implications go further: they suggest that people have limited capacity to recognize their projections and that, in some way, this must structure their experience of the world, at the same time reflecting the constructs of the world that they have absorbed, consistent with the existence of the social unconscious (Hopper and Weinberg 2011, 2016). If this is the case on a universal scale, it is not surprising that human beings have such difficulty agreeing on fundamental aspects of life, generating the complex panoply of morals, values and prejudices in which we are all implicated. An aspect of this is splitting, a cognitive process we tend to associate with a primitive mentality in which the polarities of good and bad, idealized and denigrated, are rigidly divided in people's minds. Sometimes, in discussions of the paintings, splits were apparent, sometimes hinted at or concealed, sometimes filtering through the discourse. This is not the province of the present project, but the strength of projection the paintings unleashed cannot go unmentioned.

Another observation that may be linked is the sense of people's difficulty in facing problematic or painful stimuli or situations. This came up with some of the darker, more disturbing imagery. It was not altogether surprising given anhedonic subjects such as *The Deserted City*, with its associations of the pandemic, also some of the more ambiguous and troubling doll figures. However, the turning away from such images – literally fleeing in a few cases – seemed part of a process of avoidance, splitting and repudiation. It can be understood as "flight": the trope described by Bion (1961) as a defence against overwhelming anxiety.

I am aware that I am giving a different picture here from that of the generous, creative and insightful contributions that I previously noted. Mostly, the group responses were perceptive, rounded and reflective. But there was a marked vein of projection and avoidance that wove through some of the contributions, adding complexity to the discourse.

Implications for psychotherapy

That the project was not undertaken with psychotherapy in mind still stands, but at the same time, the unexpected therapeutic benefits must be noted. Much of this is attributable to the group experience, given the powerful resonance and mirroring in the groups, with a particularly high degree of universality, one of the classical group therapeutic factors (Yalom and Leszcz 2005). Their activation in these groups explains in part, at least, some participants emphasizing how much they gained, to the extent of learning more than they had in their own psychotherapies, and others saying how much they would like to participate in ongoing events of this sort. Of course, it was not the group alone that had this effect: it was the presentation of the paintings and the narrative that stimulated and touched people, adding a strong focus to the discussions and cohesion to the groups. But the holding, facilitating quality of the group itself added distinct value.

While highlighting the group-specific factors, there are also insights into the psychotherapeutic process generally. These relate to the traditionally hierarchical structure of the therapeutic relationship. The conventional role distinction between analyst and patient puts the analyst in the expert role and requires that he/she divulges very little on a personal level. Although this schema of a therapeutic relationship has its merits, clarifying boundaries and providing a safe structure for the treatment, it also loses the benefit of greater flexibility. In my talks, I presented myself as the expert in some respects, but I also stepped out of the conventional role by speaking much more personally than I would in formal psychotherapy. I also consistently invited feedback and associations from the group audience. This created an interactional field of communication rather than a one-way process between expert and client. There is little doubt that this was of benefit to the inquiry generally and to me personally.

In psychoanalytic history, Firenczi is well-known for his experiments with "mutual analysis" (Rudnytsky 2021). That these ran aground is important since they highlight the complications of reversing the patient-analyst relationship. At the same time, Ferenczi's attempt at a full reversal of the analytic relationship in the psychoanalysis of the time (1930's) may have been doomed to failure. He was subject to a dominant, conformist institutional culture, as well as the built-in inequalities of the one-way psychoanalytic interpretive processes. In the present day, with the emergence of relational psychoanalysis and other intersubjective approaches (Malone 2018; Mitchell and Aron 1999; Schulte 2000), this type of reversal may be less a reversal and more a recognition that members of the dyad (or group) contribute equally to an ongoing interactional process and that transparency, rather than concealment and constraint, is therapeutic.

A further point concerns the therapeutic value to *myself*. I have described the project as being transformative. I need to clarify how this happened. I believe that the responses of the group, varied, empathic, yet also challenging, surprising and unexpected in many cases, had a freely associative function, opening up whole areas of the unthought known (Bollas 1987). The important difference was that the associations came from a group, whether online or real, rather than from me on the couch or in the patient's chair. As highlighted before, this was a reciprocal, interactional process – I fed narratives and images to the group: the group questioned and associated in an ongoing cycle: a virtuous circle. This not only supports group analytic principles but shows how the group provides an important auxiliary resource – rather like the auxiliary ego in psychodrama (Karp 1998).

I acknowledge my initial doubts about the approach. I was anxious about the exposure to which I was opening myself: exhibiting whole series of paintings and revealing highly personal information while taking on the challenge of online group work and the daunting venture of my convergence as psychologist and artist. I was ready for the challenge but recognised that I had entered novel, untried territory, different from the familiar constraints of day-to-day professional psychotherapeutic practice. These constraints are not to be ignored or repudiated: appropriate constraints add integrity and reliability to our work. But I was, and am, keen to invigorate the practice: to find a way between the requirements of therapeutic responsibility and the potential in our work to take greater risks, to experiment, to *play*.

The uncanny

While adopting a phenomenological-heuristic approach as the framework for my project and finding clarity about several questions, I at the same time recognise how much remains elusive. In part, I associate this with the quality of the uncanny that exists in some of the painting themes, as well as in specific paintings. This applied particularly where the blurred line between real and unreal, animate and inanimate, created discomfort for people. I link this to Freud's observations of the uncanny in art, as well as the contemporary concept of the "uncanny valley" (Cheetham et al. 2011).

Although the uncanny is featured strongly in the dolls paintings, I believe that it filtered into many of my other paintings. In *The Deserted City*, for example, I think it was the uncanny sense of whole cities emptying out during lockdown and creating a mysteriously unfamiliar environment of empty streets and embattled buildings. Some people were disturbed not only by the depiction of a town in the grip of a plague but by a sense of the uncanny. Was this real? Could it have happened and how did it happen? Why choose this as subject matter for painting? I suggest that, in some way, all my series of paintings reflected this quality as an expression of my own journey through the unfamiliar. Fragile nature, although conveying a spirit of containment and hope, includes scenes that hint at the mysterious and the unknown in nature, the secret life of the woods, the underground world of forests, the spirit of plants and animals in complex symbiosis. This sense of the uncanny lurking in the shadows of experience, whether human or in nature, was with me through much of the painting.

I am aware of how as a psychologist/psychotherapist, I am often dealing with a sense of the ineffable, the un-understandable in my work. I was glad to have an opportunity in these paintings to explore this dimension. At the broadest level, there is something uncanny about life itself, suspended as we are in a chasm of existence between birth and death, of relentless change and loss, of the sense of being a speck in an unfathomable universe. My phenomenological inquiry, although revealing and productive, in a sense ended where it began – at a point of uncertainty and wonder.

References

Balint, M. (1968). *The Basic Fault: Therapeutic Aspects of Regression*. London: Tavistock.

Becker, E. (1975). *The Denial of Death*. London: Macmillan Publishing.

Benjamin, W. (1935). The work of art in the age of mechanical reproduction. In Arendt, H. (Ed.), *Illuminations*, 1969. New York: Shocken Books.

Berman, A., and Avrahami, L. (2022). London: The tree and the rhizome and the horizontal and vertical axes – reflections on individual and group psychotherapy following Deleuze and Guattari. In Asbach, S., and Berman, A. (Eds.), *Sibling Relationships and the Horizontal Axis in Group Analysis*. London: Routledge.

Bion, W. F. (1961). *Experiences in Groups*. London: Routledge, 1989.

Bollas, C. (1987). The transformational object. In *The Shadow of the Object: Psychoanalysis of the Unthought Known*. London: Free Association Books.

Bollas, C. (1989). *Forces of Destiny: Psychoanalysis and Human Idiom*. London: Free Association Books.

Combs, G., and Freedman, J. (1996). *Narrative Therapy: The Social Construction of Preferred Realities*. London: Norton.

Deleuze, G., and Guattari, F. (1987). *A Thousand Plateaus*. Minneapolis: University of Minnesota Press, 2007.

Denborough, D. (2014). *Retelling the Stories of Our Lives: Everyday Narrative Therapy to Draw Inspiration and Transform Experience*. New York: W W Norton and Co.

Elias, N. (1994). *The Civilising Process: Sociogenetic and Psychogenetic Investigations*. Oxford: Blackwell Publications.

Erikson, E. (1959). *Identity and the Life Cycle*. New York: W W Norton and Co., 1994.

Ferro, A. (1999). *Psychoanalysis as Therapy and Story Telling*. London: Routledge, 2006.

Foulkes, S. H. (1948). *Introduction to Group Analytic Psychotherapy*. London: Karnac, 1983.

Foulkes, S. H. (1964). *Therapeutic Group Analysis*. London: Routledge: Routledge, 1984.

Freud, S. (1916). *Leonardo da Vinci: A Psychosexual Study of an Infantile Reminiscence*. New York: Moffat, Yard, and Co.

Freud, S. (1917). Morning and melancholia. In *The Standard Edition of the Complete Psychological Work of Sigmund Freud*. Vol. X1V. London: Vintage, 1999.

Freud, S. (1919). The "uncanny". In Freud, S. (Ed.), *The Standard Edition of the Complete Psychological Works of Sigmund Freud*. Vol. XVII. London: Vintage, 1999.

Friedman, R. (2015). The soldier's matrix. *Group Analysis*, 48(3), 239–257.

Frost, R. (1923). Nothing gold can stay. New Haven, Connecticut. *The Yale Review*, October.

Gans, J. (1997). Review: The anti-group: Destructive forces in the group and their creative potential (Nitsun, M, 1996). *International Journal of Group Psychotherapy*, 47, 531–534.

Gans, J. (2006). *Endorsement: The Group as an Object of Desire: Exploring Sexuality in Group Psychotherapy* (M. Nitsun, Ed.). London: Routledge.

Gerada, C. (2019). The making of a doctor: The matrix and self. *Group Analysis*, 52(3), 350–361.

Glasser, M. (1979). Some aspects of the role of aggression in the perversions. In Rosen, I. (Ed.), *Sexual Deviations*. Oxford: Oxford University Press.

Goldberg, R. (2011). *Performance Art: From Futurism to the Present*. London: Thames and Hudson.

Golinelli, P. (2021). *Psychoanalytic Reflections on Writing, Cinema, and the Arts*. London: Routledge.

Greer, G. (2009). Degas's dancers are studies in cruel reality. *The Guardian*, newspaper article, January.

Grotstein, J. S. (2004). The seventh servant: The implications of a truth drive in Bion's theory of O. *International Journal of Psychoanalysis*, 85, 1081–1101.

Hashmi, S., Vanderwert, R. E., Price, H. A., and Gerson, S. A. (2020). Exploring the benefits of doll play through neuroscience. *Frontiers in Human Neuroscience*, 14, 560176. https://doi.org/10.3389/fnhum.2020.560176

Hitchens, C. (1995). *The Missionary Position: Mother Teresa in Theory and Practice*. London: Versa.

Hopper, E. (2003). *Traumatic Experience in the Unconscious Life of Groups: The Fourth Basic Assumption*. London: Jessica Kingsley.

Hopper, E. (2018). The development of the concept of the Tripartite Matrix: A response to 'Four modalities of the experience of others in groups', by Victor Schermer. *Group Analysis*, 51, 97–206.

Hopper, E. (2022). From remorse to relational reparation and mature hope and communication in our response to social conflict and the virus as a persecuting object. *Contexts*, Issue 95.

Hopper, E., and Weinberg, H. (Eds.). (2011). *The Social Unconscious in Persons, Groups and Societies. Volume 1: Mainly Theory*. London: Karnac.

Hopper, E., and Weinberg, H. (Eds.). (2016). *The Social Unconscious in Persons, Groups and Societies. Volume 2: Mainly Foundation Matrices*. London: Karnac.

Jung, C. G. (1956). Symbols of transformation. In Adler, G., Fordham, M., and Read, H. (Eds.), *The Collected Works of C G Jung*. London: Routledge.

Karp, M. (Ed.). (1998). *The Handbook of Psychodrama*. London: Routledge.

Kingsley, M. J. (2021). From being different to making a difference: developing the role of clinical health services in the public arena. *Unpublished Doctoral Dissertation*, Middlesex University.

Kohut, H. (2009). *The Analysis of the Self: A Systematic Approach to the Psychoanalytic Treatment of Personality Disorders*. Chicago: Chicago Universities Press.

Lasch, C. (1987). *The Culture of Narcissism: American Life in an Age of Diminishing Expectations*. New York: Penguin.

Lorca, F. G. (1933). *In Search of Duende*. New York: New Directions, 1998.

Malone, J. C. (2018). Relational psychoanalysis: Not a theory but a framework. In Charles, M. (Ed.), *Introduction to Contemporary Psychoanalysis: Defining Terms and Building Bridges*. London: Routledge/Taylor & Francis Group, pp. 208–226.

McNeilly, G. (2005). *Group Analytic Art Therapy*. London: Jessica Kingsley.

Merleau-Ponty, M. (1962). *The Philosophy of Perception*. London: Routledge and Kegan Paul.

Merwin, W. S. (2007). To a leaf falling in winter. In *In Present Company*. Port Townsend, WA: Copper Canyon Press.

Miller, A. (1983). *The Drama of the Gifted Child: The Search for the True Self*. New York: Basic Books.

Milner, M. (1950). *On Not Being Able to Paint*. Madison, CT: International Universities Press.

Misselhorn, C. (2009). Empathy with inanimate objects and the uncanny valley. *Minds and Machines*, 19(3), 345–359.

Mitchell, S., and Aron, L. (Eds.). (1999). *Relational Psychoanalysis: The Emergence of a Tradition*. Vol. 14. New York: Routledge.

Morris, J. (1974). *Conundrum*. London: Faber and Faber.

Moustakas, C. E. (1990). *Heuristic Research: Design, Methodology, and Applications*. London: Sage.

Munch, E. (1882/1982). Holland. In Gill, J. (Ed.), *The Private Journals of Edvard Munch*. Madison: University of Wisconsin Press.

Nitsun, M. (1988). *The Hospital Relations Technique: Assessing the Relationship to Care and Treatment*. Unpublished Projective Technique.

Nitsun, M. (1991). The Anti-group: Destructive forces in the group and their therapeutic potential. *Group Analysis*, 24(1), 7–20.

Nitsun, M. (1996). *The Anti-group: Destructive Forces in the Group and Their Creative Potential*. London: Routledge.

Nitsun, M. (1998). The organizational mirror: A group analytic approach to organizational consultancy, part 1 – theory. *Group Analysis*, 31, 245–270.

Nitsun, M. (2006). *The Group as an Object of Desire: Exploring Sexuality in Group Psychotherapy*. London: Routledge.

Nitsun, M. (2015a). *Beyond the Anti-group: Survival and Transformation*. London: Routledge.

Nitsun, M. (2015b). Group analysis and performance art. In *Beyond the Anti-group: Survival and Transformation*. London: Routledge.

Nitsun, M. (2019). Writing as rebellion. In Weegman, M. (Ed.), *Psychodynamics of Writing*. London: Routledge.

Noah, T. (2016). *Born a Crime: Stories from a South African Childhood*. New York: One World.

Ogden, T. H. (1992). *Projective Identification and Psychotherapeutic Technique*. New York: Routledge.

Parks, R. (1992). *My Story*. New York: Penguin.

Pazcoguin, G. (2021). *Swan Dive: The Making of a Rogue Ballerina*. New York: Pan MacMillan.

Picasso, P. (2021). Every act of creation is first of all an act of destruction. In *Picasso Quotes*. San Francisco: Goodreads.

Piotrowski, Z. A. (1950). A new evaluation of the TAT. *The Psychoanalytic Review*, 195(2), 101.

Rhyne, J. (2021). Gestalt art therapy. In Rubin, J. A. (Ed.), *Approaches to Art Therapy: Theory and Technique*. New York: Routledge.

Rilke, R. M. (1918). The Spanish dancer. In *Poems by Rainer Maria Rilke (1918)* (J. Lamont, Trans.). New York: Tobias A Wright.

Roberts, J. (1983). Foulkes' concept of the matrix. *Group Analysis*, 15(2), 111–126.

Rudnytsky, P. L. (2021). *Mutual Analysis: Ferenczi, Severn, and the Origins of Trauma Theory*. London: Routledge.

Schama, S. (2009a). Picasso: Modern art goes political. In *The Power of Art*. London: Bodley Head.

Schama, S. (2009b). Rothko: The music of beyond in the city of glitter. In *The Power of Art*. London: The Bodley Head.

Schama, S. (2009c). Van Gogh: Painting from inside the head. In *The Power of Art*. London: The Bodley Head.

Schaverien, J. (2015). *Boarding School Syndrome: The Psychological Trauma of the 'Privileged' Child*. London: Taylor and Francis.

Schermer, V. L. (2018). Four modalities of the experience of others in groups. *Group Analysis*, 51, 175–196.

Schlapobersky, J. (2016). *From the Couch to the Circle: Group-Analytic Psychotherapy in Practice*. London: Routledge.

Schulte, P. (2000). Holding in mind: Intersubjectivity, subject relations and the group. *Group Analysis*, 33, 531–544.

Searles, H. (1965). *Collected Papers on Schizophrenia and Related Topics*. London: Hogarth Press.

Segal, H. (1952). A psycho-analytical approach to aesthetics. *International Journal of Psychoanalysis*, 33, 196–207.

Sehgal, T. (2012). *The Unilever Series: These Associations*. Tate Modern Exhibitions. London: Turbine Hall.

Sela-Smith, S. (2002). Heuristic research: A review and critique of Moustakas' method. *Journal of Humanistic Psychology*, 42, 53–88.

Snell, R. (2021). *Cezanne and the Post-Bionian Field*. London: Routledge.

Stern, D. (1985). *The Interpersonal World of the Infant*. New York: Basic Books.

Storr, R. (2016). *Intimate Geometries: The Art and Life of Louise Bourgeois*. London: Thames and Hudson Ltd.

Tuttman, S. (1991). The Anti-group: An historical and ideological breakthrough. *Group Analysis*, 24, 483–484.

Van der Kolk, B. (1990). *The Body Keeps the Score: Brain, Mind, and Body in the Healing of Trauma*. New York: Penguin.

Volkan, V. D. (1981). *Linking Objects and Linking Phenomena: A Study of the Forms, Symptoms, Metapsychology and Therapy of Complicated Mourning*. Madison, CT: International Universities Press.

Waller, D. (1999). *Becoming a Profession. A History of Art Therapy 1940–82*. London: Routledge.

Waller, D. (2014). *Interactive Art Therapy. Its Use in Training*. London: Routledge.

Weegman, M. (Ed.). (2019). *Psychodynamics of Writing*. London: Routledge.

Weisel-Barth, J. (2020). *Theoretical and Clinical Perspectives on Narrative in Psychoanalysis: The Creation of Intimate Fictions*. Los Angeles: Routledge.

Winnicott, D. W. (1953). Transitional objects and transitional phenomena. In *Playing and Reality*. London: Pelican, 1974.

Winnicott, D. W. (1967). Mirror-role of the mother and family in child development. In P. Lomas (Ed.), *The Predicament of the Family: A Psycho-Analytical Symposium*. London: Hogarth.

Winnicott, D. W. (1974). Playing: A theoretical statement. In *Playing and Reality*. London: Pelican.

Wright, K. (1991). *Vision and Separation between Mother and Baby*. London: Free Association Books.

Yalom, I., and Leszcz, M. (2005). *The Theory and Practice of Group Psychotherapy*. New York: Basic Books.

Zinkin, L. (1983). Malignant mirroring. *Group Analysis*, 16, 113–126.

Index

Note: page numbers in *italics* indicate a figure on the corresponding page.

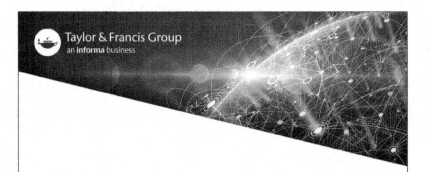